RACIAL
INNOCENCE

RACIAL INNOCENCE

UNMASKING LATINO ANTI-BLACK BIAS AND THE STRUGGLE FOR EQUALITY

TANYA KATERÍ HERNÁNDEZ

BEACON PRESS • BOSTON

Library of Congress Cataloging-in-Publication Data
Names: Hernández, Tanya Katerí, author.
Title: Racial innocence : unmasking Latino anti-Black bias and the struggle
for equality / Tanya Katerí Hernández.
Description: Boston : Beacon Press, [2022] | Includes bibliographical
references and index. | Summary: "Bringing to light stories of Latino
anti-Black racism and how they matter for the societal pursuit of
equality"—Provided by publisher.
Identifiers: LCCN 2022010993 | ISBN 9780807012741 (paperback) | ISBN
9780807020142 (ebook)
Subjects: LCSH: Hispanic Americans—Attitudes. | Racism—United
States. |
African Americans. | United States—Race relations.
Classification: LCC E184.S75 H477 2022 | DDC 305.800973—dc23/
eng/20220509
LC record available at https://lccn.loc.gov/2022010993

*This book is dedicated to the late Miriam Esther
Jiménez Román, the bold leader of Afro-Latin@ Studies.
I have tried my best to remember all that she taught me
and model her fearlessness in addressing how "some 'Browns'
are browner than other Browns, that some Blacks are
also Latinos, and that many Latinos are victims
of racial—as well as cultural—discrimination"
("Real Unity for AfroLatinos," AfroLatin@Forum.org).*

*And to James Quentin Walker,
for everything always.* ✝

CONTENTS

CHAPTER 1

WHAT IS LATINO ANTI-BLACKNESS?

Even before I understood the word "nigger,"
I heard "negro" in Spanish.
—JOSÉ LUIS VILSON, Afro-Latino educator[1]

Wherever the Negro goes, he remains a Negro.
—FRANTZ FANON[2]

Latinos can be racist. Some may be startled to hear this. After all, our national conversations about racism appear oblivious to this fact, and some civil rights leaders are also seemingly reticent to "air the dirty laundry" of the bias that exists within communities of color, lest it distract from the "real racism" of White supremacy. However, all the while Afro-Latinos and African Americans suffer from discrimination at the hands of Latinos who claim that their racially mixed cultures immunize them from being racist. I call this the "Latino racial innocence" cloak that veils Latino complicity in US racism. In turn, public ignorance about Latino anti-Blackness undermines the ability to fully address the interwoven complexities of US racism in developing public policies and enforcing antidiscrimination law. Judges, in addition to the rest of society, need to learn that Latinos can be prejudiced toward both Afro-Latinos and African Americans.

The pervasiveness of anti-Black violence, still so pronounced decades after the achievements of the civil rights movement, cannot be readily understood nor addressed with the traditional sole focus on White non-Hispanic (non-Latino White) actors. According to the US Census Bureau, non-Hispanic Whites are declining in number. The 2020 census reported the first decline in the White non-Hispanic population since the introduction of the national survey; White non-Hispanics now represent 57.8 percent of the population, down 8.6 percent from the 2010 census.[3] Moreover, White non-Hispanics are predicted to decline to 15 percent by 2060.[4]

The continued vibrancy of White supremacist attitudes thus cannot be explained exclusively by the perspectives of the declining number of White non-Hispanics. The ongoing upkeep and silent acceptance of anti-Blackness implicates many other racial and ethnic groups in the United States as well as across the globe.[5]

Exploring Latino complicity in anti-Blackness is particularly helpful. As a multihued ethnic group, Latinos are often viewed as free of racism or, at the very least, free of its most exclusionary forms. Examining how anti-Blackness still does manage to manifest itself among the racially mixed rainbow of Latinos (who currently comprise 18.7 percent of the population and are predicted to increase to 28 percent by 2060), is thereby a powerful illustration of how people of color can fortify racism.[6]

All the same, when I tell people that part of my research is on the topic of anti-Blackness in Latino communities (and explain "Yes, that is a thing"), light-skinned and fair-skinned Latinos often react by telling me that most Latinos and African Americans get along and frequently live in neighboring areas or the very same buildings. In other words, they're conveying that they do not believe anti-Blackness is a real issue in Latino communities like it is in White non-Hispanic communities.

While it would certainly be ideal if Latinos were all truly color-blind and incapable of committing racist acts, as an Afro-Latina myself I do not have the luxury of indulging in the fantasy of a Latino racial mixture utopia. As I share in the epilogue, the visibility of my family's Black ancestry means I literally have "skin in the game" of accurately assessing the operation of racism in its many forms. Consequently, this book excavates the voices of Afro-Latinos and African Americans who have actually experienced Latino anti-Black bias, in an effort to help disrupt the public ignorance and Latino disinclination to grapple with Latino anti-Blackness. The need for such an intervention is usefully demonstrated by a consideration of the Latino adoration of Afro-Cuban Queen of Salsa, Celia Cruz.

When Celia Cruz died on July 16, 2003, her wake in Miami attracted at least one hundred thousand fans. Later, when her body was brought to New York City, thousands waited to see her body, exceeding the crowds that honored Judy Garland and Ed Sullivan at the very same funeral home. Anyone viewing the news footage of all the racially diverse Latinos expressing their love for Celia would find it difficult to envision any of those mourners as also harboring anti-Black bias.[7] Indeed, the Latino mourners themselves would be quick to denounce such an accusation. And yet, absolute love for the art that Black individuals create can coexist with the hierarchical impulse to generally denigrate Blacks as intellectually inferior and socially dangerous.[8] This dualism is readily apparent in the profound US worship of African American pop star Beyoncé, simultaneous with the pervasive killing of unarmed African Americans presumed inherently dangerous.

However, anti-Black racism that arises outside the unfortunately familiar US frame of White non-Hispanic versus African American bias can be mystifying for many people. This is in part because US Blackness is primarily conceived of as embodied solely by English-speaking African Americans. In turn, anti-Blackness is popularly understood as a uniquely US phenomenon affecting those English-speaking African Americans (with occasional recognition of the racialized struggles of Africans and others in the African diaspora).[9] This skewed vision is only compounded by how Latino communities themselves marginalize or entirely erase the existence of Afro-Latinos.

Notably, the seminal volume "The Afro-Latin@ Reader: History and Culture in the United States" highlights this marginalization in its opening definition:

> Afro-Latin@? What's an Afro-Latin@? Who is an Afro-Latin@? The term befuddles us because we are accustomed to thinking of "Afro" and "Latin@" as distinct from each other and mutually exclusive: one is either Black or Latin@.
>
> The short answer is that Afro-Latin@s belong to both groups. They are people of African descent in Mexico, Central and South America, and the Spanish-speaking Caribbean and by extension those of African descent in the United States whose origins are in Latin America and the Caribbean.[10]

So to be clear, Afro-Latinos are simultaneously ethnically Latino and racially Black.[11] In daily life few people are preoccupied with how and when ethnic identity differs from racial identity. Indeed, there are those who view the concepts as the same, or at least are cognizant of how much they can overlap as social constructs. Some researchers even prefer the hyphenated term "ethno-racial" to refer to the overlap.[12] But for Afro-Latinos living at the intersection of Blackness and Latinidad (a vision of a panethnic Latino community), the two terms usefully highlight important differences. As Afro-Peruvian writer Kayla Popuchet Quesada, notes, "All Latinos are nationally oppressed, but not all Latinos are racially or ethnically oppressed."[13]

Generally speaking, ethnicity refers to how individuals are associated with a social group based upon cultural markers like language, religion, customs, traditions, food, geographic origin, and so on, and not primarily their physical appearance.[14] Within an ethnic group, physical appearance can vary widely. Accordingly, when this book refers to "Latinos" without a racial qualifier such as White or Afro, it is a reference to the general ethnic group of Latinos.

Race is more directly rooted to imposed social hierarchy based upon physical differences or presumed physical differences from ancestral lineage.[15] Skin color is only one of the physical markers like facial features, hair texture, body shape all enveloped in a matrix of demeaning stereotypes. Unlike ethnicity, race is always about creating and maintaining a caste system.[16] The default presumptions we make about physical features automatically revealing inherent truths about a person have a pecking order.[17] That ranking is socially understood as a racial order. The racial social meanings are so deeply entrenched that even individuals without the physical markers are exposed to derogatory stereotypes when their ancestral connections are revealed.

While racial group members in particular geographic spaces can, over time, come to identify themselves as culturally different, racial groups, unlike ethnic groups, have no single culture. Thus, for example, the Black culture of US African Americans is not the same in the South as in the North, and is also distinct from that of Afro-Colombians, Afro-French, Afro-Koreans, and so on. But across all those distinct cultural spaces, racialized physical markers create common experiences of social marginalization.

Racial Blackness and the term "Blacks" in this book thus includes not only African Americans but Afro-Latinos as well. Afro-Latino poets, novelists, and memoirists have long depicted this duality. Their numbers include but are not limited to writers like Elizabeth Acevedo, Jaquira Diaz, Junot Diaz, Dahlma Llanos-Figueroa, Marianela Medrano, Willi Perdomo, Spring Redd, Daniel Serrano, and Piri Thomas.[18]

Yet our national conversations about racism appear oblivious to this fact apart from a few notable exceptions.[19] This disregard is a problem. The lack of public awareness cannot be justified with the presumption that the plight of Afro-Latinos simply duplicates caste system problems among other groups (such as color hierarchies among Indo-Americans or African Americans and the interethnic tensions between Serbians and Croatians, Tutsi and Hutu, or Irish Americans and Italian Americans at the turn of the nineteenth century). An important distinction is that Latino anti-Blackness is not publicly acknowledged as a problem like other caste systems, and when instances of Latino anti-Blackness are called out, they are deemed inconsequential.

Nevertheless, the societal befuddlement about who Afro-Latinos are does not change the fact that Latino life circumstances are influenced not only by the social meaning of being of Hispanic ethnic origin but also by physical markers of Blackness in skin color, facial features, and hair texture.[20] Visible facial connections to Africa racialize a Latino as also Black. Indeed, the constrained socioeconomic status of Afro-Latinos in the United States is more akin to that of African Americans than to other Latinos or White Americans. Latinos who also identify themselves as racially Black often have lower incomes, higher unemployment rates, higher rates of poverty, less education, and fewer opportunities and are more likely to reside in segregated neighborhoods than those who identify themselves as White Latinos or "other."[21] In addition, Afro-Latinos report greater racial harassment from law enforcement and involvement with the criminal justice system.[22]

Just the same, publicly identifying as Black is immaterial to how African ancestry adversely affects a Latino's socioeconomic status and psychological health.[23] (The Latino cultural pressure to reject Black racial identities will be addressed in chapter 6 in the discussion of census racial-category politics.) Those who appear to others as Afro-Latino, have meager access to health insurance and health services in ways that parallel the disparate health outcomes of African Americans.[24] These racially distinctive health-related outcomes exist among Latinos even as they share common foods and other cultural commonalities. For instance, in Puerto Rico, high blood pressure rates vary based on skin color. Those perceived as Afro–Puerto Rican have higher blood pressure levels and rates of hypertension than Puerto Ricans socially perceived as more European descended.[25] Furthermore, socially perceived Blackness is more predictive of Latino mental health status than Latino racial self-identification.[26] Given the significance of how much African phenotype, hair and skin shade, influence the socioeconomic status of Latinos, some researchers suggest that interviewer observations of racial appearance provide the most accurate tool for monitoring discrimination among Latinos of varying shades.[27] Despite mounting evidence that there are distinct social outcomes based on intermarriage, housing segregation, educational attainment, prison sentencing, and labor market access that vary for Latinos according to externally perceived racial status, the unequal treatment of Afro-Latinos is invisible in our public discourse with its reference to all Latinos regardless of appearance as "brown."[28]

Hidden from view is the way Latino disregard for Blackness plays a role in the subordinated status of Afro-Latinos and in turn the exclusion of African Americans. Latino workplace supervisors deny both groups of Blacks access to promotions and wage increases. Latino homeowners turn away Black prospective tenants and home purchasers. Latino restaurant workers block Black customers from entry and refuse to serve them. Latino students bully and harass Black students. Latino educators belittle Black students. Latino police officers assault and kill Blacks. Most heinous are the Latinos who join violent White power organizations and harm Blacks. However, even when Latinos do not racially identify as White, like a White Supremacist, their identities as solely Latino do not mitigate the aforementioned instances of anti-Blackness.

Yet, many Latinos deny the existence of prejudice against Afro-Latinos and any "true" Latino racism against African Americans. This denial is rooted in the Latino *mestizaje* (racial mixture discourse) cultural notion that as a uniquely racially mixed people Latinos are incapable of racist attitudes. In turn, Latino *mestizaje* situates anti-Blackness as a culturally foreign North American construct learned only once in the United States when "racially innocent" Latinos encounter racist thinking for the first time.[29]

Latino racial innocence thus characterizes negative interactions with African Americans as either strictly moments of cultural misunderstanding, disputes over scarce resources, or generic interest-group political skirmishes. This stance of denial about Latino anti-Black racism is frequently accompanied with a reference to anecdotal descriptions of the many times Latinos and African Americans get along, collaborate, and live in neighboring areas. At the same time, Latinos dismiss the reported instances of discrimination against African Americans by Latinos as inconsequential as compared to the enormity of White non-Hispanic racism. In California, even the murder of African Americans with no gang involvement for the explicitly stated purpose of keeping Latinos segregated from Blacks has been characterized by Latino commentators as unrelated to histories of Latino anti-Blackness. In fact, there was a virulent Latino reaction when in a *Los Angeles Times* op-ed I dared to characterize the California murders as "Latino ethnic cleansing of African Americans from multiracial neighborhoods."[30] For example, one reader, Mario Ashla, wrote in to say:

> I take exception to [the writer's] conclusion that Latino-Black tensions are mainly rooted in Latino prejudice. A major flaw in [the writer's] thinking is equating Latino "racism" to the historical racism of the United States. Moreover, the majority of Latinos in the U.S. are racially mixed.[31]

Reader Adriana E. Padilla agreed and accused the op-ed writer (me) as being "way off" because "her historical analysis is irrelevant" to the context.[32] The hate mail I received was similarly imbued with outrage by my assertion that Latino anti-Black bias exists. Closer examinations of the violence suggest a more complex racial reality influenced by many factors and varying by context.[33]

Nonetheless, anti-Blackness persists as a relevant factor. For instance, when Latino-immigrant racial attitudes are compared to those of non-migrant Latinos still residing in the Dominican Republic, there is little difference in the degree and nature of anti-Black racial attitudes.[34] Thus, negative attitudes toward Blackness in general and Black Americans in particular develop long before immigrants land in the United States.

Strikingly, the negative racial stereotypes that Latino immigrants harbor can exceed those of US native-born Whites. Dominican immigrants in Boston and New York are significantly more likely to view Blacks as preferring to live off welfare.[35] Even younger generations with US bicultural frameworks have negative racial views shaped by their older relatives.

Yet, when any public or scholarly attention is focused on the subject of Latino–African American race relations, the predominant interest is in exploring the presumption that African Americans harbor resentment and bias against Latinos for "leapfrogging" over them in a competition for jobs and resources.[36] In fact, the disproportionate focus on African Americans as the cause of any perceived hostilities between Latinos and African Americans can itself be understood as part of the pervasiveness of anti-Blackness that quickly attributes the cause of bad attitudes as emanating from African Americans.[37] For this reason, I seek to balance the picture by exposing the role of Latino agency in manifestations of anti-Blackness.

I intentionally bring together the Latino discrimination against Afro-Latinos and African Americans for the purpose of disrupting the narratives that dismiss the significance of the bias each group experiences. First, the Latino bias against Afro-Latinos is dismissed as merely a part of the hierarchies internal to Latino communities that is not like the "real racism" that White non-Hispanics commit against African Americans. Second, the Latino bias against African Americans is dismissed as simply in-group favoritism or common interethnic group competition that is also distinct from the "real racism," that White non-Hispanics commit against African Americans. Unifying the analysis of Latino discrimination against both Afro-Latinos and African Americans helps illuminate the significance of Latino anti-Blackness as a contributing factor to the exclusionary actions Latinos take against *all* groups of Afro-descendants.

Given the state of denial about Latino anti-Black bias and the confusion about the existence of Afro-Latinos amid demonstrable harms to Black bodies caused by Latinos, it is crucially important to disrupt the status quo. In this book, I seek to intervene by introducing the world of law cases into the sociopolitical discussion of Latino racial attitudes. Why is that helpful?

News stories alone cannot be a corrective to ignorance about Latino anti-Blackness. Media outlets provide inconsistent coverage. And when journalists do choose to direct their attention to instances of Latino anti-Blackness, many Latinos and others dismiss the accounts as isolated incidents overblown by the press. Even firsthand accounts of Latino anti-Blackness provided in social media outlets have not fully disrupted the deficiencies of the public discourse on Latino racial attitudes. These social media sites include but are not limited to the *Black Latinas Know Collective* blog, the *Radio Caña Negra* podcast, and the Latinx Racial Equity Project training center.[38]

Bringing in legal case stories to be considered alongside the news stories dispels the notion that Latino anti-Blackness is a made-up problem. Civil rights law is the domain in which narratives about racial discrimination are formulated and its language is effectively deployed to clarify what is racially motivated bias. The language and grammar of antidiscrimination legal cases illuminate what is often obfuscated in societal deflection from the realities of racism. The book's cases navigate instances of individual-focused bias in addition to structural forms of discrimination, because Latino anti-Blackness is manifested in both forms.

This is not to say that law is perfect and always precise in its articulation. Nevertheless, the legal domain has the advantage of being the space in which long-standing attended focus has been dedicated to formulating devices for identifying and describing discrimination. In short, legal cases help illuminate the contours of Latino anti-Blackness because it is the public space dedicated to exposing and naming the harms of discrimination. As such, law has much to contribute to the limited number of sociopolitical discussions of Latino anti-Blackness that currently exist.

At the same time, I will also assess those instances in which judges misconstrue the manifestation and salience of Latino anti-Blackness. The jurisprudence of US antidiscrimination law has long understood Black to be solely a reference to African Americans and has viewed non-Latino Whites as the primary agents of discrimination. Within that context, Afro-Latinos asserting discrimination by other Latinos presents a conundrum that does not fit the traditional narrative of US discrimination. Afro-Latinos can thus be an enigma for the United States courts of law, just as the Latino expression of bias against African Americans can be judicially misunderstood. I aim for the book to deepen our understanding of the evolving challenges to antidiscrimination law in the face of the growing significance of Latino racial attitudes.

To be sure, educating legal actors and the greater public is not a cure-all, but it can certainly be part of the solution. Yet, assisting people in becoming literate in the existence of Latino anti-Black bias can be a tool for change only if it is accompanied by a critical engagement with how such bias adversely affects Afro-Latinos and African Americans in sustaining White supremacy. Social media campaigns to raise awareness about patterns of Latino preferences for identification with Whiteness and disinclination for Blackness, as much of the Afro-Latino consciousness-raising has done to date on Twitter, Facebook, and Instagram, is just the start of what is needed. In isolation, such information only serves to situate Latino anti-Blackness as a cultural prejudice detached from systems of racism. This is encapsulated by the adage that people of color can be prejudiced but they cannot be racists because they do not create or control systems of racism. The stories of discrimination in this book implicate a revision of that assumption.

When Latinos, and other people of color, for that matter, are active participants in the denial of access to an important life opportunity (a home, a job, an unimpeded education, entrance into public spaces, and freedom from violence) based on race, they are no longer just passive holders of an anti-Black cultural prejudice. They are part of the problem of racism. Certainly none of the victims of anti-Black bias in the narratives of discrimination shared in this book would be placated with the disclaimer "Your experience is not an example of racism because Latinos don't have the systemic power to be racists in White non-Hispanic created structures." One can immediately envision such a victim replying, "Oh, yeah? That so-called nonracist Latino is the one who oppressed me for being Black." A Latino claim of racial innocence in the racist world White non-Hispanics created in the United States is a thin reed of moral superiority when a Latino hand is the one forcefully slamming the door to Black inclusion.

Thus, this book is more than just a call for recognizing that Latinos can be prejudiced too. Rather, it is an entreaty for all future interventions into matters of racism to critically engage how Latinos (and many others) collaborate and sustain structures of racism. By recognizing they are part of the problem, interventions can also address them as part of the solution. Judges and juries can be taught to desist from being distracted by the "I can't be racist, I'm Latino" defense by instead using a critical race theory focus on the race-based patterns of exclusion and systemic inequality involving Latinos.[39] In short, dismantling racism in the United States requires that every component of its structures be taken apart—even the ones articulated in Spanish.

THE ORIGINS OF LATINO ANTI-BLACK BIAS

It is useful to first summarize Latin American and Caribbean perspectives about Afro-Latinos, that is, their own Afro-descendants, before discussing how those perspectives also inform Latino attitudes toward African Americans in the United States. The presentation of Latin American/Caribbean race ideology is not meant to suggest that all Latinos are racist and harbor these racialized perspectives or to insinuate that all Latinos think a particular way. Admittedly, group-focused discussions always run the risk of suggesting a fixed essentialized view of a group.[40] The research about Latino racial perspectives is provided to demonstrate the nature of Latino racial stereotypes of which legal actors in the United States may otherwise be ignorant. Recognizing and effectively addressing the discriminatory conduct of Latinos necessitates understanding how Latinos act upon such stereotypes and tolerate structures of racial inequality.

Racism, anti-Black racism in particular, is a pervasive and historically entrenched fact of life in Latin America and the Caribbean (even across the region's historical and sociopolitical variation).[41] Over 90 percent of the approximately 10.7 million enslaved Africans who survived the Middle Passage voyage were taken to Latin America and the Caribbean, whereas only .036 percent were taken to the United States.[42] As such, the legacy of slavery in Latin America and the Caribbean is similar to that in the United States: having lighter skin and European features increases the chances of socioeconomic opportunity, while having darker skin and African features severely limits social mobility.[43] The poorest socioeconomic class is populated primarily by Afro-Latinos, while the most privileged class is populated primarily by Whites; an elastic intermediary socioeconomic standing exists for some light-skinned (mixed-race) "Mulattos" and "Mestizos." For example, until the Cuban revolution in 1959, certain occupations used explicit color preferences to hire Mulattos to the complete exclusion of dark-skinned Afro-Cubans, based on the premise that Mulattos were superior to dark-skinned Afro-Cubans though not of the same status as Whites. Even with the socialist revolution's eradication of formal racial barriers, anti-Blackness continues to plague the lives of Afro-Cubans today.[44]

White supremacy is deeply ingrained and continues into the present. In sociologist Edward Telles's meticulous empirical investigation into contemporary racism in Latin America, his team of researchers found that skin color is a central axis of social stratification even when one controls for educational level and socioeconomic status.[45] In other words, the darker a person is in Latin America, the worse their access to opportunity as compared to those with lighter skin and the same educational level and socioeconomic status.[46]

Notwithstanding these racialized patterns, many people in Latin America point to the ubiquitous use of loving phrases referencing

Blackness as cultural evidence of the absence of racial discrimination. For instance, affection is expressed by stating, "that's my Black person" or calling someone "my little Black person." Even compliments directed toward those who are Black are reserved for those presumed to "supersede" their Blackness by having other "superior" traits. Such racialized compliments include "he is Black but has the soul/heart of a white"; "she is Black but good looking"; "he is Black but well-groomed and scented." This use of racialized language in terms of endearment, unconsciously invokes the paternalism of slavery's past. While such statements are not meant to carry racial malice, they still activate racial stereotypes about the inferiority of Blacks. In fact, these perspectives about persons of African descent are so embedded in the social fiber of Latin American societies that Blacks' subordinated status in society is viewed as natural and logical.

Even in Puerto Rico, where US antidiscrimination laws have been available because of this Spanish-speaking island's territorial status with the United States, Latin American racial pathologies persist. In a survey of college students in Puerto Rico, the overwhelming majority described "Puerto Ricans who are 'dumb' as having 'dark skin.'"[47] Conversely, the same students correlated light skin color with a description of "Puerto Ricans who are physically strong." Such racialized perspectives about African ancestry are not limited to college students. In 1988, when the presiding governor of Puerto Rico publicly stated, "The contribution of the Black race to Puerto Rican culture is irrelevant, it is mere rhetoric," it was in keeping with what social scientists describe as the standard paradox in Puerto Rico: Puerto Ricans take great pride in the claim of being the Whitest people of the Caribbean islands, while simultaneously asserting they are not racist. The pride of being a presumably White population is a direct reaction to the Puerto Rican understanding that "Black people are perceived to be culturally unrefined and lack ambition."[48]

Over thirty-one years later, another Puerto Rican governor would again be revealed as a racist in the debacle known alternatively as "Telegramgate," "Chatgate," and "RickyLeaks." On July 8, 2019, Puerto Rico's Center of Investigative Journalism released over eight hundred pages of a group chat between then governor Ricardo Rosselló and members of his staff on the messaging application Telegram.[49] Included within Governor Rosselló's homophobic and sexist message exchanges were racist comments about Afro-styled Black hair and the use of Aunt Jemima imagery to belittle the female mayor of San Juan, Carmen Yulín Cruz, whom he opposed. Protests broke out regarding the sexist messages that predominated. The Puerto Rican public was particularly galvanized to protest the jokes Rosselló made about impoverished islanders who died during Hurricane Maria. Because of the political scandal Rosselló resigned, but the racialized stereotypes he made use of continue to flourish. In this respect, the Puerto Rican example is emblematic of the racial attitudes throughout the Caribbean and Latin America.[50]

Moreover, as in the United States, those who disparage Black identity are not limited to Mulattos, Mestizos, and Whites but also extend to darker-skinned Afro-Latinos who can harbor internalized racist norms. Internalized racism can mean either internalized feelings of superiority and privilege or feelings of being less worthy, and racialized group members may experience all at the same time.[51] The Afro-Latino internalization manifests itself in a widespread concern among Afro-Latinos with the degree of pigmentation, width of nose, thickness of lips, and nature of one's hair—with straight European hair denominated literally as "good" hair. This concern with European skin and features also influences Afro-Latinos' assessments of preferred marriage partners. Marrying someone lighter is called *adelantando la raza* (improving the race) under the theory of *blanqueamiento* (whitening), which prizes the mixture of races precisely to help diminish the existence of Afro-Latinos.

Even in the midst of Latin American nationalistic emphasis on having individuals identify solely by their country of origin rather than by racial ancestry, distinctions are made about the diminished value of Blacks and Blackness. Indeed, it is even common within Latin America and the Caribbean to rank order the prestige of countries based on a color spectrum in which each country is racially identified.[52] In this way "nationality is a proxy for race" that embodies White supremacy. As a result, countries with a large percentage of Whites are valued while those with a large percentage of Blacks are discounted as "less cultured."[53] The attribution of a racial identity to countries, with nationality serving as a proxy for race, also permits a schizophrenic ability to cast racial aspersions about a person's background without ever openly discussing race. These proxies for race are deeply ingrained in Latin American/Caribbean national cultures.

FAMILY RACIAL TRAUMAS

As disturbing as is the anti-Black aspects of Latin American/Caribbean national cultures, for many Afro-Latinos the deepest racial scars are those inflicted within intimate familial structures.[54] When it comes to Latino racism, the family is the scene of the crime. Racial trauma is instilled when Latino parents show preferential treatment to children with lighter skin,[55] and consistently make negative appraisals of Black racialized facial features, skin color, and hair texture.[56] Contemporary Afro-Latino memoirs are replete with recollections of racialized familial slights and injuries targeting the darkest person in even the most diverse array of family skin shades. Afro–Puerto Rican sociologist Eduardo Bonilla-Silva describes the racially negative familial interactions as affecting a "soft segregation" of separation between darker- and lighter-skinned family members.[57] Large family gatherings like weddings are emblematic of this soft segregation that has darker family members seated at separate tables from lighter-skinned family members. Families thereby operate their own intuitive Jim Crow systems. The implicit justifications for the racial segregation are continually reinforced with racist comments about Black family members and Blackness in general. Bonilla-Silva recalls some of his aunts and even his own mother saying, "Eduardo, those [Black] people do not have class," and "You know, your [Black] aunt does not know better because she is accustomed to living in shit." Similarly, Marta I. Cruz-Janzen poignantly describes how her White Puerto Rican family members denigrated the Blackness of her Afro–Puerto Rican father and her siblings that inherited his brown skin tone, African facial features, and curly hair:

> We were *una pena* (a disgrace, sorrow, and shame). Both sides of the family continually judged our looks; whoever had the most clearly defined White features was considered good-looking. I was constantly reminded to pinch my nose each day so it would lose its roundness and be sharper like those of my [Whiter] brothers and sisters. My younger sister was openly praised for her long flowing hair while I was pitied for my *greñas* (long mane of tangly hair).[58]

Cruz-Janzen often overheard her White-skinned Puerto Rican relatives ask her mother in relation to her darker-skinned daughters: "How are you going to get them married?"[59] In a related vein, Cruz-Janzen's family constantly reminded her of her responsibility to marry someone lighter or, hopefully, White to improve the family's status. At the same time, she was also aware that for White Puerto Rican families "to actually bring a Black woman into the family through the sanctity of marriage is an unbearable public nightmare, . . . a real threat to the family's purity and public *honra* (honor)." Fellow Afro–Puerto Rican Lillian Comas-Díaz also recounts instances of family racial trauma starting from early childhood when her lighter-skinned brother repeatedly called her *moyeta* (Black and ugly).[60] In fact, Comas-Díaz identifies the Latino family as the major source of "racial rejection" of family members with visible African ancestry.[61] As Afro–Puerto Rican scholar Hilda Llorens notes about the Puerto Rican context, "Thousands of girls and women whose hair is other than straight suffer great psychic and psychological distress."[62]

Family dynamics often filter interactions through a screen that imbues Blackness as the source of all things negative. For example, when a colicky baby is disparaged as "*Esa prieta majadera*" (that bothersome Black female baby), the family thereby hammers in the denigration of Blackness.[63] This is also the case when family caregivers yell invectives such as "*Maldito sea este pelo*" (Damn this hair) while combing curly Afro-descended hair, and "*Cierra esa bemba*" (Close your large African lips) when silencing Black children,[64] or when the backs of babies' ears are examined for the dangerous development of future dark skin color.[65] In short, dark skin, curly hair, and African bodily features evoke familial expressions of ridicule, rejection, and hostility whereby the family nucleus is the incubator for inculcating anti-Blackness. Indeed, even Latino children as young as four years old have higher risks for mental health problems the darker their skin is.[66]

Upon adolescence, the familial vigilance against Blackness is intensified in the Latino project of pursuing and/or maintaining a semblance of Whiteness. The obsession with *mejorando y adelantando la raza* (improving and advancing the race) by marrying lighter and ideally Whiter partners means each potential suitor is sorted out for taints of Blackness. Afro–Puerto Rican anthropologist Maritza Quiñones Rivera keenly felt the familial pressure to date only White men. Yet, when she met the family of her first White Puerto Rican boyfriend, they called her "unintelligent, *negra sucia* dirty Black woman, and slut."[67] These racial boundaries are so deeply internalized that they transcend parental supervision and extend into the modernity of online dating.

In a study of Latino internet daters in Los Angeles, New York, Chicago, and Atlanta, it was found that across these diverse cities with Latinos from different ancestral countries of origin, Latinos prefer dating Whites and exclude dating Blacks at about the same rates. Fifty-seven percent of the Latinas and 44 percent of the Latinos in the study excluded Blacks as possible dates.[68] These rates approximate those of White non-Hispanic daters, where 66 percent of White non-Hispanic women and 56 percent of White non-Hispanic men exclude dating Blacks. To the extent that the study did not control for the skin shade or racial identity of the Latino respondents, it is also quite possible that the Black rejection rate is even higher among White-identified Latinos. For as Angela Jorge notes about family lessons in racism, "Any intimacy with a Black American . . . is absolutely taboo."[69] Indeed, a qualitative study of young adult children of Latino immigrants in Los Angeles suggests that immigrant parents send strong racialized messages about African Americans that deter their US-born Latino children from dating African Americans.[70]

It should not be surprising, then, that migrants from Latin America and the Caribbean travel to the United States with their familial and national culture of anti-Black racism well intact. In turn, this facet of Latino culture is transmitted to some degree to younger generations.[71] In one ethnographic study of Dominican racial identity within the United States, all the Dominican preoccupations with skin color and European phenotype honed in the Dominican Republic were readily apparent among the Dominican diaspora in the United States.[72] Similarly, interviews of Dominican clients at a hair salon in Washington Heights, New York, demonstrated the pervasive Latin American/Caribbean racialized denigration of curly African hair as "bad" and straight European hair as "good," along with the distaste for dark skin.[73] Thus, when Latinos are surveyed, Afro-Latinos indicate higher rates of racial discrimination based on their skin color as opposed to their socioeconomic status.[74]

Despite the long histories of anti-Blackness among Latin American and Caribbean populations, there is an inability, or perhaps an unwillingness, to perceive Latino racism in the United States. In US public discourse there is often a blanket acceptance of the Latin American myth that racism does not exist in Latin America and that racism is thus not part of the Latino migrant legacy across generations.[75] In turn, Latinos and the commentators who describe their racial attitudes tend to accept the related notion that any anti-Black sentiment expressed by Latinos in the United States is a consequence of learning the cultural norms of the United States and its racial paradigm.[76] However, a growing social science literature discredits that premise.

LATINO SOCIAL DISTANCE FROM AFRICAN AMERICANS

While the COVID-19 pandemic experience, beginning in 2020, made us all unfortunately familiar with the general idea of *social distance*, the term also has a particular meaning within studies of discrimination. The sociological concept of social distance measures the social unease that an ethnic or racial group has in interactions with another ethnic or racial group.[77] While social science studies of Latino racial attitudes are few and sometimes dated, those that do exist depict a consistent picture of a general Latino preference for maintaining social distance from African Americans.[78] It should be noted, however, that these studies rarely disaggregate their findings about Latino attitudes by Latino skin shade or racial identity apart from their Latino ethnicity.

Notably, immigrant status has been identified as influencing racial attitudes. The social distance level is largest for recent Latin American immigrants. A survey of six hundred Latinos (two-thirds of whom were Mexican, the remainder Salvadorian and Colombian) and six hundred African Americans in Houston, Texas, found that African Americans had more positive views of Latinos than vice versa.[79] While a slim majority of US-born Latinos did use positive identifiers when describing African Americans, only a minority of foreign-born Latinos did so. Of the foreign-born Latino respondents a typical statement was "I just don't trust them. . . . The men, especially, all use drugs and they all carry guns." It is thus not surprising that this same study found that although Latino immigrants live in residential neighborhoods with African Americans in the same proportion as US-born Latinos, 46 percent of Latino immigrants report almost no interaction with African Americans whatsoever.[80]

A later study of Houston-based Latinos continued to find that living in integrated areas with African Americans did not increase

Latino social contact and friendship with African Americans.[81] White non-Hispanic Houston residents were twice as likely as Latinos to have a Black friend, and four times as likely when compared to Houston's Latino immigrant population. Similarly, the Los Angeles Survey of Urban Inequality found that recent and intermediate-term Latino immigrants held the most negative stereotypes of African Americans.[82]

The social distance of Latinos from African Americans is consistently reflected in Latino responses to other survey questions.[83] In a survey of five hundred residents of Durham, North Carolina (equally divided among Latinos, African Americans, and White non-Hispanics), Latinos' negative stereotypes of African Americans exceeded those held by White non-Hispanics.[84] Specifically, a majority of Latino immigrants in the study—58.9 percent—said that few or almost no African Americans are hardworking. Fifty-seven percent said few if any African Americans could be trusted, and nearly one third said few if any African Americans are easy to get along with. In contrast, of the White non-Hispanics in the study, 9.3 percent said few African Americans work hard, 9.6 percent said African Americans could not be trusted, and 8.4 percent said African Americans were difficult to get along with.

US-born Latino racial attitudes are not so distinctive from that of Latino immigrants. More established communities of Latinos in the United States are also characterized by their social distance from African Americans. In interviews with Latinos living in New Orleans in 2015, the number of years lived in the United States did not impact Latino social distance from African Americans.[85] Regardless of place of birth or years living in the United States, the New Orleans Latinos interviewed who had lighter skin were the least prone to perceive commonality with African Americans while at the same time feeling little to no economic competition with them.

Mirroring such negative attitudes, Los Angeles Latinos are quicker to reject African Americans as neighbors compared to members of other racial groups.[86] Across the nation, Latinos indicate that African Americans are their least desirable marriage partners.[87] In contrast, African Americans are more accepting of intermarriage with Latinos.

Similarly, Latinos state they have the most in common with White non-Hispanics and the least in common with African Americans.[88] In contrast, African Americans respond that they feel they have more in common with Latinos and the least in common with Whites and Asian Americans. It is ironic that African Americans, who are publicly depicted as being averse to coalition building with Latinos, provide survey responses that are actually more in accord with socioeconomic data that demonstrates the commonality of African American and Latino communities. Meanwhile, Latino responses fly in the face of all the socioeconomic data demonstrating African American and Latino parallels.[89]

Although some might equate the Latino preference for White non-Hispanics over African Americans with the competition they perceive from African Americans in the labor market, the fact is that Latinos more frequently identify other Latinos as economic competitors rather than African Americans.[90] However, the greater the social distance Latinos prefer to maintain from African Americans, the more likely they are to see African Americans as competitors.[91] In other words, anti-Black animosity facilitates the perception of African Americans as an economic threat because prejudice contributes to perceptions of group threat and economic competition. This is particularly evident in the US South where African Americans are more numerous and the one region in which Latinos view African Americans as a greater source of economic competition.[92] In contrast, African Americans have a lower rate of viewing Latinos as economic competitors.[93] Latinos also attribute disorder to predominantly African American neighborhoods much more readily than do other racial or ethnic groups.[94] In fact, Latino stereotypes about African American neighborhoods more powerfully shape perceptions of disorder than actual observations of disorder.

There is a Latino affinity for White non-Hispanics over African Americans that is part and parcel of the Latino identification with Whiteness. Indeed, in contrast to the many reports of a Latino proclivity for mixed-race census racial categories, there is a strong Latino preference for the White racial category, and some Latino groups, like Cubans, disproportionately select that category.[95] When Latinos select a single fixed category, they disproportionately select White, as did 81 percent of Latino single-race box checkers on the 2020 census and as 92.3 percent did the decade before.[96] The White racial category is particularly preferred by recent immigrants of all skin-color shades.[97] And when later generations do move away from the White racial category, they do so in favor of collective national ethnic labels like "Latino" or "Hispanic."[98] This is exemplified by the 42.2 percent of Latinos on the 2020 census and the 36.7 percent on the 2010 census who selected the "some other race" option to write in an ethnic label like "Latino" or "Hispanic" or a national origin like "Peruvian" or "Guatemalan," rather than any other racial category.

In addition, when Latino census respondents alter their choice of racial categories from one census decade to another, they primarily do so by moving from "some other race" to White. For instance, 2.5 million respondents who said they were Hispanic and "some other race" on the 2000 census later told the census in 2010 that they were Hispanic and White.[99] In their pursuit of Whiteness, Latinos are the largest race or ethnic group to alter their selection of racial categories from one census year to another.

No wonder then that the default Latino media visual representation of Latino identity is a White face.[100] Even for those Latinos who do acknowledge their African ancestry, there is cultural pressure to emphasize their Latino ethnicity publicly as a mechanism for distancing themselves from public association with the denigrated societal class of African Americans.[101] This truism is highlighted by the popular refrain "The darker the skin, the louder the Spanish."[102]

The one area in which Latino anti-Black racism has at least
been raised in the United States is with respect to the apparent
racial caste system of Spanish-language television that presents
Latinos as almost exclusively White and Afro-Latinos as "margin-
ally Latino."[103] The Univision Afro-Latina newscaster unicorn Ilia
Calderon has Latino viewers who post social media messages saying, "Hispanics aren't black, YOU don't represent us on TV."[104]
Because of the scarce but derogatory images of Afro-Latinos in
the media, activists once lobbied the Puerto Rican Legal Defense
and Education Fund to consider a lawsuit against the two major
Spanish-language networks to challenge their stereotyped depiction of Afro-Latinos.[105] Some Latino activists see a direct parallel
between the Whiteness of Spanish-language television and Latino
politics. One such activist states:

> Latino leaders and organizations do not want to acknowledge
> that racism exists among our people, so they have ignored the
> issue by subscribing to a national origin strategy. This strategy
> identifies Latinos as a group comprising different nationali-
> ties, thereby creating the false impression that Latinos live in a
> color-blind society.[106]

Many concrete examples demonstrate that Latinos are not
color-blind. To begin with, darker-skinned Latinos and self-
identified Afro-Latinos in the United States experience color
discrimination at the hands of other Latinos. Tellingly, while
64 percent of them report experiencing discrimination, 41 percent indicate that the victimization is caused by other Latinos.[107]
Furthermore, despite variations across regions and ethnic groups,
the commonality of Latinos social distance in relations with African Americans remains constant. What follows is an exploration
of the social science literature that demonstrates the consistency
of anti-Black sentiment in various Latino communities across the
United States.

RACIAL ATTITUDES AMONG LATINOS ACROSS
ETHNIC GROUPS AND REGIONS

Of all the Latino ethnic subgroups, Mexican Americans have the largest demographic presence within the United States. As of 2020, the Census reports that of the sixty-two million Latinos who are 18.7 percent of the U.S. population, approximately 62.3 percent are of Mexican or Mexican American origin.[108] This large demographic presence represents not only contemporary immigration flows from Mexico but also the generations of Mexican Americans who trace their roots to the incorporation of Mexican lands into the United States after the 1848 Treaty of Guadalupe Hidalgo, which ended the Mexican American War.[109]

The development of Mexican American racial identity in the United States has been subject to a variety of influences. Prior to the Chicano movement of the 1960s, Mexican American leaders claimed that Mexicans were Caucasian and therefore deserving of the same social status as White non-Hispanics.[110] Latino race scholar Ian Haney López notes, "The Mexican American generation saw themselves as a White group. This self-conception both drew upon and led to prejudice against African Americans, which in turn hindered direct relations between those two groups."[111] A contemporary observer of the Chicano movement developments was Ruben Salazar, a *Los Angeles Times* journalist. Importantly, he noted that at the time many Mexican Americans still held on to "the idea that Mexican-Americans are Caucasians, thus White, thus 'one of the boys.'"[112] In addition, Salazar decried that "several of the more conservative Mexican-American leaders strongly [opposed] any 'mixing' of Mexican-American and Negro grievances."[113] Only after widespread police brutality and judicial mistreatment of Mexicans in the wake of the Black civil rights movement did a Chicano movement that stressed a non-White Chicano identity emerge.[114] Yet, this non-White identity focused upon Chicanos' indigenous ancestry and completely submerged their African ancestry.[115] Moreover, the social distance and negative attitudes about Blackness and African Americans continued.[116]

Chicanos in California and the Southwest in the 1960s and 1970s expressed feelings of cultural superiority with respect to African Americans that adversely affected intergroup interactions.[117] At the time, one Chicano college student summed up this sentiment when he wrote:

> We're not like the Negroes. They want to be White men because they have no history to be proud of. My ancestors come from one of the most civilized nations in the world.[118]

After the 1965 Watts urban uprising, such sentiments in turn fed Chicano resentment about the allocation of government funds in Los Angeles to service agencies catering to what Chicanos described as "less needy" African Americans.[119] Such perspectives have not greatly changed in the new millennium. In Los Angeles, where a predominant number of Latinos are Chicano, it has been observed:

> Many Latinos fail to understand the complexity and severity of the Black experience. They frequently bash Blacks for their poverty and goad them to pull themselves up like other immigrants have done. Worse, some even repeat the same vicious anti-Black epithets used by racist Whites.[120]

Thus, Fernando Oaxaca, a prominent Mexican American business executive and commentator in Los Angeles who founded the Republican National Hispanic Assembly and died in 2004, accounted for the difference in Latino and African American economic conditions with the explanation, "We have a work ethic."[121] Oaxaca's racialized attitudes exemplify the continuing ill effects of the historic positioning of Mexican Americans as racially White.[122]

Younger generations are not immune to anti-Black sentiment. Latino high school students in the Los Angeles town of Inglewood have brawled with African American students over several Black History Month celebrations.[123] The source of the violence is Latino teens' resentment at the month-long celebration of Black culture. In one instance, the principal of Inglewood High School simply decided to cancel the Black History Month celebration to avoid a repeat of the violence.[124]

Unfortunately, the interethnic teen violence has not been limited to Inglewood, in as much as "ethnic and racial tension comes to Los Angeles as regularly as the Santa Ana winds."[125] When Latino and Black students violently clashed at Poly High School in Long Beach in 2019, Black parents noted that it mirrored experiences they had at the same high school a generation before.[126] Many also recall the horror of the one-hundred-student fight at Jefferson High School in South Los Angeles between Latinos and Blacks in 2005.[127] Similar incidents have been reported at other area schools in South Los Angeles, the San Fernando Valley, San Bernardino County, Oakland, Rialto, and San Jacinto.[128]

Los Angeles Latinos have even proposed having block association meetings that exclude the African American residents of the block, prompting one African American resident to state, "It seems like the Latinos don't even want to try to forge neighborhood unity."[129] This social distance extends to congregations in which Latino and African American parishioners who share the same church attend separate services, serve on separate parish councils, and never meet.[130] It is interesting to note that notwithstanding when African American congregations in other areas of the United States have actively made it part of their ministry to reach out to their Latino neighbors, the social distance with Latinos remains.[131]

Ethnographic studies of Mexican Americans in Chicago and the southern states uncover the same disdain for African Americans.[132] As a Chicago-based Latino high school student said, "It's crazy. But a lot of the Hispanic kids here just don't want to be friends with the Blacks."[133] Adult Latinos in the South have mirrored this same racial hostility. In the North Carolina pork industry's rigid racial hierarchy, with job tasks assigned by race, Latino employees have aimed their venom at their African American coworkers rather than the injustice of all-White management ranks.[134] For instance, in reflecting on the hardships of working on the slaughterhouse assembly line, Mrs. Fernandez, a Mexican worker stated, "Blacks don't want to work. They're lazy." Her husband agreed and added, "I hate the Blacks."

A broader study of Latino racial attitudes in the rural South uncovered similar Latino anti-Black attitudes, exemplified by the observation "Hispanics come to this country and want nothing to do with Blacks. We don't want to socialize with them and be part of that world. Even in our own countries, we learn this. We learn we don't want to be a part of their community."[135] Metropolitan southern locations mirror the Latino anti-Blackness of rural ones. Thus in surveys of Latinos in Richmond, Virginia, the researchers found indicators of social distancing by Latinos in relation to Blacks and little interaction between the groups.[136]

The rare exception to the generalized pattern of anti-Black attitudes are when Afro-Latinos are solicited for their opinions. Thus, in interviews of Latinos in Winston-Salem, North Carolina, it is an Afro-Mexican man who uniquely states, "I've got a lot of Black friends. Black people here, they treat you like a friend, like a brother. White people here, they just treat you like another guy."[137]

Nor have the racial relations of Cubans with African Americans in Florida been much better. In fact, Miami (a city in which Cubans and other Latinos predominate and hold political power) has the distinction of being the only city that was the locus of four separate race riots in the 1980s.[138] The immediate causes of all four riots were police shootings of African Americans in which two directly implicated Latino police officers. Although police brutality against African Americans is endemic throughout the United States, Miami is a city with many Latino police officers and, more alarmingly, a Latino population seemingly indifferent to anti-Black police brutality.

When Colombian immigrant police officer William Lozano was found guilty of manslaughter for killing African American motorcyclist Clement Lloyd, the Latino community came out to protest the conviction.[139] Furthermore, Latinos publicly denounced the urban uprisings that marked each affront to the humanity of African Americans as the work of the "criminal element."[140] This is typical of how Latinos in Miami associate African Americans with crime, along with "an invidious comparison between Hispanic economic advancement—attributed to hard work, family values, and self-reliance—and Black dependency on welfare and other social programs."[141]

In contrast, studies of Puerto Rican relations with African Americans in the northeastern United States have often characterized the interactions between Puerto Ricans and African Americans as comparatively less contentious.[142] The larger presence of Afro–Puerto Ricans and culturally Black-identified Puerto Ricans in New York is one factor that mitigates the rates of anti-Black attitudes measured in surveys.[143] Puerto Ricans who also identify as Black more frequently live in neighborhoods with African Americans.[144]

Nonetheless as is so often the case with broad-based comparisons, important nuances can be underappreciated. The social distance between African Americans and Puerto Ricans and all other Latino ethnic groups is also affected by the situational and historical particulars in different regions.[145] In Miami and Los Angeles, the residential sprawl of the landscapes results in Latinos being typically more spatially segregated from African Americans. Whereas in New York, the urban density of the built environment has historically contained Puerto Ricans and African Americans in closer proximity to one another in ways that have fostered greater interaction and community.[146] The settlement of Puerto Ricans in New York also contrasts with the Midwest urban context of Chicago, where government officials sought to disperse Puerto Ricans into predominantly White neighborhoods on the city's North Side with the hopes of deterring the formation of "problematic"

Latino ghettoes.[147] The proximity of Puerto Ricans and African Americans in New York facilitated collaborative political activism during the 1960s' War Against Poverty and the struggle for quality public school education.[148]

However, even in New York and elsewhere, Puerto Ricans manifest anti-Black racism. Angela Jorge noted early on that Puerto Ricans are taught within their family circles to dislike African Americans.[149] Because of the anti-Black prejudice they harbor, Puerto Ricans are not eager to be identified with African Americans.[150] When Afro–Puerto Ricans are not part of the analysis, the measure of residential segregation between non-Black identified Puerto Ricans and African Americans in the United States is high.[151]

One observer of the civil rights coalitions historically formed between Puerto Ricans and African Americans has even gone so far as to claim that the coalition "was more of a strategic device than a factual description of the true nature of the relationship between the groups. Puerto Rican participation in civil rights organizations and on picket lines was lower than for Whites."[152] Indeed, Puerto Ricans from New York and the northeast were only 1 percent of the peaceful demonstrators at the 1963 March on Washington for Jobs and Freedom.[153] Furthermore, even though Puerto Rican youth organizations like the Young Lords in the 1960s and 1970s modeled themselves after the Black Panthers, some commentators report that the groups never had much contact with Black Power organizations.[154] As in New York, Chicago has also been the site of racial tensions between Puerto Ricans and African Americans over the competition for housing rehabilitation, in which Puerto Ricans have depicted African Americans as presumed gang members, criminals, and generally the cause of the tightening housing market.[155]

The concern with racial tensions between Latinos and African Americans does not dissipate when one examines Dominicans, who are frequently viewed as Black themselves.[156] In fact, Latinos with more pronounced African ancestry, such as Dominicans, more readily cite color discrimination as an explanation for the

bias they experience from other Latinos.[157] Yet, despite often sharing the more visible facial imprint of African ancestry with African
Americans, Dominicans and African Americans have a high level
of residential segregation from one another in New York City.[158]
Moreover, Dominicans have been reported to resent job competition from African Americans.[159] Incidents of high school violence
show Dominican youth and African American youth involved in
fierce clashes as well.[160]

In sum, much of the research regarding Latino racial attitudes to date indicates a lingering problem with Blackness across
various Latino communities. Nevertheless, this is a truth that
many Latinos do not acknowledge or view as significant. In turn,
US government public policies are developed in the absence of
a full understanding of Latino racial realities to the detriment
of racial progress. I seek to address the gap that exists between
the research regarding Latino racial attitudes and the politics of
how racial equality is addressed in public policy and law. In the
chapters that follow I examine legal cases and personal accounts
of racial discrimination that elevate concrete examples of how
Latino anti-Blackness is manifested in the contexts of schools,
public accommodations, the workplace, housing market, electoral politics, and the criminal justice system. Together, all the
narratives of individual and structural discrimination illuminate
the necessity for a critical consideration of Afro-Latino racial status, the anti-Blackness of Latinos, and the juridical "Latinos can't
be prejudiced" pseudo defense to racism. In the global effort to
dismantle all aspects of racial hierarchy and subordination, these
Afro-descendant discrimination stories need to be heard and considered. "Never again a world without us."[161]

A NOTE ABOUT THE TERM *LATINO*

This book uses the Spanish language term *Latino* for pragmatic
ease of presentation rather than all the current alternatives of *Hispanic, Hispano, Latina/o, Latin@, Latine,* or *Latinx.* The simplicity

of *Latino* as a term is also more inclusive of Latinos across generations and geographic spaces that have yet to embrace the explicitly
gender-inclusive *Latina/o* and *Latin@* or the gender-neutral *Latinx*
that has come to be adopted by college students and inhabitants
of some large cities.[162] Indeed, the Pew Research Center 2019 National Survey of Latinos found that only about 3 percent of Latinos use the term *Latinx*, while another 75 percent have never even
heard of the term.[163] *Latinos* also offers greater clarity for an audi-
ence not as familiar with the evolution in the multiplicity of identity terms.[164] The choice then to use the Spanish language *Latino*
is in no way a rejection of the inclusivity that the *x* suffix is meant
to offer but rather a recognition of its awkward English language
imposition on the architecture of the Spanish language.[165] My
hope is that all readers, regardless of their own choice regarding
terminology, will be able to appreciate what the book has to offer
at the same time that my own Mami recognizes her Afro-Latina
reality in its pages.

In addition, an honest account of Black realities also requires that
the linguistic details of how anti-Blackness is expressed be elaborated. However, this book uses "n———r" (and, for the audiobook,
the term "the N-word") rather than articulating the full racist expletive that is a constant feature of the narratives set forth within
the book. Recognizing how the unremitting use of the expletive
can feel like a racial assault for victims of racism, this book attempts not to participate in the cycle of racial trauma.

CHAPTER 2

"NO JUEGUES CON NIÑOS DE COLOR EXTRAÑO"

PLAYING AND LEARNING IN "WHITE" LATINO SPACES

Diciendo a su hijo de cinco años,
No juegues con niños de color extraño.

Telling her five-year-old son,
Don't play with children of a strange [non-White] color.[1]

Latinos learn the Latin American/Caribbean-style racial hierarchy rules in public leisure spaces and schools, the two spheres in which the rules are most intensely indoctrinated outside the home. These two spaces where people play and learn are intimately intertwined because even before a child begins school, they are first immersed in how public spaces are racialized. That some public spaces are understood and unquestioned as White spaces is implicitly established at a very young age (as mediated through adult caregivers) and serves to normalize school-based racial hierarchies.

The Latino formation of White Latino spaces in the United States is influenced by Latinos' implicit awareness of how Latin American and Caribbean geographies are racially structured and regulated. Latino White ruling elites, such as politicians, business leaders, and property owners, structure access to the spaces they own and frequent both in Latin America and in the United States. Indeed, traveling in much of Latin America and the Caribbean in a Black body can be disconcerting.

At the same time that there is great pleasure in seeing the vast numbers of Afro-descendants traversing the streets, there is also the jarring dislocation of noting their remarkable absence as consumers from many public spaces of leisure and entertainment. While the popular explanation for this duality is the entrenched convergence between skin color and socioeconomic status, there is also an active racial policing of public spheres that maintains them as elite White spaces. What is encouraging is that growing numbers of antidiscrimination law cases in Latin America challenge the exclusion of Afro-descendants in public accommodations such as dance clubs and banks.[2] What is telling, though, is how closely the Latin American case stories parallel the narratives of Latinos cultivating White Latino spaces in the United States and its territories.

The US territory of Puerto Rico is an appropriate place to begin to unpack the complexity of Latin American–influenced Latino construction and preoccupation with White spaces under US law. A possession of the United States since the Spanish-American War ended in 1898, and accorded United States citizenship pursuant to the 1917 Jones Act, Puerto Rico is subject to US federal civil rights laws. Like the rest of the Caribbean and Latin America, Puerto Rico has a long history of racial stratification stemming from its use of chattel slavery.[3] Puerto Rico's Spanish settlers extensively relied on chattel slave labor after having decimated the indigenous population in the early 1500s.[4] As a Spanish colony, Puerto Rico did not abolish slavery until 1873. Thereafter, the colonial racial hierarchy continued with a privileged White elite, an intermediate "buffer" class of persons of African ancestry with physically apparent European ancestry and a sizeable population of disempowered darker-skinned African descendants.[5] Indeed, when US troops invaded Puerto Rico during the Spanish-American War of 1898, they were warmly greeted by Puerto Ricans of African descent with US flags pinned to their clothing.[6] But after becoming subject to US governmental authority, Puerto Rican society continued to be racially stratified—and is so today.[7] This is the case despite the fact that Puerto Rico's legislature had instituted a variety of measures to address race discrimination as early as 1943, long before the US federal government enacted the Civil Rights Act of 1964.[8]

Puerto Rico has long occupied a legal and cultural hybridity. It is a Spanish-speaking territory with its own codified local laws influenced by the Spanish Civil Code, and it also is subject to US federal law, such as US antidiscrimination legislation.[9] This is why Puerto Rican cultural practices of racism can be vetted with an application of US–based civil rights law. Let us consider then how this is manifested in the legal mandate for racially equal access to public spheres for socializing, known as "public accommodations law" (encompassing restaurants, night clubs, hotels, service centers, and recreational facilities).[10]

Fridays in Puerto Rico are affectionately called "Viernes Social" (Social Friday), when coworkers and friends meet after work to socialize over a cocktail and sometimes dinner. One such Friday, friends Héctor Bermúdez Zenón, Jaime Tosado Martínez, and Pedro Mantilla met at Restaurante Compostela in San Juan city's center to enjoy a Viernes Social dinner together.[11] Since they were meeting after work, they were dressed in semiformal attire, as were the other patrons of the restaurant. However, this group of friends did stand out from all the other customers. Two of them were Afro–Puerto Rican and the third a White Puerto Rican. Compostela, a restaurant owned by White Spaniards Maximino Del Rey and Jose Manuel Del Rey, was like so many other upscale and elegant spaces in Puerto Rico, populated with White-presenting Puerto Ricans. Héctor Bermúdez Zenón was already accustomed to the White exclusionary spaces of Puerto Rico because of his elite professional life as an engineer on the island. However, Héctor implicitly expected that his elite education, career accomplishments, and professional attire would smooth his access into Puerto Rico's racially exclusive recreational spaces.

Therefore, Héctor and his multiracial group of friends were not alarmed when they were asked to wait in the restaurant's bar area until a table would become available for dinner. Compostela was a popular restaurant, and they understood some waiting might be required. They waited three hours. Three hours in which they were catching up on each other's news but also noticing that White patrons who arrived after them were promptly provided with seats and service. When Héctor and his friends asked why they were uniquely experiencing such a long wait, the restaurant staff then stated that the restaurant required advance reservations to be seated for dinner. Mystified as to why the restaurant had not immediately stated that this was their policy, the friends exited the restaurant. But rather than drive away, they called the restaurant and asked about being able to have dinner there that evening. No reservations were required—is what the restaurant indicated on that telephone call, moments after the group had been denied access.

Thus, just as in Latin American public accommodations discrimination cases where a race-neutral reason is articulated as the denial for Black access (reservations needed, formal attire required, private club, private function, and so forth), the Compostela restaurant engaged in similar racial sorting. Fortunately for Héctor and his friends, they were able to file a claim for discrimination in the US federal court in Puerto Rico. When the restaurant owners sought to have the case dismissed, the judge did not agree that the case was not a viable claim of discrimination and the restaurant entered into a settlement agreement with Héctor and his friends.

Unfortunately, few instances of public accommodations discrimination ever get reported and sanctioned by a court. Officially reporting an incident of public exclusion means having to acknowledge the racial insult in a way that can aggravate the pain. Many people in Puerto Rico (and elsewhere) instead choose to bury the memory of the exclusion and reorder their lives to studiously avoid encroaching upon White spaces where they anticipate not being welcome. Afro-Latina sociologist Zaire Dinzey-Flores offers a poignant account of such racial survival choices.

> One night, when I was about eleven, my sister and I and other children were picked up in a car by a classmate's mother, for whom race did not seem to matter much (for friendship, that is), for a "disco party" at a private country club called El Club Deportivo. Some of us were members, some were not. Every child was admitted hospitably, except for my sister and me. The guard at the gate told us we could not enter. Our classmate's mother drove us home. Days later, after another white parent complained, the club sent a note of apology and promised free admission to the next disco party. We did not try again.[12]

Countless instances of this kind of exclusion happen and can be devastating to a child's self-esteem and psyche.

Notably, the Latino racial sorting of public spaces is not limited to the White Latino environs of Puerto Rico. Latino-dominated public spaces in the continental United States, like Miami and New Mexico, have also been beset by reported Latino anti-Black exclusionary tactics. Miami is a city long known for the density and growth of its Latino population. In 2019, the US Census Bureau estimated that Latinos constitute 72.7 percent of the city's population.[13] As of the 2020 Census, Latinos are 68.7 percent of all of Miami-Dade County.[14] With such Latino demographic presence, it is understandable why Miami is referred to as the "capital of Latin America."[15] As in Latin America, in Miami White Latinos attain higher economic outcomes than Black Latinos.[16] Moreover, the socioeconomic advantage of White Latinos persists even when their educational attainment is only slightly higher than that of Black Latinos. The racial replication of Latin American racial spaces in Miami is why Latino racial attitudes are integral to understanding how racial discrimination unfolds in the city. Indeed, when political scientist Mark Sawyer sought to explain the

particularities of Miami's Latino racism, he began the essay with a
public accommodations discrimination vignette.

> In Little Havana, Miami, a young Afro Cuban woman went
> into a "Cuban" hair salon seeking to make an appointment. She
> politely asked in Spanish how she might make an appointment
> to have her hair done. The proprietor of the salon snapped
> back in English, "We don't work on Black hair here—you will
> have to go somewhere else." The women in the salon went
> back to conversing in Spanish and the Afro Cuban woman left
> dejected.[17]

The following legal account of how discrimination in a national restaurant chain surfaced "Latino style" in a Miami location
further elaborates the details of Latino anti-Blackness. Four years
after the national restaurant chain Denny's agreed to pay $54 mil-
lion to settle the discrimination lawsuits of thousands of African
American customers who had been refused service or had been
forced to wait longer or pay more than White customers, one of
its Miami Latino-run branches continued its racially exclusionary practices. Despite the national court order and the company's
diversity training for its employees, along with a newly consti-
tuted in-house monitoring system for random checks, Latino
anti-Blackness at Denny's continued.[18] In 1994, the Denny's settlement was the largest and broadest settlement under the federal
public-accommodation laws, thereby making the 1998 Miami incident that much more disturbing.

On January 2, after working a four p.m. to midnight shift as
correctional officers at the Everglades Correctional Institution, a
group of nine uniformed coworkers gathered at a Miami Denny's to celebrate the holidays together. Six of the nine coworkers
were African American (Nicole Channer, Sylvia Clinch, Clifford
Fortner, Vickie Kendrick, Maryline Laroche, and Aaron Wright)
and the other three, White (Daniel Carpenter, Francis Tulino,
and Alma Waters). After they were seated the server returned to

their table and claimed that the restaurant was out of food. Such a claim was belied by the restaurant's own records, which indicated that customer traffic was sparse at the time and only eight customers had been served between midnight and 1:00 a.m., despite the restaurant's capacity for 143 customers. Because the group could see that other customers were being served and that cooks were preparing food in the kitchen, they asked to speak to the manager for further explanation. Inopportunely, it was Latino Carlos Ibarra who was the manager on duty at that time. Rather than following the established Denny's "Don't Fight, Make It Right" instructions for handling customer complaints, Ibarra escalated the situation.

Ibarra insisted that the restaurant was completely out of food, that the group could call the restaurant's 1-800 number if they had a complaint. He then informed the group that he would not speak with them any further, the restaurant was now closed, and they would "have to leave." No explanation was provided for why the restaurant was closing when its hours were posted as being open twenty-four hours a day or why they were initially seated after the presumable closing hours. Ibarra then physically escorted the group out of the restaurant and locked the door, as he said to them "You don't look right together." As the coworkers were all still in their correctional officer (CO) uniforms, the most significant difference in their appearance was their skin color and gender. Yet, while many of the customers inside the restaurant were surely mixed-gender groups, none of them were African American. Moreover, when CO Laroche called the restaurant from the parking lot after the group was ejected from the premises, the restaurant employee on the telephone stated that the restaurant was indeed open but that a few items on the menu were not available. While waiting in the parking lot, the coworkers observed a group of five or six White Latina customers arrive, for whom Ibarra unlocked the door, then ushered them into the restaurant. All of which had African American CO Fortner reconsider what he had been told a month earlier, when he had previously tried to eat there and was told that "the stove was broken."

Given Denny's earlier national notoriety with racial discrimination, it would be easy to attribute manager Ibarra's behavior to the chain's previous manager training in how to deal with "blackout," the company code word for what they felt were too many Blacks in the restaurant at one time.[19] However, after Ibarra banished the multiracial group of COs from the restaurant, three of the African American COs headed over to another Denny's location in the suburban Miami Lakes area. There the African American COs were admitted and served without question that same evening. It appears that only the Denny's Ibarra managed was now barring Black patrons in Miami. As part of its management training, Denny's had provided Ibarra two separate sessions on its nondiscrimination policies, along with instruction on the corporate policies of protocols for customer incident reports and never improperly locking restaurant doors. Ibarra flagrantly violated all these Denny policies and lied to the COs about the nonexistence of food that evening, as he insisted that the multiracial gathering of friends "don't look right together." When the COs filed their lawsuit for discrimination, Denny's chose not to defend Ibarra. Instead, Denny's regional manager suspended Ibarra. After Denny's conducted an investigation they terminated Ibarra. All of which underscores the significance of Ibarra's actions as a Latino manager separate from Denny's prior history. As a result, the court awarded each of the COs financial compensation for the racial exclusion they experienced.

While no other city in the contiguous United States has a nickname akin to Miami's "capital of Latin America," others do have significant Latino populations in which anti-Black sentiment can influence how public space is regulated. In fact, as early as the 1930s, Afro-Cuban Evelio Grillo observed how the Cuban émigré clubs in Tampa, Florida, did not admit Afro-Cubans.[20] When the new century arrived, it was accompanied by the same White Latino exclusion of Afro-Latinos in Tampa and elsewhere.[21]

Like Tampa and Miami, Chicago is a city with a density of Latino residents living and working in Latino enclaves. Within such ethnic enclaves, Latino ownership of restaurants and shops is not unusual. Unfortunately, the Latino ownership of such venues of leisure and commerce has also been accompanied by a Latino culture of anti-Blackness against Afro-Latinos and African Americans alike.

Afro-Latino Eric Trujillo felt the chill of anti-Black animosity when he sought to have lunch at the Mexican restaurant Cuauhtemoc.[22] Upon seating himself at a table, Eric waited for forty-five minutes while the Latina owner, Martha Perez, and a waitress looked at him and whispered between themselves rather than approach his table for service. After observing at least ten other patrons who appeared to be of Latino descent enter the restaurant after he did and be greeted politely and served quickly, Eric raised his voice to attract the waitress's attention. When the waitress asked Eric for his food order, she did so from a distance of three feet from his table. When the food arrived, the waitress pushed it across the table as if Eric was diseased. None of the non-Black Latino patrons were treated with the discourtesy aimed at Eric, the only person of African descent in the restaurant. While Eric did not suffer any out-of-pocket expenses from the long wait for service, the Chicago Commission on Human Relations concluded that the racial humiliation the restaurant caused him warranted financial compensation to him along with paying the City of Chicago its maximum fine.

In addition to compensation for emotional distress and administrative fines, victims of discrimination can also be awarded punitive damages when the racist conduct is especially outrageous. Edna Pryor and Emma Boney are two Chicago residents who experienced such outrageous conduct when attempting to shop at Cirilo Echevarria's retail clothing store Passion for Fashion/ Casa Echevarria.[23] When Edna, a Jamaican woman, entered Casa Echevarria, store owner Echevarria demanded that she check her bag. Edna explained that she did not have any bags and was only carrying her purse, which she did not wish to check. Rather than acknowledge Edna's common-sense concern for the security of her purse contents (a wallet, identification, and personal items), Echevarria instead ordered Edna out of the store, stating that he did not want "N——rs" in his store. When Edna later returned with her friend Emma Boney (who is African American), Echevarria escalated into declaring that his business was not for Black people, and again stating that he did not wish to have "N——rs" in his store. He refused to talk to Edna and Emma, and instead shouted at them to "get out," as he escorted them to the door.

Even though neither Edna nor Emma incurred any out-of-pocket expenses from the incident, the Chicago Commission on Human Relations decided that Echevarria's egregious display of Latino anti-Blackness warranted the imposition of a financial penalty for the emotional distress Echevarria caused to both Edna and Emma. Moreover, the commission awarded punitive damages to both Edna and Emma, along with imposing a fine on Echevarria payable to the City of Chicago.

Chicago Latino anti-Blackness is not restricted to establishments that Latinos own but also infects Latino operations of national and local chain establishments. Bernie Andrews was an African American slapped with the indignity of Latino anti-Black exclusion and hostility when he entered a McDonald's franchise located in the Jefferson Park area of Chicago's North Side.[24] While Jefferson Park has long been noted as a vibrant Polish American residential neighborhood with a sizeable number of Irish Americans as well, the Latina manager of the local McDonald's seemingly took it upon herself to police the space as a *Whites-only* eatery.

Bernie was able to enter the restaurant and eat his meal. However, the law is still violated when a customer is treated differently due to race after being admitted and served. Once he finished his meal, Bernie entered the restroom, and while there its Latina manager entered and sarcastically asked him if he was taking a bath. She then told him, "Get out, n——r," and exited. As Bernie continued to wash his hands, two other female employees opened the door to the men's room, and through the open door he saw the manager speaking to a Latino patron. Upon speaking with the manager, the Latino patron entered the bathroom and bumped Bernie. He then placed his right hand in his coat pocket, feigning that he had a weapon, while interrogating Bernie with the questions: "Why are you bothering that lady, Old Pop? N——r, why don't you go back to the South Side where you belong?"

When the McDonald's franchise owner attempted to have the case dismissed as lacking merit, the Chicago Commission on Human Relations disagreed and refused to dismiss the case. The commission concluded that it could be reasonably inferred from the allegations not only that the Latina manager had racially harassed Bernie with her verbal assault but that she also had requested or condoned the Latino patron's racial harassment. After the commission refused to dismiss the case, the parties decided to forgo further proceedings, as is often the case when litigants resolve a claim among themselves with a settlement agreement.

Unfortunately, patrons like Bernie can be accosted by Latino anti-Black bias even outside cities like Chicago and Miami, which are known for having a density of Latino residents living and working in Latino ethnic enclaves. For instance, Carlsbad, New Mexico, is a city whose mineral-extraction-based economy and state parks tourism are not accompanied by the same acclaim as Miami. Yet, it too is populated with a significant number of Latinos. The 2000 census listed Latinos as 36.7 percent of the Carlsbad population.[25] By the 2010 census that number increased to 42.5 percent, and the 2019 American Community Survey estimated an increase to 51.5 percent.[26] While Carlsbad may not be confused for Miami, its Latinos are numerous enough to influence how racism is experienced. Grant Pirtle is an African American resident of Carlsbad who felt the sting of Latino anti-Black exclusion despite being married to a light-skinned Latina woman.[27]

One Saturday afternoon, Grant Pirtle entered Allsup's Convenience Store located on National Parks Highway and attempted to make a purchase, the total cost of which was $7.63. Grant handed over a five-dollar bill and three one-dollar bills from change he had received during an earlier purchase at a Chevron gas station.

When presented with the eight-dollar tender, the White Latina cashier, Mary Jane Celaya, examined the five-dollar bill in the light and stated that the bill was counterfeit. Grant then offered her a ten-dollar bill and twenty dollars. Celaya then proceeded to rub the bills with her hand and concluded that all of Grant's money was "counterfeit and no good," even though she did not examine the one-dollar bills.[28] Nor did she employ any of the official store protocols she had been taught for dealing with suspected counterfeit bills (and which were conveniently listed on a poster next to her cash register). The protocols include different features for detecting counterfeit bills and the actions to take, such as "Keep the bill from the passer," "Delay the passer with some excuse if possible," "Telephone the police or the U.S. Secret Service," and "Write your initials and the date on the border of the bill and surrender the note only to the police or Secret Service." Celaya's failure to follow any of these store procedures suggests that her stated concern with counterfeit bills was itself manufactured. She then topped off her performance by removing the items Grant wanted to purchase out of his reach and behind the counter.

Blocked from any means of making a purchase at the store and mortified by Celaya's deep-seated suspicion of him as a customer, Grant left the premises. Plagued by the public humiliation that Celaya subjected him to, Grant decided to return to the Chevron convenience store at which he received the proclaimed counterfeit bills. Grant related the difficulty he encountered with Celaya, and the Chevron clerk examined the money and used a special marker to determine if the bills were counterfeit. Using the marker, the Chevron clerk was able to definitively conclude that the bills were not counterfeit. In fact, when Grant entered a different convenience store that day, he successfully made a purchase with the same bills Celaya had refused to accept.

Grant then returned to Allsup's Convenience Store and asked Celaya how Allsup determines counterfeit money. Celaya responded that there is no formal method in place and that she could tell "just from the feel of it."[29] Grant asked to speak to a manager, and Celaya obstructed him at every turn by first claiming there was no manager in the store, that there were no managers at any of the other Allsup's locations, and finally that she could not call over the assistant manager who was actually in the store, because he was busy and could not talk to Grant. Celaya's coup de grace was to order Grant to leave the store.

Grant went home to his wife, Yolanda Pirtle, and told her about the incident that was still upsetting him. Yolanda decided to return to the store and see whether Celaya would treat her any differently as a light-skinned Latina. Celaya not only refrained from asking Yolanda any questions about the bills she tendered, she also accepted the bills and permitted Yolanda to successfully complete her purchase. The bills Celaya accepted from Yolanda without question, were the very same bills she rejected outright from Grant as presumably counterfeit. Grant submitted a complaint to the New Mexico Human Rights Division. The division conducted their own investigation and concluded that there was probable cause to assert a discrimination claim. Thereafter, Grant filed a lawsuit in federal court, and a settlement agreement was reached.

Viewed as a whole, the public accommodation case examples demonstrate that elite and nonelite Latino-dominated public spaces, from upscale gourmet restaurants to midlevel chain restaurants to highway convenience stores, are all subject to being racially policed. Yet, when confronted with accounts of discrimination, people often respond with expressions of hope that education and the progression of time will effectuate social change. That reaction may be sincere and well intentioned, but it misses how even the educational context can be riddled with hierarchy producing anti-Blackness. What the following narratives underscore is that unraveling the roots of racial discrimination must be intentional to be effective, because the status quo operation of our educational environments are not always equipped to disrupt Latino anti-Black bias.

THE EDUCATIONAL SPACE

While college campuses often pride themselves as being at the forefront of promoting public conversation about racial diversity, Afro-Latino college students have reported that on campus "Latino spaces have always been the most violent."[30] A 2017 study of Afro-Latino college-student interviews, blog posts, and focus groups found that most had strong feelings of social exclusion from other Latinos in their colleges. As one participant noted:

> My entire life, Latino spaces have always been the most violent for me. To this day, I can't enter a space where there are only Latinos. Even though everyone knew I was on the board [of a Latino college student group], I'm at every meeting, this one girl looked uncomfortable with my presence, but I don't think she really realized that that's what her face looked like as soon as I walked into the room, but it's like I know that face well enough to know exactly what you're thinking right now and what your discomfort means in this space and why.[31]

Similar findings were found again in 2020 interviews of Afro-Latino students attending a small, urban, commuter public college in the New York Metropolitan area.[32] The common theme across all the interviews was the anti-Blackness the students experienced from their fellow Latino students who mocked them as being *too Black* in appearance to claim a Latino identity. "They'd make fun of me, like you aren't Latina."[33]

This also accords with research that indicates that Latino student involvement in majority-Latino college-student organizations significantly increased the odds of in-group harassment.[34] Such insights help explain earlier findings that the skin color of immigrant Latina college students impacts their self-perception.[35] The darker-skinned Latina-immigrant college students had lower self-esteem as compared to the lighter-skinned Latina-immigrant college students.

As an antidote, education researchers recommend specific interventions. They exhort higher education practitioners to become knowledgeable and aware of both colorism within the Latino community and microaggressions against Afro-Latino students. With this knowledge, educators will be empowered to intentionally foster learning environments that challenge anti-Black racism among Latino students. In addition, it is advisable to encourage "collaboration and dialog between Latino and Black student groups [particularly because] those who are themselves victims of discrimination can also be victimizers of others who are perceived to hold even more racially subordinate positions."[36]

Similar interventions have also been recommended with respect to tensions between Latino and African American college students. Patricia Literte's study of public university students in California observed that racial stereotyping among the Latino students fostered anti-Black sentiments. "Nancy, a Mexican American student, described the stereotypes: 'Basically, Blacks are very loud and always pick fights.'"[37] Literte concludes that universities should be proactive in easing Latino versus African American tensions by implementing conflict resolution and peace-building programs. Case filings data indirectly suggests that such conflict resolution programs are desperately needed. But first a few words about the case records.

US federal and local laws protect the privacy of students who file discrimination claims, and for that reason the public records about the lawsuits are quite barebones. Absent consent from the complainant, government agencies, like the federal Office of Civil Rights in the Department of Education that administer the discrimination claims, are prohibited from publicly disclosing the complainant's name and personal information.[38] As a result, the publicly available data for the Office of Civil Rights (OCR) lists all pending cases only by the name of the institution sued.[39] Searching for Latino-specific claims in the public OCR data is thus impracticable. Public access becomes feasible only when complainants (or minors represented by their parents) decide to use their resources to continue their fight in federal court and to disclose their identity.

Local agencies that enforce state and municipal antidiscrimination law often refrain from even publicly posting their list of pending cases. After a Freedom of Information Law (FOIL) request for further information, one such agency, the New York State Division of Human Rights, indicated privacy law permitted them to release only a list of cases the agency had reached a final determination on. Between 2010 and 2020, the agency flagged forty-five final determinations related to Latino bias against Afro-Latinos and African Americans. That still leaves an entire universe of pending cases. But one immediate pattern is evident—at least 58 percent of the relevant final determinations were cases filed in the higher education setting, whereas only 42 percent related to the K–12 setting. All of which suggests that the higher education setting could greatly benefit from the Latino-Black conflict resolution interventions that commentators have recommended. This is underscored by the anti-Blackness of Latino college educators that Afro-Latino peers have witnessed.[40]

However, the K–12 educational context presents an even more aggravated set of circumstances. The educational studies literature has tended to focus on how Latino and African American communities are pitted against one another as competitors for scarce resources in under-resourced schools into which children of color are segregated from White students in better funded public schools.[41] Educational scholarship has spent less time discussing the physical clashes between Latino and African American students. Yet in California in particular, at least ten different high schools as described in chapter 1 have been the center of Latino versus Black violence that has had little to do with the strategic skirmishes of leaders of color seeking political control of public institutions.[42] In other words, segregated public schools can be "a venue for the negotiation of power, resources, and control among minority populations within a community," but that is not what directly instigates the inter-racial violence among student populations.[43]

One incident that especially stands out as an example is that of Samohi High School in Santa Monica, California, where in 2005 it took twenty-six police officers half an hour to settle a riot with the aid of police reinforcements from other area police departments.[44] Initially there was a fight in the school cafeteria between an African American student and a Latino student, after which a crowd of two hundred students rushed the scene for what they expected would be another lunchtime fight between African Americans and Latinos as had occurred in the past. This was not related to gang-on-gang violence. One African American student expressed fear for his safety because Latino students "who have graduated from Samohi often get involved, showing up after school and line up waiting to pick a fight with black kids. They just don't like each other. It ain't never gonna stop." Indeed, thereafter then mayor Antonio Villaraigosa himself had to intervene after more high school brawls broke out between Latinos and African American students.

These concerns are not limited to California. In fact, education specialist David Stovall cautions that it is very important to note regional specificities when examining the issue of Latino anti-Blackness in school settings.[45] Historical migration patterns and the variation in segregated spaces across the country influence when, how, and against which Afro-descendant populations Latino anti-Blackness is manifested. In Chicago, where Professor Stovall has both researched and worked as a K–12 teacher, he has observed waves of clashes between Latino and African American students, from the late 1990s, 2000s, and again in the 2010s. With each wave of violence, Chicago public school officials would attempt to mitigate the racialized confrontations by designating separate school entrances for students arriving from the south of Chicago and those arriving from the north of Chicago. The intense residential segregation of Chicago guaranteed that the separate entrances would act as de facto "African American

only" versus "Latino only doors" for these students arriving from
separate sections of the city.

Yet, there are occasions when ad hoc administrative attempts
to contain racial conflict are insufficient within and outside Chicago such that news agencies are made aware of them. Several
notable news accounts include the 2014 lunchtime fight between
African Americans and Latinos at Streamwood High School in
a suburb of Chicago. The fight involved at least forty students
across two different floors and offices.[46] Educators note that racialized lunchtime school spaces are "where the trouble usually
happens."[47] Another such lunchtime melee that reached news outlets was that of Canyon Springs High School in Las Vegas. It was
notable because the police felt compelled to use pepper spray to
quell the fight between Latino and African American students.[48]

Apart from large-scale school melees, Latino anti-Blackness
also crops up in individual instances of bullying. Alma Yariela
Cruz, an Afro-Latina student in Puerto Rico, was eleven years
old in 2018 when two classmates taunted her for two years with
racial slurs such as *"negra sucia"* (dirty Black girl), *"negra asquerosa"* (disgusting Black girl), *"negra dientúa"* (big-tooth Black girl),
along with racist commentary about her Afro-descended hair.[49]
The racial harassment Alma experienced parallels that of another
Afro-Latina middle schooler in Denver. While traveling to school
she was excited about having had her hair professionally done for
the first time. But when she arrived at school, her Latino classmates told her that despite what she did to herself she was still
ugly and undesirable. They threw water all over her new clothes
and hair and called her "ape man, jungle bunny, and monkey."[50]

When African American Kavin found herself the target of
race-based bullying at the public school she attended in Marion,
Texas, part of the racially hostile environment she experienced
from the majority White non-Hispanic population included an
assault by two Latina students.[51] The two Latinas surrounded Kavin at her locker and began taunting her, punched her, and threw
her back against the locker. The two Latina students could have

chosen to abstain from the White non-Hispanic student campaign to terrorize Kavin and her two sisters as the few African
Americans at the school. Instead, they chose to actively throw
their lot in with the White non-Hispanic anti-Black racial harass-
ers who repeatedly hurled racial insults and ostracized Kavin on
the White non-Hispanic-dominated cheerleading team she was
nominally a part of. Such racial allegiances are not so difficult to
comprehend when one considers that the anti-Blackness learned
in Latino family settings surfaces as early as preschool. Sili Recio,
an Afro-Latina living in Orlando, Florida, in 2015 recalls how her
preschool daughter was called "black and ugly" by a fellow Latino
preschool classmate.[52]

As distressing as biased classmate bullying can be, school-based
Latino anti-Blackness does not end there. Latino school officials
are also part of the problem. In fact, anti-Blackness by Latino instructors has been documented as early as 1884. That was the year
that Afro–Puerto Rican bibliophile Arturo Schomburg was told
by his fifth-grade schoolteacher in Puerto Rico that "Black people
had no history, no heroes, no great moments."[53] (It was that White
Latina's anti-Blackness that inspired Schomburg's lifelong dedi-
cation to amassing an archive of African diaspora literature and
letters now housed by the New York Public Library's Research
Division at the Schomburg Center.)[54]

Over a century later, Latino-instructor anti-Blackness continues to be a problem. After twenty years of being an educator,
Afro–Puerto Rican Noemí Cortés still sharply recalls how a fellow
Latino teacher in Chicago ostracized his Black students.[55] Because
this (White Cuban) middle-school literacy teacher automatically
assumed all his Black students were deficient, he refused to interact with them directly and instead segregated them into a separate
corner of the classroom for instruction exclusively with a special
education aide. Cortés also noted that the teacher's racialized perspectives about his Black students also informed his perception of
a twelve-year-old girl as impossible to work with because she was
"such an adult." ("Adultification" of Black youngsters as a racist

dynamic will be more fully elaborated below.) For these Black students in Chicago, the classroom ostracism by their Latino teacher was all a part of the racial trauma they experienced in school: Latino students freely used the N-word in the building and the Puerto Rican security guard openly shared his presumption that all Black students were behavior problems to be closely monitored and regulated. For this reason, Cortés found it necessary to provide classroom time and space for these Black students to decompress from the stress of navigating the anti-Black minefields of the predominantly Latino school.

Strikingly, Cortés is not alone in her concerns about Latino teacher anti-Black attitudes in Chicago. David Stovall has directly observed how Latino administrators in Chicago rely on anti-Black racial stereotypes when deciding to accord discipline for school infractions committed by African American students that, in contrast, are excused as inconsequential when committed by Latino students.[56] Stovall vividly recalls how one Latina school principal in particular was so wedded to her racially biased views of African American students as inherent behavior problems who could never be trusted that she would across-the-board refuse to consider the perspectives of African American students. Each of her interactions with African American students was hostile, and this was also reflected in how she denied them school benefits (admission to special school programs, appointments with guidance counselors, appointments with college recruiters, access to school trips, and so on).

This is a dynamic that extends beyond Chicago. Consider the reflections of Afro-Dominican José Luis Vilson, who taught math for fifteen years, from 2005 to 2020, at a New York City public school in Washington Heights that was densely populated with Latinos, particularly from the Dominican Republic. During his entire fifteen-year tenure, Vilson repeatedly witnessed the Latino school administrators treat dark-skinned students as inherently incompetent and prone to misbehavior.[57] This reliance on Black racial stereotypes also resulted in disproportionate punishments for Black students. However, the racial bias was seemingly imperceptible to the Latino school administrators.

Latino anti-Black attitudes surface early in training of teachers. Roberto Montoya, an instructor of student teachers at the University of Colorado Denver's School of Education since 2012, has repeatedly observed his Latino students express anti-Black attitudes and interact negatively with their fellow Black education students.[58] Especially worrisome to Montoya is that when he attempts to intervene and create a teachable moment regarding Latino anti-Blackness in the classroom, many of the Latino student teachers dismiss it as irrelevant to them. These then are the unteachable teachers sent off to instruct the nation's young people. In short, the anti-Blackness of Latino teachers and school administrators has material consequences despite being effectively invisible in public discourse. And this invisibility adversely affects even the most well-meaning of school reform attempts.

Contemporary Providence, Rhode Island, provides a useful case study. It is a school district in which Latino students are 65 percent of the K–12 public-school student population, and Black students are 16 percent.[59] During the school year, the students are taught primarily by White non-Hispanic teachers who continually subject students of color to school discipline for infractions that other students also commit without the same disciplinary consequences.[60]

However, during the summer months, the Generation Teach program offers these same middle-school students an academic enrichment program that specifically seeks to end racial injustice and inequity in education.[61] The instructors are intentionally more racially diverse and directed to endorse the program's anti-racism mission. And yet Latino instructor anti-Blackness manages to encroach upon even this carefully crafted educational space. Time and again, teachers observed a Latina program leader reprimand African American students for the very same infractions lighter-skinned Latino students committed without chastisement.[62] The Latina program leader's differential treatment extended to reprimanding the African American students for behavior as innocuous as purchasing food items from the school vending machines rather than eating the food provided in the cafeteria. The racial disparity was particularly noticeable because the entire student population of all backgrounds used the vending machines as an alternative to the cafeteria food they did not like.

Equally concerning, a junior Latina instructor was observed over-sexualizing her African American and Afro-Latino middle school students in problematic ways that were never addressed by the program.[63] The over-sexualization of the boys was manifested in the junior Latina instructor's constant touching and flirting with them, which many other teachers found inappropriate. The "adultification" of young Black girls is a topic that has only recently garnered some public attention in the conversation about intersectional discrimination (the vortex where race and gender combine).[64] However, adultification is just as detrimental to the formation of boys of color. Interacting with children of color as if they were much older, based on racial stereotypes about their inherent sexual prowess, not only deprives those children of an actual childhood characterized by adult nurturing and guidance but also exposes them to being more harshly disciplined. Adultification is where the school-to-prison pipeline begins.

The junior Latina instructor's fellow teachers believed she was operating under such Black racial stereotypes, given her proclivity for inserting into a conversation the non sequitur of how much she wanted to date Black men by starting with light-skinned men and then "working her way up" to dark-skinned men. It appeared to her coworkers that the inappropriate behavior this Latina teacher had with her Black male students was a dress rehearsal for launching her fantasy of dating Black men. Educational programs that ignore the Latino deployment of racial stereotypes create hostile learning environments for children of African descent.

Unfortunately, the Latino sexualization of Black students is not limited to this single example of a Latina Providence educator. Education specialist David Stovall has noted the same problem with Latino sexualization of Black female students in Chicago.[65] In fact, a 2018 report by the *Chicago Tribune* revealed that the Chicago school district was the site of massive sexual abuse and assault of its students, and the reports of sexual abuse continue.[66] Notably, a significant number of the victimized students who were profiled by the *Chicago Tribune* exposé were Black. Inasmuch as Latinos and Afro-Latinos together constitute 20.9 percent of the Chicago school district population of teachers, they are not excluded from the concerns of racialized sexual abuse.[67]

Nor is the racial climate across the country much better among Latino educators themselves. At a meeting of Latino educators in Colorado, Afro-Latina Marta Cruz-Janzen was met with great hostility and was told, "Some Hispanics don't want you to be one of them because you represent everything they don't want to be. How dare this black woman speak Spanish and claim to be one of us? They see you as black and they don't want to be black. They want you to stop saying that you're like them."[68]

In short, the tales of Latino anti-Blackness in public spaces of recreation and education all resound a consistent theme. Across diverse geographic locations what remains consistent is the manner in which Latinos regulate public spaces to exclude and demean Blackness. Playing and learning in White-dominated Latino spaces is where Afro-Latinos are taught the rules of Latino racial hierarchies, and African Americans are informed that they are unwelcome. In the next chapter I consider how all this permeates the work context.

·━●●·━·

CHAPTER 3

WORKING IN THE USA

Popular culture often depicts "diverse" workplace settings as racial utopias where people of all races and ethnicities happily coexist. For instance, the Golden Globe Award–winning television show *Brooklyn Nine-Nine*, which aired from 2013 to 2021, depicted its New York City Black, Latino, and White fellow police officers as free of any racial acrimony. Like so many other media portrayals, it did not delve into the quotidian realities of racial coexistence that occur across a much more complex spectrum. At the same time, such romanticized media depictions (mis)inform our societal conceptions of what racial diversity truly means.

In contrast, legal narratives of what individuals experience and perceive when racial conflict occurs provide a picture grounded in the complexity and messiness of actual diverse contexts. What the stories reveal with regard to Latinos, is that anti-Blackness is an ongoing phenomenon that adversely affects Afro-Latinos, African Americans, and Africans alike, even against a richly diverse landscape where interracial cooperation exists simultaneously with racial conflict. The stories that these legal claimants tell have much to teach us about the complexity of racially diverse Latino workplaces.

Edward Olumuyiwa, a Nigerian American and a Brooklyn resident, was hired as a security guard with Harvard Protection

Services, a company based in New York City that provides security services to corporate clients. Unbeknownst to Edward, at
that time a racialized wage structure existed at the company where
Latino and Yugoslavian employees received 50 percent more than
Edward and the African American security guards. In addition,
the company also gave the Latino and Yugoslavian workers more
favorable work shifts and hours.[1]

However, Edward learned of the racial hierarchy only after
having become the target of racial harassment from his Latino
supervisor, Jason Ortiz. The racial bias was evident because supervisor Ortiz directly stated that he did not like Edward because
he was Nigerian. His campaign of racial harassment included the
overtly discriminatory remarks: "Why is your Black ass sleeping
here?! I am going to deduct two hours pay from your Black-ass
paycheck!" and "We Hispanics run this office!" The racially in-
flammatory comments were accompanied by actions that sought
to demean Edward further.

While Harvard Protection had a general policy of having a
supervisor appear at a job site only once per night, supervisor Ortiz showed up at Edward's job site approximately six times and
harassed him with the taunt "I'm going to catch you!" Moreover,
Edward was required to work longer hours than any other security
guard employed by Harvard Protection. On at least ten occasions,
he was directed to work sixteen consecutive hours. Even when
Edward advised Vice President Camacho that he had a heart con-
dition and needed four days off to have surgery, Camacho flatly
denied the request. In fact, the harassment was condoned by the
Latino-dominant management at the security company and its
Latino vice president, Ron Camacho.

Only after filing a discrimination claim in court was Edward
able to successfully reach a settlement agreement to address his
adverse treatment. Indeed, the Latino anti-Black discrimination
cases that are most frequently resolved in favor of the Black complainant (whether they be Afro-Latino, Afro-Caribbean, African
American, or an African immigrant) are cases like Edward's in

which there is clear preferential treatment of Latino employees at
the expense of identifiable Black employees who are demeaned, in
addition to cases of overt anti-Black racial harassment and intentionally unfavorable treatment.[2]

Nonetheless, the virulence of Latino anti-Black statements
can be particularly violent when aimed at Afro-Latinos in particular, because the epithets are often delivered in a double dose
of both Spanish and English. Afro-Latino Eloy Cruz had such a
bilingual attacker when he was a warehouse manager at a company
in Hialeah Gardens, a city in Florida's Miami-Dade County. Sales
manager Jorge Fernández was the Latino who made it his mission
to repeatedly berate Eloy with a barrage of racially hostile terms:
"n——r," "stupid n——r," "Head N——r in Charge," "spigger"
(short form for "spic n——r"), "*negro*" (n——r), "*negro estupido*"
(stupid n——r), "*negro maricon*" (gay n——r), and "*negro mierda*"
(shitty n——r).[3] Adding to the racially hostile environment were
Fernández's threats to physically harm Eloy and make his job
"hell," ultimately resulting in Eloy being fired. Like Edward Olumuyiwa, Eloy was able to successfully obtain a settlement agreement to resolve his lawsuit.

In the antidiscrimination law context, civil rights lawyers view
settlement agreements to be a success. This is because the vast
majority of racial discrimination claims are dismissed by courts
without the opportunity for a trial.[4] From 1979 through 2006,
federal claimants won only 15 percent of job discrimination cases.
By comparison, in all other civil cases, the win rate was 51 percent.[5] Commentators attribute the low success rate to the growing
hostility with which courts approach allegations of discrimination.[6] Courts seemingly believe that the passage of civil rights
laws alone has wrought a post-racial society in which instances
of intentional discrimination are rare. As a result, when a judge
refrains from dismissing a racial discrimination claim as legally
insufficient on its face, lawyers understand it as if "a judge has
given quasi-approval to the complainant's case," which in turn facilitates the legal parties to reach a settlement agreement.[7] This is

why settlement agreements are often understood as "wins" for the complainant in racial discrimination cases.

Unfortunately, not every tale of racist conduct within Latino-dominant workplaces like Edward Olumuyiwa's is successfully resolved by the judicial system.[8] Many instances of discrimination never even reach a judge. In fact, economists have documented that Latino managers often refrain from hiring African Americans at rates similar to those of White non-Hispanic managers.[9]

Nor are Latinos more receptive to African ancestry when an Afro-Latino employee seeks advancement in Latino-dominated workplaces. What follows is José Arrocha's story of the challenges Afro-Latinos can encounter in Latino workplaces. Like Edward, José Arrocha lived and worked in New York City and as a dark-skinned Afro-Panamanian felt similarly excluded by his Latino superiors.

José worked for two years as an adjunct instructor for City University of New York Medgar Evers College campus (MEC) in the Spanish language program of its Languages, Literature, and Philosophy Department. After having been reappointed as an adjunct instructor three semesters in a row, José's contract was not renewed after he received a single lukewarm review from the departmental evaluator, Professor Iraida Lopez.[10] Despite having been rated as satisfactory (3 on a 1–5 scale) during prior performance evaluations, Professor Lopez lowered his rating to 2.5 and stated:

> The one-hour class I observed covered too much material. . . .
> Students need to play a more active role. A more creative use of
> the exercises should be made to challenge students & encourage them to use language in an active way. The instructor relies
> on the textbook explanation and exercises.

Based on this dubious commentary from a single hour of class observation, José's contract was not renewed. Given the sparseness of the basis for José's termination, he was upset and disturbed to discover that the eight instructors who were reappointed instead of him were White. In José's view it reflected "a disturbing culture of favoritism that favor[ed] the appointments of *White* Cubans, Spaniards and *White* Hispanics from South America, . . . [with] the use of an evaluation process used to discredit my work and exclude me from the Spanish faculty only because I am Black. Medgar Evers does not have a *Black* professor of Spanish because of the blatant racism of *White* Hispanics toward *Black* Hispanics. In my opinion, *Black* Hispanics do not have an equal opportunity to teach Spanish." As a result, José filed a legal claim asserting that the Latino heads of the Medgar Evers College Spanish Department discriminated against *Black* Hispanics like himself.

However, unlike Edward Olumuyiwa, José was unable to persuade the court that his termination was the result of discrimination. While the disproportionate favoring of White Latino candidates over José based on observing a single one-hour class is quite suggestive of racialized decision-making, it held little weight with the judge.

José's judge immediately rejected that possibility of discrimination because five of the eight adjunct instructors who were reappointed instead of José were natives of other South or Central American countries, such as Argentina, Peru, and Mexico, as well as the Dominican Republic. Simply because the college reappointed natives from other Latin American countries, the judge treated all Latinos as racially and ethnically interchangeable and thus incapable of discrimination against other Latinos. This is made starkly evident by the judge's statement that "*diversity* in an employer's staff undercuts an inference of discriminatory intent," (emphasis added) presumably because in hiring many Latinos, the employer's diverse hires manifest an egalitarian corporate culture. For whom exactly, though, was the Spanish Department a nonracialized "diverse" workplace?

Consider that this judicial equivalence was only possible by overlooking the ways in which Latino culture fuses a racialized hierarchy onto the list of Latin American and Caribbean nations. As discussed in chapter 1, countries perceived as European are viewed as more advanced than those more significantly populated with people of indigenous descent or those of African descent. In the list of countries the judge thought equivalent, Latin American racial constructs would rank Argentina as a highly valued White country, followed by Peru and Mexico with their indigenous populations, followed by the Dominican Republic and José's own country of origin, Panama, because they are populated by more people of African descent.

Imbued into the racial taxonomy of Latin American countries are derogatory notions about the inadequacy of Afro-inflected Spanish. The closer a nation's association with Whiteness, the more its inhabitants are presumed to speak a cultured and refined Spanish. As Frantz Fanon importantly noted, the subjects of postcolonial societies often wield language as a tool for imposing racial hierarchy.[11] Fanon's observations about the French-language racial pecking order in Martinique are just as salient to Latin American notions about "civilized," proper Spanish-speaking nations. For José, the Spanish Department was its own postcolonial society looking down on the presumed "Black" origins of his Panamanian Spanish and in turn the legitimacy of his ability to teach others proper (White Castilian) Spanish.

To be sure, for Latinos influenced by Latin American racial paradigms where each country has a racial identification, a diverse workforce of Latinos is not the immediate equivalent of a bias-free context. Nor is color preference divorced from a racialized ideology within the Latino context. Thus when José specifically enumerated the Hispanic countries of origin from which the favored candidates emanated, it was as part of the story of how racial hierarchy played out in the workplace. However, for the judge, José's Latino ethnicity erased his Black racial identity and the judge's ability to see any racial difference among the various Latino candidates. The judge's intuitions were seemingly validated by the absence of racial identification in the employees' personnel files. Specifically, of the eight adjunct instructors that were reappointed, only one self-identified as White, while three others failed to supply any racial identification, another three characterized their race as "Hispanic," and the final instructor said he was a Mexican with a brown skin color. In effect, the Latino disinclination to specify a race was allowed to act as a judicial veil around the particulars of Latino racial differentiation. As a result, the judge permitted the jury to assess only whether it was uniquely a skin-color discrimination case.

Yet, what was left for the jury to examine? The judge's compartmentalized approach to assessing color, race, and ethnicity as independent dynamics misses how Latino racism is a deeply intertwined intersection of biases based upon color, race, and ethnicity. Pull apart the strands and the picture of how Latino racism operates is incomprehensible. With the search for visible skin-color gradations in the workplace decontextualized from any understanding of Latino racialized meanings, it is not at all surprising that José Arrocha failed to persuade the jury that his ostracism was an act of color discrimination.

In short, the existence of a so-called diverse Latino workplace operated as a veil around possible racial discrimination, despite Supreme Court case authority explicitly warning against the presumption that intra-ethnic and intraracial discrimination cannot exist.[12] The *Arrocha* court instead mistakenly treated the panethnic identifier of Latino/Hispanic as precluding discrimination between various Latinos. Lawyering Latino anti-Black claims thus requires educating juries and judges about Latino racial attitudes.

Learning about the features of Latino anti-Black bias also necessitates a consideration of how racial bias can additionally manifest itself in a sexualized manner, in what has come to be called intersectional discrimination.[13] Intersectional discrimination occurs when multiple sources of bias (such as race and gender) converge for a person as a single experience of discrimination with interactive stereotypes. As is often the case when African Americans are targeted for workplace harassment, Afro-Latinos are also victimized by other Latinos based upon racial stereotypes regarding the sexualized attributes of Blackness. The following two narratives illustrate how the racialization of the Black body is sexualized by Latinos.

Cruz Young, a banquet server at the Marriott Phoenix Airport hotel is an Afro-Dominican woman who fell into the vortex of intersectional Latino discrimination when coworker Jose Herrera began to harass her.[14] Herrera made repeated references to Cruz as having a large butt and being a "fucking *puta*" (a prostitute or sexually wanton woman) with a "fucking N——r" for a boyfriend, all while forcibly touching her against her will. In this way, Herrera's sexual-harassing conduct was fixated upon the Latino cultural objectification of the Black body. Latino literature, music lyrics, film, television, and public discourse all depict the Black body as the embodiment of sex and sexual prowess. Buttocks are not merely a body part when viewed on a Black body. They are sex itself. In turn, Juan Jones was not merely Cruz's boyfriend but instead envisioned by Herrera as literally a "fucking N——r."

The rest of Cruz's Latino coworkers who witnessed the harassment and Cruz's tears interpreted it through the Latino, racially sexualized lens of Herrera "wooing her or courting her." Only in a Latino cultural context that equates Blackness with sexual availability and wantonness would a man who forcibly touched, grabbed, dragged, and verbally assaulted a woman as a racial object still be viewed as innocuously engaged in "courtship." Indeed, when Cruz filed her claim of discrimination, her Latino manager, Raul Peña, referred to her as "that garbage" who should "go back to the Dominican Republic" (which Latinos characterize as a backward Black country).

Fortunately for Cruz, the judge assigned to her case was not persuaded to dismiss the case based upon the employer's claim that the events were caused by a "personal dispute" rather than discrimination that continued unabated for the better part of a year, if not longer. While the judge did not explicitly refer to the discrimination as intersectional, he did use a nuanced analysis that considered both its gendered and its race-based aspects. After the judge noted that the employer's explanation of a personal disagreement was "without merit," a jury decided discrimination occurred and granted Cruz financial compensation. Such compensatory damages are designed to pay victims for out-of-pocket expenses caused by the discrimination (such as costs associated with a new job search or medical expenses) and compensate them for any emotional harm suffered (such as mental anguish, inconvenience, or loss of enjoyment of life).[15]

Afro-Latina women are not alone in being subject to Latino racialized sexual-harassment discrimination. Latino racial discourse also sexualizes Black male bodies based on their Blackness. Chris Bartholomew, an Afro-Caribbean, experienced that directly as the darkest of all the employees at the Martin Brower Company in Puerto Rico. After twelve years of employment at the company, during which time Chris worked his way up from warehouse worker to transportation supervisor, the arrival of two new upper-management supervisors radically altered Chris's work environment.

Chris's new supervisors were two "light-skinned men of Latin American origin," named Loscar Mejía and Bismark Márquez, who immediately began calling Chris "Blackie."[16] Mejía and Márquez then launched a three-month campaign of racial abuse centrally focused on the presumed sexual attributes of Chris's body, with references to his genitalia as "sausage," "*morcilla*" (blood sausage), and the remark that he had "three legs" (given the presumed length of his penis). They compounded the verbal abuse with visually graphic emails and texts to Chris bound up in the racial stereotype of Black men as having large genitalia and being oversexed. One image included a large penis attacking a woman, with the label "Chris attack." Another image depicted Chris as a sausage and another as Spiderman with a huge penis. Rather than being a worker worthy of respect, Mejía and Márquez reduced Chris to a racialized sexual object for their own entertainment. After the judge refused to dismiss the case and set it on track for a jury trial, the parties reached a private settlement and Chris was financially compensated for the harm he endured.

However, for some judges, just raising the issue of Latino anti-Black bias can be considered a racist act itself. When Maybell Webb, an African American title clerk in a predominantly White-Hispanic car dealership in Miami became concerned that her Latino supervisors seemed to be reprimanding her for being "rude" when Latino employees were not disciplined for their curt behavior, the judge refused to entertain her claim.[17] The judge rejected outright Maybell's concerns and the employer's repeated use of the Spanish term *la negra* (the Black girl) in her presence, with the following warning to anyone who might file a similar interethnic racial discrimination claim:

> Over the years, work environments have come to reflect our increasingly multi-cultural world. With the coming together of numerous diverse ethnicities and cultures in the common workplace, there are bound to be not only many instances of cultural harmony but also some occasions of *cultural friction*. . . . While this Court sincerely hopes that all employees of all cultures will choose to exercise common respect and courtesy, it cannot allow Title VII to be used as a sword by which one culture may achieve supremacy in the workplace over another—[by filing a discrimination claim!].

Even more striking is when organizations dedicated to addressing discrimination are themselves sites where Latino anti-Black bias is alleged, and courts are still disinclined to find the allegations credible. Maxine Sprott, an African American woman who worked as a deputy director of the New York City Housing Authority's (NYCHA) Office of Equal Opportunity alleged that her Latina supervisor, office director Rosalind Reyes, harassed her with derogatory comments about her work performance despite Maxine repeatedly earning positive performance evaluation ratings like "good" and "very good."[18] Director Reyes insinuated that even though Maxine had attended several Equal Employment Opportunity Studies courses at Cornell University, she still did not have a grasp of the nature of her work as it related to identifying and investigating acts of discrimination. Each positive performance evaluation rating from Reyes was then followed with commentary about Maxine's lack of leadership skills in her role as deputy director.

Even Maxine's proposal that the office purchase multimedia instructional material on sexual harassment was not deemed by Reyes as a sufficient indicator of leadership initiative. The director also singularly harassed Maxine about her timesheets and excluded her from various office functions and meetings. When Maxine could no longer withstand the onslaught of derogatory commentary about her competence, she filed a claim of discrimination with the general manager of NYCHA. Exactly three days after Maxine filed her discrimination claim, Reyes submitted a performance evaluation that for the first time rated Maxine as "marginal," and as a result, Maxine was denied a managerial merit salary increase.

Any expectations that Maxine might have had that working for a city Equal Opportunity division focused on addressing discrimination in public housing would be a more racially enlightened workplace were shredded when her employer not only failed to investigate her allegations but then retaliated against her for filing a discrimination claim. In fact, it was yet another Latino NYCHA official, its chairman Ruben Franco, that discriminatorily retaliated against Maxine. Specifically, when Maxine refused to accept NYCHA's proposed terms for settling her discrimination claim regarding Reyes, Franco informed Maxine that she was being transferred to another office where her material responsibilities were diminished, and she was moved from a well-furnished private office into an open cubicle. This was yet another instance of retaliation for Maxine's exercise of her right to assert her claim of discrimination. Only when Maxine filed suit in court was she able to reach a settlement agreement with NYCHA and receive financial compensation.

While any number of concerns may have influenced Maxine and her attorney to settle the case rather than move forward with a jury trial, one contributing factor could very well have been the great significance the judge placed upon office racial diversity as mitigating claims of discrimination. For the judge, it was immaterial that when chairman Franco transferred Maxine to an effectively lesser position in a cubicle, he simultaneously terminated two other African American female employees, all as part of his ostensible reorganization plan. Instead, the judge concluded that such facts failed to raise an inference of discrimination because "the new Director is an Hispanic woman. . . . There are now two deputy directors—one African-American and one Caucasian. . . . The remaining staff is comprised of twenty-four Hispanics, twenty-three African Americans, nine Caucasians, and one person categorized as 'other.'" Thus, the judge accorded a diverse Latino workplace and the supervisor's Hispanic status great power to circumvent racism. Herein, then, is the judicial presumption that Latino coworkers in diverse workplaces cannot be bearers of racism.

Other workplace narratives seem to suggest that decision makers may instead read Latino anti-Blackness as instances of mere cultural misunderstanding. A report from a human resources director provides a helpful illustration:

> I was called in because a small work team in a laboratory was not meeting deadlines on an important project. On the surface it looked like a time management issue to their supervisor when in fact, two Hispanic employees on the team had issues that were culturally rooted—one being Puerto Rican and the other being Dominican. Their issues were getting in the way of the team's progress. While unfortunate and inaccurate, people who were working with and supervising these employees never thought something diversity-related was going on. It never came up on their radar screens because they saw both employees as "Hispanic."[19]

This workplace case study illustrates two separate aspects of the opacity of interethnic disputes for decision makers. First, the supervisor concludes that the conflict is simply a mere personality conflict between two Latino employees because of the presumption that Latinos are a monolithic group. Then the human resources director, who is African American and asserts knowledge about the existence of intraracial bias within racial groups, is better able to appreciate that two Latinos from different ethnic subgroups can harbor group-based bias against one another. Yet even this human resources director presumes that the conflict is simply "culturally rooted" rather than informed by Latino racial ideology about the "inherent racial differences" between Puerto Ricans and Dominicans, rooted in Latino stereotyping of Puerto Rico as a "Whiter" island distinct from the Blackness of the Dominican Republic. Thus, even when a workplace HR office identifies interethnic conflicts, it is not necessarily schooled to appreciate that Latino "culture" is not divorced from Latino racism.

LATINO JUDGES

Some might attribute the confusion about Latino discrimination in legal cases to the fact that US judges and juries are typically not racially or ethnically diverse.[20] Jury pools are created from voter registration lists and Department of Motor Vehicles records, which frequently do not parallel the racial diversity of any given city. In addition, the socioeconomic burden of missing work for jury service is not racially or ethnically proportionate.

Yet, Latino jurors and judges themselves can be equally confounded by allegations of Latino anti-Black discrimination when they presume that Latino workplaces are not as susceptible to racial discrimination because of the predominance of Latino employees. Latino cultural attitudes presume that racism is a North American phenomenon that is more exceptional in Latino contexts. This Latino juridical attitude is particularly evident in cases of discrimination filed in the US federal courts of Puerto Rico, where US federal antidiscrimination laws are applied to the US territory by a cadre of elite White Puerto Ricans. In the District of

Puerto Rico's (DPR) twenty-one-year history, there is not a single recorded instance of an Afro-Latino judge. One seventeen-year veteran employee of the DPR court system never saw a Black judge in the courthouse until an African American judge was flown in as a temporary visiting judge for a number of weeks.[21] Afro-Latino employees are primarily men relegated to the hyper-masculinized law enforcement space as courthouse US marshals and court security officers (roles matching the Latino racial stereotyping of Black men as physically strong brutes).[22]

Consider the plight of Victor Omar Portugues-Santa, a self-identified Black Puerto Rican trying his best to tell his story of discrimination within the contemporary racial caste of the DPR.[23] Victor was forced to contend with one Puerto Rican judge's inappropriately oppressive demands for evidence of violent expressions of anti-Blackness (like a frozen picture of 1940s Jim Crow US racism) that could be deemed the equivalent of *real racism*. Before a trial could even be held, the judge dismissed Victor's racial discrimination claim with the conclusion that he was not subjected to severe or pervasive racial harassment that materially altered the conditions of his employment, despite his compelling story of ill treatment.

Victor worked as the director of sales and marketing for beer and liquor with B. Fernandez Hermanos, Inc. (BFH), a distribution company that operates a wholesale facility in Bayamon, Puerto Rico. Victor's primary responsibility was to market Anheuser-Busch beer products to the gay community in Puerto Rico with a "Bud Light Alternative" campaign. In fact, Victor initiated and brought the campaign to Puerto Rico.

As the only self-identified Black Puerto Rican among his peers, Victor was targeted with racialized commentary that focused on treating him as a racial inferior who had elevated himself beyond his proper station. The racial comments included being called "a White Black person" and "Black guy with a Mercedes Benz" and described as the "Black guy who parts his hair." Within the Puerto Rican context, such phrases were meant to disparage Victor as a

Black man inappropriately putting on the airs of a White racial superior. This racialized commentary was accompanied by exclusionary actions that Victor felt affected his work experience significantly.

After repeated requests, Victor was denied a laptop computer in contrast to all the other White directors who had one. Racial distinctions were also apparent in the refusal to permit Victor to hire a replacement for a departing staff member, in contrast to his White Latino counterparts who were allowed to hire additional support staff. The company also refused to permit Victor to attend a work convention in Las Vegas, Nevada, at the same time that they financed a White Latino coworker's trip to the convention. Victor missed out on opportunities to apply for promotions because the company failed to publicly post the positions on the company bulletin boards and instead used racially exclusive, informal dissemination of the openings, which Victor did not have access to.

In four years at the company, Victor never received a performance evaluation or a salary increase. When the company decided to reorganize as part of a cost reduction plan, it terminated Victor's position. Yet when Victor asked if he could be placed in another position at a lower salary, his request was rejected, and he was replaced with a White coworker instead. As such, Victor felt he was the victim of racial discrimination.

Antidiscrimination law certainly permits an employer to respond to such allegations and explain how its actions had legitimate nondiscriminatory justifications. Yet, a jury was never allowed the opportunity to assess the credibility of the allegations or the company's justifications, simply because the presiding Latino judge, Francisco Besosa, rejected the sufficiency of Victor's allegations altogether. The judge's threshold for what could be deemed discriminatory was set so high that few if any claims would count as discrimination for legal purposes.

To begin with, Judge Besosa disdained the significance of the racialized commentary that victimized Victor, because Victor could not prove that any of his supervisors were present when the comments were made. However, established antidiscrimination law does not require that, in order to hold a company responsible for negligently permitting a racially hostile work environment, that the employee who used the racist language or was present to hear racist commentary must have been a supervisor.[24] Once the misconduct is reported to the employer or otherwise made evident, the employer has a responsibility to investigate and address the discriminatory conduct.

Equally erroneous is Judge Besosa's depiction of discrimination as manifested only when part of a violent context. The judge explicitly states, "While the language used might very well have embarrassed [Victor] Portugues, just as it may have been premised upon unsavory racial stereotypes, it was not overtly aggressive or excessively derogatory. The racial references were not combined with any physical activity." As a result, Victor's dismay at being denied a laptop computer in contrast to all the other White directors who had one is minimized by Judge Besosa as "a minor inconvenience." Rather than easily discerning how the racially disparate treatment in the allocation of standard office equipment communicated an unequal status not warranted by job station, the judge instead scolds Victor for not explaining "why or how a laptop would have been of significant importance to him in his position." Judge Besosa's demand for "more" is also imposed on Victor's observation that he was denied support staff, unlike other directors. In response, the judge chastises Victor for his failure to provide information as to why he needed the support staff.

Judge Besosa similarly excuses the employer for its failure to post job promotion opportunities on the company bulletin boards simply because the employee handbook says only that such job openings "*may* be posted on the bulletin boards" rather than "*must* be posted on the bulletin boards." The racial exclusivity of the choice the company made for disseminating job openings was immaterial to the judge, despite the fact that established case law frowns upon word-of-mouth-style hiring practices that keep racial minorities unaware of job openings in nondiverse workplaces.[25] It was also immaterial to the judge that Victor was denied the opportunity to attend a work conference in Nevada that a White coworker was allowed to attend, because on a prior occasion the company sent Victor to another convention. Here the possibility of racialized decision-making on one occasion is judicially deemed expunged by the existence of equal treatment on a prior occasion.

Finally, Judge Besosa never questions the company's cost-reduction reorganization justification for terminating Victor, despite its refusal to consider keeping Victor on with his offer to remain working at a lower salary to help the company reduce its costs. In short, this judge viewed racial discrimination as so exceptional in contemporary Puerto Rico in comparison to the historical Jim Crow narrative of violent US segregation, that he set forth a higher threshold for proving discrimination than actually exists in mainland United States courts today.

The extremity of this judge's perspective is further highlighted by how far removed it is from the US government agency model for assessing discrimination, formulated by the Equal Employment Opportunity Commission (EEOC). While EEOC guidelines are not laws that judges are obligated to follow, they are interpretive regulations that judges have long deferred to. In fact, in the same year that Victor's judge would only accept evidence of "aggressive or excessively derogatory" language and physical violence as adequate proof of racial discrimination, the EEOC, in contrast, sued and successfully reached a financial settlement with a Puerto Rican furniture company whose store manager verbally taunted a sales associate about his dark color and questioned why he was "so Black."[26] As the government agency that articulates national guidelines for evaluating the validity of discrimination claims, the EEOC made no demand for evidence of physical violence. For the EEOC, the racialized commentary in the Puerto Rican furniture store was a sufficient indicator of a racially hostile environment warranting investigation and action.

Being out of step with the racial expertise of the EEOC is not limited to Latino judges operating within the US territory of Puerto Rico. Latino judges within the contiguous United States can be just as captured by the presumption that Latino anti-Black bias is exceptional, even in work environments riddled with anti-Black Spanish epithets and actions. A contemporary example out of Texas provides a useful illustration.

Michael Johnson worked as a carpenter for Pride Industries (a nonprofit social enterprise with the mission of creating jobs for people with disabilities) at its placement within the Fort Bliss US Army garrison in El Paso, Texas.[27] During much of his time with Pride, he was the only African American carpenter at Fort Bliss. Michael's supervisor, Juan Palomares, and many of his co-workers were Latinos, as would be expected in a city like El Paso, situated on the Rio Grande across the US-Mexico border from Ciudad Juárez. In El Paso, Latinos comprise 83 percent of the population.[28]

Although Michael was not a Spanish speaker, supervisor Palomares impressed upon Michael the racial hostility of the Spanish phrases "*pinche mayate*" and "*pinche negro*" (slang terms for "fucking n——r" and "fucking Black"), each time he hurled the epithets at him. In addition to frequently assaulting Michael with the Spanish anti-Black epithets, Palomares also violated the esteem-building company policy of only referring to employees by their names. For Palomares, Michael was not worthy of respect, and thus rather than addressing him by his proper name, Palomares called him "*mijo*." (*Mijo* literally translates to "my son" but is more generally a Latino form of address that an adult uses with any child or for referring to a person of a lower status). Because Palomares singled Michael out with the gross Spanish informality of "*mijo*" while at the same time he mistreated him in the workplace, there was no ambiguity about the hostility of the address. Like the racially loaded use of the English term *boy* for referring to full-grown Black men, the Spanish *mijo* accords the same racial paternalism and disrespect in the workplace.

Palomares's discriminatory actions included repeatedly withholding needed tools for Michael's work, hiding paperwork for a promotion on two separate occasions, telling him to "shut up" when he asked for clarification of work meeting information delivered in Spanish, and berating him and no one else for working through lunch. The harassment Palomares modeled then escalated to coworkers repeatedly vandalizing Michael's truck, stealing his personal phone and work truck keys, drilling a screw into his truck tire, and leaving a rifle magazine loaded with blanks on the bumper of his truck. Ultimately Michael was racially terrorized and forced out of working there.

Rather than allowing a jury to listen to all the evidence and render a decision, Judge Montalvo, the Latino presiding judge, dismissed the racial discrimination claim by ruling there was insufficient evidence of severe or pervasive harassment to present to a jury. In coming to this conclusion, Judge Montalvo usurped the role of the jury in assessing the facts. Instead, the judge unilaterally decided that the uses of Spanish-language racial epithets were "not in itself enough to establish a prima facie case of hostile work environment based on race." He further concluded that the use of *mijo* held "little evidentiary weight of racial discrimination." As a result, for Judge Montalvo all the physical instances of harassment were "not connected to racial discrimination."

As White-presenting (non-Black appearing) Latinos, Judge Montalvo in El Paso and Judge Besosa in Puerto Rico have likely never had to contend with Latino anti-Black bias directly targeted at them. With Latino anti-Black bias as an abstraction rather than a lived experience, Latino expressions of anti-Black bias can be dismissed as inconsequential compared to US Anglo–instigated discrimination. Hence, Judge Besosa's demand for evidence of physical assault before he would consider a workplace in Puerto Rico replete with racist language a racially hostile work environment.

For Judge Montalvo in El Paso, *mijo* simply means "my son," a term of endearment with no further context needed. In turn, *mayete* is intellectually offensive but in and of itself not racially harassing. Despite fellow coworkers corroborating supervisor Palomares's frequent use of the racial epithets, Judge Montalvo seemingly viewed them as not as demeaning as the English language N-word, and thus not as severe as discrimination instigated by US Anglos. In fact, Judge Montalvo's presumption that no reasonable jury could find that Michael was the victim of racial discrimination ignored established law as if it applied only to US Anglo–instigated discrimination.

Judge Montalvo's contravention of established law in Michael's case was so significant that the EEOC made the unusual choice to submit an amicus curiae (friend of the court) brief to support Michael's request to overturn Judge Montalvo's dismissal of his case. Notably, the EEOC detailed both relevant court decisions that articulate the rule that frequent use of racial slurs is sufficient to create a severe or pervasive hostile work environment and Supreme Court precedent explaining that "context, inflection, tone of voice, local custom, and historical usage" of a word like *boy* can be evidence of racial animus.[29] Unfortunately, neither Michael nor the EEOC were able to change Judge Montalvo's mind.

Afro-Latinos who are unambiguously identifiable as Black do not find it so easy to dismiss the hostility of a workplace replete with Spanish racial name-calling. Nor can they disaggregate it from the informal address and hierarchy imbued in the word *mijo* uniquely directed at the one Black person at a job site victimized with differential treatment. As Cornel West insightfully states, "Race matters."[30] Unless non-Black-identified Latino judges take on the work of contending with the specifics of Latino anti-Black discrimination, they will be as prone as White non-Hispanic judges in misconstruing the import of Latino anti-Black bias.

SYSTEMIC EXCLUSION

Further aggravating the judicial incomprehension of discriminatory Latino workplaces is the structural racism of the labor market.

This is because Latino anti-Black bias shows up not only as an expression of individual Latino racial attitudes but also in systemic structures of exclusion. For instance, in 2016 Latino employees of a Chicago-based nationwide job placement agency described how their Latino supervisors trained them to exclude African American applicants from job placements in favor of Latino applicants.[31] They were instructed to automatically reject African American applicants because of the stereotype that they were not capable of working as hard as Latinos. The lawsuit, which settled in March 2020, details how dispatchers who nevertheless sent African American job seekers to a company would later be reprimanded by their Latino bosses for doing so.[32]

The placement agency would start the day by separating Latino job applicants from African Americans. They would enter the Latino applicants' contact information into a database so they could be easily reached when jobs opened up. African American applicants rarely received the same treatment. Instead, Black applicants were usually instructed to go to the agency office at dawn to wait for assignments that rarely came. One agency dispatcher noted, "If it was 10 Mexicans that would come at 1:30 p.m., and 25 African Americans that were there at 4:30 a.m. and were waiting to be sent to work, they would send the Mexicans first."[33] This Latino-run employment agency effectively ensured a secondary racial-caste system of Latinos over Blacks in an already-segregated Chicago-area labor market that privileges White non-Hispanics.

Equally problematic are the toxic effects of Latino anti-Black sentiment in the labor market when Latino business ownership dominates a particular industry and geographic area. Antonio Rodriguez was a man of Spanish ancestry who had been in the automobile business for thirty-eight years, employing close to four- to five-hundred employees in the ten automobile dealerships he owned in Fresno, California. Given his influence in the market, the local automobile industry was quite aware of his blanket refusal to hire Black people during all his decades of owning automobile dealerships. As one area sales manager stated, "It was so well known that Rodriguez did not hire the brothers that it was a joke."[34] African American applicants were repeatedly turned away, refused application forms, and lied to about the nonexistence of actual open job slots. Even Black applicants with superlative track records as proven high-volume salespersons were turned away without any consideration because of the Rodriguez-mandated embargo on Black hires. Rodriguez preferred the racial exclusivity of his company over his own financial self-interest.

Within Rodriguez's staff, the fact that the dealerships did not hire Blacks was openly discussed at sales meetings, where the N-word was used often to describe African Americans, along with the threat that any staff member who hired a Black person would be fired as a result. When a Rodriguez manager was demoted and then discharged in retaliation for opposing the established Rodriguez company policy of denying all Black people jobs, the Equal Employment Opportunity Commission (EEOC) investigated and filed a case to address the pattern and practice of systemic discrimination against Black people.

The EEOC amassed a significant amount of evidence about the owner's stated policy of not hiring African Americans as salespersons and his promotion of a racially hostile environment. The evidence included testimony regarding racist commentary at the workplace that Rodriguez condoned, such as "I don't care how good that N——r is, he will never work here." Sales meetings often contained verbal references to "N——rs." Other racially disparaging terms included "sand N——r," "large lips," "fucking N——rs," "hey buckwheat," "hey boy," "I-be," and "we-bes." The latter two terms were understood among the employees as a way to refer to stereotyped Black speech as in "I be doing this" and "we be doing that."

There was also testimony that other dark-skinned ethnic group members would only be hired upon demonstrating they were not African American. An East Indian applicant whose skin color was unfavorably contrasted against a dark-colored desk, a company test for acceptable skin color, was told that the managers might still be able to hire him because he was Indian and not African American. Similarly, a dark-skinned Mexican salesperson was saved from being fired by a manager who thought he was Black when another manager explained, "It's OK, he's not Black, he's Mexican."

Yet, despite the wealth of evidence demonstrating the company's discriminatory practices, Rodriguez asserted a Latino culturally framed defense that he could not be "prejudiced" against African Americans because he had been the subject of discrimination himself as a person descended from Spanish ancestors. Presumably his own ethnic heritage exposed him to racism and thereby inoculated him against being racist himself. Rodriguez was counting on the judge to accord significant weight to the notion of racialized groups being interchangeable (and the presumption that his family origin from Spain would be viewed as Hispanic). Absent the EEOC's meticulous investigation, judicial inattention to the White Latino sleight of hand veiling the operation of White privilege behind a presumption of Latino racial homogeneity could very well have resulted in a miscarriage of justice.[35]

Fortunately, the judge was more impressed with how "numerous witnesses, Black, White, Hispanic, male, female old, young, formerly employed, presently employed, managers and supervisors, and rank and file, testified credibly concerning their knowledge of statements and discriminatory conduct against Afro-Americans by management officials of defendant Rodriguez' dealerships."[36] The judge concluded at trial that Rodriguez was liable for the discrimination of his company, and thereafter the parties reached a settlement agreement. While the "I'm a Latino Who Can't Be Prejudiced" defense ultimately failed in this case amid the significant EEOC evidence of discrimination, Rodriguez's decision to assert his own ethnic diversity as a defense highlights the potential for continued misapplication of Latino racial innocence discourse in employment discrimination litigation if not properly identified and opposed. Indeed, Latino community organizers strongly believe that it is practically impossible to persuade a judge that racial discrimination against Latino workers supervised by Latino supervisors can occur.[37] Their intuition is strongly validated by the instances in which judges immediately equate the presence of Latino supervisors and managers as definitive proof that no discrimination has occurred.[38]

LABOR MARKET SKIN-COLOR HIERARCHIES

Further aggravating the systemic effects of Latino anti-Blackness in the workplace is the manner in which it intersects perniciously with the overarching skin-color and race bias of the labor market, in which employers prefer hiring lighter-skinned Latinos to the exclusion of Afro-Latinos and African Americans.[39] This is the case even where all the job applicants are immigrants, including Afro-Latinos and other immigrants of African descent.[40] Economists have long demonstrated that lighter skin tone can result in approximately 17 percent more earnings for immigrants, including Latino immigrants, even after controlling for educational attainment and other productivity-linked demographic characteristics like English-language proficiency, education level, and so forth.[41] Studies specific to particular Latino immigrant groups indicate similar findings. Mexican Americans with darker skin earn significantly less than lighter-skinned Mexican Americans with more European facial characteristics.[42] Even after controlling for education, English-language proficiency, occupation prior to entry in the US, family background, ethnicity, race, and country of birth, light-skinned immigrants still earn significantly more than their darker-skinned counterparts.[43]

In fact, the skin-shade penalty in wages for darker immigrants is driven exclusively by the experience of immigrants from Latin America, because the wage effects of colorism are much less pronounced among other ethnic groups.[44] One possible explanation for the significance of colorism in the wages of Latino immigrants of African descent, operating in contrast to its lack of effect in the wages of African immigrants of African descent, is the existence of separate ethnic hiring networks,[45] which enable Latino anti-Black colorist bias to operate unfettered.[46] In other words, Latinos who recruit, recommend, and hire other Latino workers help set a Latino color-based hierarchy that adversely affects Afro-Latinos in ways that African immigrants seeking jobs through separate African hiring networks are insulated from.

Even so, judges do not always fully understand the particulars of Latino colorism as a problematic aspect of racial discrimination. The color discrimination case of Carmen Felix provides a helpful example.[47] Carmen Felix, a Puerto Rican of "partial African ancestry" was terminated from employment as a secretary with the Washington, DC, office of the Federal Affairs Administration of the Government of Puerto Rico (formerly known as the Office of the Commonwealth of Puerto Rico in Washington, DC ([OCPRW]), at the behest of both the Puerto Rican administrator of the office, José Cabranes, and the Puerto Rican supervisor, Providencia Haggerty.

To prove her claim of color discrimination, Carmen introduced the personnel cards of twenty-eight fellow employees to demonstrate that only two others were as dark or darker than she. She argued that there was thus a prevailing bias against dark-skinned employees in the office in the allocation of promotions that privileged what she termed "White" employees with higher-ranked positions. The judge purported to dispute Carmen's premise of dark-skin bias by visually inspecting the photographs himself and then enumerating the employees Carmen had presumably misclassified as White, when in the judge's view they were some shade of brown.

The judge then went on to say, "These observations tend to contradict the placement of a rigid line between White and non-White employees of the OCPRW drawn by [Carmen] Felix in her testimony and reflect the fact that a substantial number of Puerto Ricans have mixed ancestry." And therein the court misperceived the actualization of colorism within Latino communities and workplaces; the persons the judge viewed as brown-skinned were perceived by Carmen, and likely her coworkers, as White by virtue of their phenotype, hair texture, and socioeconomic class and not simply because of their skin shade.

As described in chapter 1, there exists a vast literature that documents the ways in which Latinos often manifest White skin preferences in their mode of self-identification and in choice of associations that recall and mirror Latin American racial ideology.[48] What this literature demonstrates, in particular, is how Latino expressions of color bias are intimately connected with assessments of phenotype, hair texture, size and shape of noses and lips, and socioeconomic class standing. Latino race labeling thus factors in considerations of bodily features other than color that are considered to be racial signifiers of denigrated African ancestry.[49] Accordingly, when a claimant like Carmen Felix in a predominantly Latino workplace enumerates the coworkers deemed to be White, she is referring to coworkers who have achieved that racial characterization not simply because of their skin color.

What the social science literature indicates is that two individuals can be of the same light skin shade, but if one has African facial features and hair texture, a Latino would not likely categorize such an individual as White, absent indicators that the person was wealthy or of high social status.[50] In turn, the non-Whiteness attributed to that light-skinned person with African features would better position another light-skinned person with less prominent African features to be perceived as White in that context. In essence, Latinos treat racial categorization in a functional manner. In any given context, there are "functional Whites and Blacks," regardless of their degree of pigment.[51] Importantly, even though this Latino categorization scheme is fluid and context specific, it still forms the foundation for racially exclusionary conduct.[52] In other words, despite the absence of scientific precision, Latino racial categorization methods still create a tightly woven caste system that prizes approximations to Whiteness. The complexity of a Latino racial hierarchy cannot be captured by a simplistic assessment of employee skin shades. Thus, what Carmen Felix's judge failed to appreciate is how nuanced and perverse Latino/Latin American assessments of color and status are.

There is an irony in the judge failing to appropriately assess the colorism claim of the Afro–Puerto Rican Carmen after having stated that it is a particularly "appropriate claim for a Puerto Rican to present." Ironic because district court judge John Helm Pratt, until his death in 1995, was known as an important defender of civil rights and discrimination law. In 1977 and 1983 he issued orders requiring the federal government to combat bias in schools against minority groups, women, and people with disabilities.[53] Judge Pratt was a White man born in New Hampshire in 1910, but some of his most significant decisions made progress in the area of individual freedom and civil rights. Yet even this defender of US civil rights was unable to understand the racialized complexity of Latino color discrimination.

This is, in part, because the federal employment discrimination legislation of Title VII of the Civil Rights Act of 1964 provides separate categories of "race," "color," and "national origin" for what is viewed as impermissible discrimination. As a result, judges have acted as if the categories are mutually exclusive and do not relate or reinforce each other, despite the fact that the statute does not prohibit a consideration of how the categories intersect. This tunnel vision hampers judges from understanding intersectional claims where the various categories overlap in one person's experience of discrimination.[54] As a result, a "color" claim gets reduced to a simplistic consideration of skin color variation. In turn, the judiciary's sole focus on skin color completely misses how Latinos deploy racial categories informed by hair texture, phenotypic features, class, place, and space and not uniquely by skin color.

It is also interesting to note, that when African Americans or other non-Latino persons of African descent present colorism claims, courts have instead been disinclined to focus on degrees of skin color. Legal scholar Taunya Lovell Banks observes that this is because of the view that with respect to African Americans and non-Latino immigrants of African descent, one drop of Black blood makes you Black and that there are no degrees of Blackness in the US cultural mindset for persons other than Latinos.[55] In contrast, Latino colorism claims are subject to the judicial misconception of racial mixture as less prone to bias.

There is a judicial inclination to act as a color meter rather than examining how a more expansive range of racial preoccupations are deployed against Latinos of African descent within the Latino workplace. Even the color discrimination cases filed within the federal district court of Puerto Rico (in which the body of US federal civil rights laws are applied) before Puerto Rican judges are not immune from the judicial fallacy that color discrimination involves only skin color. Milton Falero Santiago encountered this problem when he was terminated from his position as a sales director because of his color.[56] In his court papers, Milton described himself as a "darker-skinned, or mulatto, Puerto Rican" and then juxtaposed his color with the White skin color of the Puerto Rican employee who took over some of his duties when Milton was terminated. The court dismissed Milton's claim as non-race-based.

Milton alleged that his White Latino supervisor called him "boy" on several occasions. As we know, there is a long racial history of Black men being called "boys" as a method to subordinate them by imbuing persons of their racial status as incapable of full human personhood.[57] The same racial dynamic occurs in Puerto Rico and Latin America. Moreover, the US Supreme Court has even acknowledged that such references can be presented as evidence of racial animus.[58] Yet, the presiding Puerto Rican jurist, Judge Perez-Gimenez, dismissively stated that "while the attributed remark is somewhat disrespectful, it seems obvious that the term 'boy' refers to a person's age and lacks racial and/or color connotations." Thus, even a Puerto Rican judge in Puerto Rico, presumably privy to the dynamics of Latino/Latin American racialization methods, is just as susceptible to misconstruing colorism when the legal cause of action is equated as solely a skin-shade matter. Judicially limiting the inquiry into color discrimination to a simplistic examination of skin color differences alone misses the multiplicity of ways racialized color hierarchies are imposed. Such an equivalence undermines the legal enforcement against discrimination perpetrated by Latinos in the workplace.

The effects of a tunnel-vision inquiry into Latino-caused workplace discrimination are not inconsequential. The racially segmented labor market means that Latinos are often employed in Latino-dominant workplaces with Latino coworkers and supervisors. Any judicial misunderstanding of Latino manifestations of anti-Blackness thus means less legal protection against racial discrimination. Over time, the growth of Latino-owned businesses that disproportionately hire Latinos and make them supervisors has increased the power of the Latino-influenced labor market. The currently available data shows that between 2012 and 2017 growth in Latino-owned businesses was more than double the national average (14 percent versus 6 percent), outstripping it in forty-one out of fifty states and in the vast majority of the nation's largest economic sectors.[59] Between 1987 and 1997, Latino-owned businesses increased 232 percent.[60] Importantly, between 2014 and 2016, employment in Latino-owned businesses increased at double the rate of employment in non-Latino-owned businesses.[61] Within the small business sector, Latino businesses are the most substantial drivers of growth. The number of Latino-owned small businesses increased by 34 percent between 2010 and 2020,[62] nearly double the Latino population growth during this same time period.[63] In comparison, non-Latino-owned small businesses grew at a rate of only 1 percent over the same decade.[64]

Put together, what all these labor statistics mean for Latinos is that despite the marginalization of Latinos in society, Latino racial attitudes are not marginal to experiences of racial bias in the workplace. In fact, Latino workers with Latino supervisors earn less money than Latinos supervised by non-Latino supervisors, whether they are employed in the informal labor sector or in the formal labor market.[65] The wage penalty of having a Latino supervisor exists regardless of education level, work experience, tenure, language skill, citizenship status, gender, firm size, or occupation. Furthermore, Latinos with Latino supervisors are less likely to hold positions of authority.[66] Taking into account that Latino workers have a greater propensity to have Latino supervisors who influence their hiring, wages, and performance evaluations, the influence of Latino racial attitudes in the labor market is considerable.[67] The next chapter shows how Latino racial attitudes are just as relevant in the world of segregated housing.

CHAPTER 4

"OYE NEGRO,
YOU CAN'T LIVE HERE"

LATINO LANDLORDS IN ACTION

Often the need for shelter can be so pressing that vindicating even the clearest cases of housing bias is less of a priority for discrimination victims who need to find a place to live. Such was the case for Quinta, an Afro-Dominican who in 2004 sought a room to rent in New York City.[1] She was a twenty-four-year–old, bilingual college graduate moving to New York for a position in government politics and needed a temporary place to stay until her husband could relocate to New York as well. Quinta considered herself fortunate that her Dominican brother-in-law alerted her to an informal Latino Craigslist-like housing network in which Latinos subleased bedrooms within their apartments in the Latino-dominated Inwood section of upper Manhattan. Arrangements were made over the phone for a week-to-week rental payment and date on which Quinta could move in.

Yet when Quinta arrived on the appointed date with her suitcase in hand, the Latina apartment dweller took one look at Quinta's brown skin and claimed that the room was not actually available to rent and that a mistake had somehow been made. Quinta's brother-in-law had never anticipated that the Latino Inwood room rental "agency" he recommended would fail Quinta in this way. Why? As a fair-skinned Latino, Quinta's brother-in-law had no experience with his racial appearance being an object of derision by fellow Latinos.

The in-person denial of a housing rental after it is offered as available on the telephone is a classic example of race-based housing discrimination. However, Quinta had a new job to start and little time for anything else, let alone filing a legal claim. So, like so many other victims of housing discrimination, Quinta simply "moved on" and located an alternative housing arrangement. Yet, over fifteen years later, as she related the details of how she was racially excluded, Quinta was still disturbed by what had happened. Quinta explained to me that having spent her childhood in predominantly White non-Hispanic spaces in Boston, she "never expected to feel at home" with White non-Hispanics but had thought she'd be more welcome among fellow Latinos. The pain of being racially excluded by her Latino and Latina compatriots then felt much more acute and perhaps too painful to process with a protracted legal proceeding. So while the Latino-dominated network of informal housing rentals does not figure into national calculations of the extent of housing segregation, such networks exert significant influence and inflict actual racial harms. Consequently, the pragmatic choice not to file discrimination claims by the Quintas of the world should not be interpreted as the absence of a Latino anti-Black discrimination problem in New York or anywhere else.

Even more disturbing perhaps is that our national law and many state laws prohibiting racial discrimination in the rental and purchase of housing purposely exempt landlords who are owner-occupiers of small-scale multiple dwelling units (such as a building of four units or fewer).[2] Legislators enacting the national Fair Housing Act wanted to protect the hypothetical "Mrs. Murphys" of the world from being forced to share their intimate settings with races they did not like. The exception was also justified with the presumption that small-scale multiple-dwelling units were not a significant share of the overall housing market. It was reasoned that this small degree of discrimination would not adversely disrupt the pursuit of racial equality. The compromise was enacted with the caveat that a real estate broker could not administer a discriminatory selection process, and public advertising for such small multiple-dwelling units could not be discriminatory in stating a preference for or an exclusion of applicants of a particular race, lest the advertising itself contribute to a societal climate of racial inequality.

While the earlier Civil Rights Act of 1866 prohibition against racial discrimination in housing does not contain a "Mrs. Murphy" exception, its reach into the informal housing market is hindered by the statute's failure to include a government enforcement mechanism.[3] The US Department of Housing and Urban Development (HUD) is legislatively tasked with enforcing the Fair Housing Act and not the Civil Rights Act of 1866 (except as it relates to housing and community development programs funded by HUD). In other words, government funding to investigate and process discrimination claims is not directed toward the "Mrs. Murphy" context. Only if an aggrieved victim has the requisite resources and wherewithal to mount their own individual Civil Rights Act of 1866 lawsuit can they seek to have a "Mrs. Murphy" sanctioned. While local state laws vary in the extent of their "Mrs. Murphy" exceptions, only a handful of states completely omit the exception.

Thus, apart from advertising, the legal system effectively authorizes discrimination in the informal housing context. What the law fails to consider is that the "Mrs. Moraleses" of the informal Latino housing market controlling access to apartment shares and basement apartment rentals are not an insignificant source of housing. Housing experts note that the private rental industry is very decentralized and includes many "disconnected, small-scale landlords who often evaluate applicants on a case-by-case basis, in-person, and without formalized eligibility criteria."[4] Independent landlords still own most rental properties and thus are of vital importance in implementing fair housing laws. Indeed, by 2018, the Latino homeownership rate rose to 47.5 percent (as compared to the national rate of 65.1 percent).[5] Against a backdrop of hyper-segregation precluding Latino access to most White non-Hispanic residential areas, the informal Latino-controlled housing networks that many Latinos are limited to take on greater importance.

Furthermore, Afro-Latinos feel the brunt of Latino anti-Blackness beyond the discrimination they experience from Latino landlords and homeowners. This is because Latino property managers and neighbors can also be agents of anti-Blackness. The Martinez family slammed right into such bias as tenants of Meridian Apartments in Cypress, California (an Orange County suburb within twenty miles of Los Angeles).

During the time that the Afro-Latino Martinez children and their African American mother, Suzy Martinez, lived there, their Latino neighbors joined with the White non-Hispanic neighbors in racially harassing the family with "persistent racial slurs, vandalism of the apartment and car, throwing of rocks, beer cans, and other matter [along with] threats of violence."[6] Moreover, the Martinez family was denied access to the complex's facilities, including the pool, courtyard, and Jacuzzi. The racial harassment was only compounded when, after reporting the discrimination to the Latina apartment complex manager, Eve Diaz, Diaz failed to take any action to address the discrimination.

By failing to take any action to halt the racial harassment, property manager Diaz and the Latino neighbors were actively complicit in fortifying the longstanding racial hostility of Orange County, California.[7] Ironically, the television show *The O.C.* visually illustrated White segregation in Orange County when it aired from 2003 to 2007, the same years Suzy was litigating her family's discrimination claim against the Meridian Apartments. At that time, the census listed the resident population of Cypress as 54.4 percent White, 3 percent African American, 0.6 percent American Indian, 31.3 percent Asian, 0.38 percent Pacific Islander, 5.2 percent other, and 4.9 percent identifying as two or more races.[8] Hispanics/Latinos made up 18.4 percent of the population (Mexican, 14.1 percent; Puerto Rican, 0.5 percent; Cuban, 0.3 percent; other Hispanic/Latino 3 percent), which was lower than the state percentage of 37.6 percent. Racially, the Hispanic/Latino population identified as 58.49 percent White, 0.77 percent Black, 1.67 percent American Indian or Native Alaskan, 1.45 percent Asian, 0.34 percent Native Hawaiian or Pacific Islander, 27.45 percent other race, and 9.8 percent two or more races. Suzy was able to receive financial compensation for the harm of the harassment when the parties reached a confidential settlement agreement on the eve of trial. However, Suzy's incident is one of the few recorded cases of Latino anti-Black housing discrimination involving Afro-Latinos in the United States.

Even Miami, with its density of Latino residents and its reputation as the capital of Cuban Whiteness, has few recorded Latino anti-Black housing discrimination cases filed by Afro-Latinos.[9] Yet, equating the absence of legal claims with the absence of instances of discrimination would be misplaced given the prevalence of discrimination accounts when Latinos are directly questioned about their life experiences. The current oral history project Black Migration into a White City: Power, Privilege and Exclusion in Miami is tracing the longstanding exclusionary tactics of White Cubans against Black Cubans in Miami.[10] Furthermore, published ethnographies of Miami parallel the narratives of exclusion illuminated in the legal cases.

In this respect, Alan Aja's interview of Afro-Cuban David Rosemond helps flesh out how the deeply entrenched racialized geography of Latino Miami normalizes discrimination and thereby discourages lawsuits. In recalling his parents' struggles when moving from New York City to Miami in the 1970s, David said, "They [Miami Latinos in Little Havana] wouldn't rent to us. It went from 'yeah the apartment is available' (over the phone) to 'we made a mistake'" once they showed up in person.[11] After feeling beleaguered from all the in-person rejection, David's mother prevailed upon a White Cuban family friend to accompany her during her search for housing, hoping her adjacency to White acquaintanceship would validate her good character and financial responsibility. Unfortunately, her strategy did not work, and the family was never able to locate housing in Little Havana despite being Cuban themselves. Instead, the Rosemond family lived in Allapattah, a once African American enclave now home to Miami's "Little Santo Domingo," populated by many darker-skinned immigrants from the Dominican Republic.

Nor is the experience of the Afro-Cuban Rosemond family singular. An early study of discrimination in rental housing in Miami found that as compared to White Cubans, Afro-Cubans were repeatedly asked to pay a higher average security deposit across Miami, including in White Cuban areas, and were more often misinformed regarding the nonavailability of vacant rental units.[12] Other studies of Miami and Susan Greenbaum's examination of Tampa, Florida, trace similar housing challenges for Afro-Cuban residents.[13] Historically, Afro-Cuban settlement across Florida from 1869 forward was subject to an anti-Black racialized geography. As Afro-Cuban Evelio Grillo recounts of his youth in Ybor City, Tampa, in the 1920s, "I don't remember playing with a single White Cuban child. . . . Black Cubans and White Cubans lived apart from one another in Ybor City."[14] Moreover, the patterns of residential segregation between White and Black Latino Florida residents continues today.[15] The echoes of the Jim Crow segregation of Afro-Cubans from White Cubans that is part of the history of Florida resound loudly in the present.[16] Miami in particular remains one of the nation's most segregated cities, and the actions of Latino landlords do nothing to mitigate this.[17] Or as one Afro-Cuban interviewee told anthropologist Michelle Hay, "The examples of [Latino anti-Black] racism in Miami is in house hunting."[18] Today, Latino anti-Black bias has an enormous ability to interfere with access to housing in Miami, given the density of Latino homeowners (and potential landlords) that exists in Miami. Unlike many other regions in the United States, in Miami, Latinos make up 67 percent of all owner-occupied homes and 70 percent of all renter-occupied homes, and thus present a vast informal, Latino-controlled housing network influenced by Latino racial attitudes.[19]

Lamentably, Afro-Latino segregation from other Latinos is not exclusive to Florida. Historian Nancy Raquel Mirabal has noted that New York City was a major destination for Puerto Ricans and Cubans from 1823 to 1957, and that the early period was marked by racial tensions and separations among the Cubans she studied.[20] Similarly, Jesse Hoffnung-Garskof's study of Puerto Rican migration to New York City before the 1920s indicates that there was little residential contact between White and Black Puerto Ricans.[21] Afro–Puerto Rican Pura Delgado's description of her arrival to New York in 1947 underscores the historical antecedents of today's intra-Latino residential discrimination.

> I remember vividly a cousin who made arrangements for me to rent a room when I arrived in New York City from a Puerto Rican woman who was her friend. But when I arrived, she refused to allow me to stay in her home because I was dark. She had assumed I was the same [light] complexion as my cousin.[22]

In essence, Pura is Quinta's ancestor across the generations of continued Latino anti-Black bias in New York City. Should it be so surprising then that Latino anti-Blackness in housing also extends to African Americans?

To begin to understand contemporary Latino housing discrimination against African Americans, consider a city like Chicago, consistently ranked by the census as one of the top five most segregated cities in the United States and the most segregated in the state of Illinois, more than fifty years after the Fair Housing Act outlawed housing segregation.[23] While Chicago certainly comports with the historical non-Hispanic Black-White vision of segregation, it has also become the fourth in segregation between Latinos and African Americans. The ranking is especially noteworthy when one considers that the three metro areas ahead of it (Milwaukee, Detroit, and Cleveland) all have fewer Latinos and significantly smaller total populations. However, the degree of Latino-Black residential segregation cannot be understood simply

from the census data. Contemporary personal accounts of racial
exclusion help illuminate how a group, like Latinos, that is discriminated against by White non-Hispanics in the housing market can then turn around and discriminate against another group,
African Americans.

The housing experience of African American Chicago tenant
Mitchell Keys provides a useful example. Mitchell discovered that
his rental agreement was more onerous than that of the other
tenants in his Chicago apartment building. When he confronted
his Latino landlord, Francisco García, about the matter, García
stated that he had a preference against renting to African Americans like Mitchell. Given the clarity of the anti-Black bias in the
landlord's conduct, the secretary of Housing and Urban Development (HUD) brought an administrative case on behalf of Mitchell.[24] García failed to provide a nondiscriminatory reason for his
actions and agreed to settle the case without a hearing before an
administrative law judge. The settlement agreement required
García to financially compensate Mitchell. Importantly, García
was also permanently prohibited from "discriminating on the basis of race, sex, color, religion, national origin, handicap, or familial status against any person and/or renter in any aspect of the
rental of a dwelling unit." HUD monitored García's compliance
by examining his HUD-mandated monthly reports regarding his
reasoning for accepting or rejecting tenants. Thus, by all metrics,
Mitchell won.

Mitchell ironically was benefitted in his claim by how brazen
García was in verbalizing his anti-Black bias and by Mitchell's own
ability to contest the racial discrimination after having obtained
housing, albeit at a discriminatorily inflated rental rate. Other victims of Latino anti-Black bias who have been excluded by landlords more savvy about obscuring their true racialized motives
are not as well positioned to challenge racism that has not been
made obvious but has completely blocked their access to housing. Similarly, those Black people who have been physically chased
out of Chicago neighborhoods by Latino residents never have the

opportunity to seek housing there, let alone file housing discrimination claims regarding their racial exclusion.[25]

At the time Mitchell filed his discrimination claim, Chicago, Illinois, had a population of 2,783,726, which was 45.4 percent White non-Hispanic, 39.1 percent Black, .3 percent American Indian, 3.7 percent Asian or Pacific Islander, and 11.5 percent other.[26] Ethnically, Latinos made up 19.6 percent of the population. While not a majority, the Latino homeownership rate in Chicago was 37.8 percent (as compared to the citywide average homeownership rate of 46.1 percent).[27] By 2018, the Latino homeownership rate in Illinois as a whole rose to 54 percent (as compared to the national average rate of 64.8 percent).[28] The density of the Latino population in Chicago then and now means that the existence of Latino anti-Black bias can have a significant effect in a housing rental market that is already virulently segregated.

Even more concerning, then, are those contexts in which Latinos are an even greater proportion of a local population with the potential for outsize influence on the home rental market (either by renting or selling properties they own or by renting rooms in apartments or homes they occupy as renters themselves). Elias and Patricia Tulsen's experience searching for a home in Latino-dominated Brentwood, New York, is thus very illuminating. Elias and Patricia are an African American couple who wished to pursue their dream of homeownership in Brentwood. The white frame house on Hewes Street greatly interested them, given its location on a quiet residential street in the suburban community of Long Island. Near the time of their search, the Census Bureau reported that there were 53,917 people living in Brentwood.[29] The population broke down racially as follows: White, 47.7 percent; Black, 18.1 percent; American Indian, 0.6 percent; Asian, 2.0 percent; Pacific Islander, 0.1 percent; other, 25.4 percent; and two or more races, 6.1 percent. Significantly, the city was 54 percent Hispanic/Latino (Mexican, 0.9 percent; Puerto Rican, 15.3 percent; Cuban, 0.4 percent; other, 37.7 percent) and 45.7 percent non-Hispanic/Latino, with 42 percent of the total

Hispanic/Latino population identifying racially as White. This marked a significant increase in the Hispanic/Latino population of the area from 34.7 percent just one decade earlier.[30] Perhaps it was this large demographic of Latinos that emboldened Latino homeowners (father and son) Thomas and Andrew Clemente to flagrantly assert their anti-Black bias.

While Elias and Patricia Tulsen toured the basement of the home, Latino seller Thomas Clemente asked his real estate agent, Lisa McNell, to stay upstairs with him. Thomas Clemente then informed the agent that he did not want to sell the property to any Black person, and the only way he might consider doing so is if they paid 3 percent above the stated sale price (despite an absence of counteroffers from any other would-be purchasers). After Thomas Clemente spoke on the phone with his son Andrew Clemente (a co-owner of the property), Thomas reaffirmed to the real estate agent their joint disinterest in selling to Black people absent a payment premium that he increased to 5 percent above the publicly listed price.[31]

In effect, the Clementes wanted to impose a "Black Tax" on Elias and Patricia, presumably for the hardship of selling to Black people and having them present in the neighborhood.[32] In addition to being discriminatory, the Clementes' bias against having Blacks seemingly taint the neighborhood is ironic, given that it was a time in which Brentwood was experiencing a surge in crime caused by Latino gang activity.[33]

Fortunately for Elias and Patricia, real estate agent Lisa Mc-Nell sacrificed her potential to earn a commission in favor of following the law, which prohibits real estate agents from facilitating the racial discrimination of sellers. McNell instead informed the real estate agency's owner about the Clementes' anti-Black comments, and in turn the agency severed its relationship with the Clemente family. In the face of such irrefutable evidence, the Clementes agreed to settle the case without a hearing or adjudication.

As a result, the Clementes paid Elias and Patricia financial compensation and agreed not to (1) retaliate, coerce, intimidate, or interfere with any individual because of their exercise or enjoyment of any right granted or protected by the Fair Housing Act; (2) make statements that indicate preferences, limitations, or discrimination against any individual(s) in the rental of property based upon any of the protected classes under the act, including, but not limited to, race and national origin; and (3) discriminate against persons because of race or national origin or any other protected class pursuant to the provisions of the act. Less than three months later, Elias and Patricia were able to purchase another home within the same price range and located within the same zip code and school district, but on an even larger lot size than the one owned by the Clementes. Meanwhile, it took the Clementes seven months to sell the property they wanted to maintain as exclusively White.

While the large numbers of Latinos living in Brentwood, New York, may have emboldened the Clementes to overtly express and act upon their anti-Black bias, similar forms of blatant Latino anti-Black exclusion have also occurred in locations where Latinos are numerically a small percentage of the population in comparison to White non-Hispanics and African Americans. When Andre Echols and Jacqueline Ash were seeking apartments in Davenport, Iowa, it had a population of approximately ninety-eight thousand.[34] It was 83.7 percent White, 9.2 percent Black or African American, 0.4 percent American Indian, 2.0 percent Asian, 2.3 percent other, and 2.4 percent two or more races. Hispanics/Latinos were only 5.4 percent of the population (Mexican, 4.5 percent; Puerto Rican, 0.2 percent; other, 0.7 percent). Racially, 44.40 percent of the Hispanic/Latino population identified as White. Despite the smaller demographic presence of Latinos in Davenport, Iowa, when Jacqueline and later Andre sought to rent an apartment from Latino landlord Frank Quijas, he felt completely free to loudly vocalize his prohibition against renting to Black people.

When Jacqueline saw Quijas's newspaper advertisement for a vacant apartment, she called to inquire about the available unit, and Quijas immediately asked: "Are you Black or White? I don't rent to Blacks."³⁵ Nor was Quijas's racial brazenness confined to this telephone conversation. Andre had the offensive experience of having Quijas contemptuously tell him to his face that he didn't rent to Black people. Andre was so shocked that he asked Quijas to repeat what he had just said so that his mother, who had accompanied him, could hear it as well. Quijas then nonchalantly repeated, "I don't rent to Blacks."

Given how egregious Quijas's expression of anti-Black bias was for both Jacqueline and later Andre, they were each awarded financial compensation, and Quijas was obligated to submit a written apology to each of them. Moreover, Quijas agreed to sell all three of the duplexes he owned as rental properties in the area and never participate in the real estate business. For Quijas, it was preferable to discontinue earning money as a landlord when the judge prohibited him from any further anti-Black discrimination.

Even Latino landlords who live nowhere near the properties they rent out still insist on maintaining their rental units as racially exclusive White spaces. A Latino couple, Jaime and Graciela Barberis, were living in Ecuador yet vigilantly policed the racial occupancy of their rental property in Rockville, Maryland, despite their use of a property management company to lease the premises for them in their absence.³⁶ Gilmore Thompson Sr. sought to rent the four-bedroom house for himself and his family as part of their move from the US Virgin Islands. When Gilmore signed the rental agreement with the property manager acting for Jaime and Graciela, he also paid the first month's rent and security deposit and was informed that Jaime and Graciela had orally agreed to rent him the house. But after Jaime and Graciela discovered Gilmore was Black, they rejected his lease.

Jaime and Graciela refused to admit they acted in a discriminatory fashion. Nevertheless, the US Department of Housing and Urban Development (HUD) concluded, based upon the witness interviews they conducted and documents they reviewed, that Jaime and Graciela had violated the Fair Housing Act in using race to deny Gilmore and his family the rental home. After HUD presented its final report and issued a charge of discrimination, Jaime and Graciela then decided to settle the case and pay Gilmore monetary compensation.

Despite the absolute clarity about the racial motivation of such Black exclusion, public commentators tend to characterize Latino anti-Black bias as simply an unfortunate outgrowth of the racism against African Americans learned in the United States. However, the presumption that Latinos are racial innocents is undercut by the very same anti-Black bias that is evident in Latino distaste for renting and selling to other Latino compatriots who happen to be Afro-Latino. Yet, the lack of public attention to Latino anti-Black bias translates into a jury pool that is not well informed to recognize its manifestations when presented in a court case. In fact, there are times when the Latino involvement in anti-Black bias makes the discrimination more vexing and difficult to address in court.

Eddie Frazier, an African American man, was thus thwarted in his efforts to combat the housing discrimination he and Diane Treloar, his White non-Hispanic girlfriend, encountered when seeking an apartment in the Long Island, New York, suburb called Smithtown (forty-three miles from New York City).[37] Like the racial segregation that Suzy Martinez had to navigate in the Orange County suburb of California, Smithtown is a town of hyperracial segregation. At the time Eddie was seeking an apartment, the Census Bureau reported that Smithtown was predominantly White (96.8 percent), the rest of the population was Black (0.8 percent), American Indian (0.1 percent), Asian or Pacific Islander (1.9 percent), and other races (0.4 percent).[38] The town was 2.6 percent Hispanic/Latino (Mexican, 0.2 percent; Puerto Rican, 1.1 percent; Cuban, 0.1 percent; other 1.2 percent) and the racial makeup among Hispanic/Latino people was White (83.13 percent), Black (0.98 percent), American Indian (0.70 percent), Asian or Pacific Islander (0.64 percent), and other (14.53 percent). Significantly, the Ku Klux Klan played a significant part in the founding of the town and was just publicly reviving its presence in New York near the time of Eddie's apartment search.[39]

Nevertheless, when Eddie's offer to rent a Smithtown apartment was rejected and his telephone calls were unreturned, while the unit remained vacant another three months until it was rented to a White tenant, the jury that heard his claim refused to conclude it was because of racial discrimination. Notably, the owners of the unit that rejected Eddie included Anna Maria Rominger, a woman the judge described as a "Brazilian with dark skin," who stated in court that the accusation of discrimination was unfounded because she was "of mixed-race heritage and that numerous of her [Latino] relatives were black, Indian, and Italian."[40] In essence, the Latina landlord advanced a Latina shield of immunity against being biased—and the jury seemingly accepted it in a way that would otherwise be viewed as implausible had a White non-Hispanic landlord said it.

Small wonder, then, that of the sizeable number of persons who indicate in surveys that they have experienced Latino anti-Black bias, few actually file legal claims. Further aggravating the disinclination to file legal claims are the limited resources that fair housing centers have for enforcing antidiscrimination law. Fair housing centers are nonprofit organizations across the country that help provide evidence of housing discrimination by investigating claims and by sending out individuals of different races and ethnicities to pose as renters or buyers for the purpose of testing for unlawful housing discrimination.

Kate Scott, the executive director of the Equal Rights Center in Washington, DC, supervises fair housing testing, and she laments that "there's no way that we have the resources to capture all of the discrimination that's happening."[41] Moreover, the discrimination that does get investigated is primarily "as a result of us being very affirmative in our outreach efforts . . . [within] the priorities of leadership at these various organizations." Given the intransigence of White non-Hispanic housing discrimination against African Americans, Amber Hendley, a fair housing testing coordinator in Chicago, notes that fair testing centers have prioritized non-Hispanic White-Black testing, without the more

complicating nuance of White Latino-Black test designs.[42] Re-
latedly, when landlords and homeowners who might be Latino,
based on their surnames, are investigated, Boston fair housing tes-
ter Catherine LaRaia has observed that the testers who are sent
out rarely specify the ethnicity and race of the landlord.[43]

Still, Latino anti-Black bias in the United States informs
and, in turn, is structurally shaped by residential segregation.
Afro-Latina scholar Zaire Zenit Dinzey-Flores powerfully reminds us from her work detailing how anti-Black racism informs
the trend to create gated communities in Puerto Rico's public
spaces: "In Puerto Rico, in the United States, in Latin America,
and in much of the world, homes and residential neighborhoods
have been a vehicle for race, ethnic, and class exclusion. Housing
and neighborhoods frame race. Space, the built environment, exposes the activated racist contours of its imaginations."[44] Today's
matrix of racially exclusive housing also implicates Latino agents
of anti-Black bias. As the legal case stories in this chapter have
shown, Latino landlords and home sellers have been direct instru-
ments of anti-Black residential exclusion against Afro-Latinos and
African Americans alike.

Residential segregation is crucial to concerns with racial equality, because the racialized ordering of neighborhoods, unfortunately, determines how community and educational resources are
allocated or not allocated. In fact, the Fair Housing Act of 1968[45]
is commonly referred to as the "last plank of the Civil Rights
Movement."[46] Thus, the existence of both stark White non-
Hispanic segregation from non-Whites and segregated proximity
of non-Whites with one another is key to understanding the current racial dynamics that exist.

Large-scale studies on US segregation patterns have detected
an additional racial barrier imposed on Latinos with apparent African ancestry compared to other Latinos.[47] For example, Puerto
Ricans perceived as "Blacker" are more segregated from White
non-Hispanics than are White Puerto Ricans and other Latino
groups.[48] Dark-skinned Mexicans and Cubans experience a lesser

degree of residential segregation from White non-Hispanics because dark-skinned Puerto Ricans are more likely to be perceived
as Afro-descendants.[49] White Latinos experience less segregation
from White non-Hispanics than do Black Latinos.[50] Hence, it is
not just skin color that penalizes Latinos in the housing and rental
market but specifically Blackness. Anti-Blackness is what under-
pins the fact that Latinos who are White–presenting, or whose
dark skin is not attributed to African ancestry, consistently are
shown to experience less intense levels of residential segregation
from White non-Hispanics. In short, Latino anti-Black bias exists
within a universe of White non-Hispanic segregation that rewards
the appearance of Whiteness and confines non-White-identifying
Latinos and African Americans to neighboring non-resourced,
non-White spaces. This helps explain why light-skinned Latinas
prefer White non-Hispanic neighbors when choosing places for
their families to live.[51]

Thus, while Latinos and African Americans often reside near
one another, that racial diversity is geographically segmented in
ways that preserve traditional segregation of Whites and non-
Whites. In fact, neighborhoods demographically categorized as "integrated" can resemble "worlds of strangers."[52] This is because when
Latino residents choose to limit their interaction with Black neighbors to fleeting contacts, racial stereotypes are left undisturbed.[53]

By the same token, being segregated from White non-Hispanics
heightens the impulse of socially derided Latinos to seek social
status through "turf defense" exclusion of the denigrated group,
African Americans. Further heightening the adverse consequences
to equality from housing discrimination is how residential segregation also facilitates interethnic violence. The next chapter examines the notable instances of Latino anti-Black violence in the
United States and how the criminal justice system has responded.

CHAPTER 5

PHYSICAL VIOLENCE

THE CRIMINAL JUSTICE SYSTEM'S "BROWN" VERSUS BLACK DYNAMIC

For most spectators, what was most notable about the Charlottesville, Virginia, August 2017 Unite the Right Rally was the alarming vision of marchers proudly identifying themselves as neo-Nazis, neo-Confederates, neofascists, White nationalists, and Ku Klux Klan members. Violence erupted. One of those White supremacists accelerated his car into a crowd of counter-protesters, killing thirty-two-year-old Heather Heyer and leaving nineteen others injured, five critically.

LATINO WHITE SUPREMACISTS

The White supremacists who caused the Charlottesville violence were not solely White non-Hispanics. Alex Michael Ramos, a Latino from Marietta, Georgia, also took part in the White nationalist rally and then joined five other White nationalists in surrounding a Black man, DeAndre Harris, in a parking lot and beating him with wooden boards and a metal pipe. Ramos defended his attack on this special education teacher's aide in a video on his Facebook page, saying that he couldn't be a racist because he was Spanish, specifically Puerto Rican.[1]

With that single statement, Ramos encapsulated the perversity of Latino anti-Black violence—the Latino Teflon shield against racism charges while being racist. Latino community leader Rosa Clemente noted at the time that "although Ramos expressed and enacted the most vile and violent form of White supremacy, his thinking is not uncommon among a minority of Puerto Ricans."[2] Nor is such thinking restricted to Puerto Ricans.

When Peruvian American George Zimmerman killed unarmed Black teenager Trayvon Martin for walking in his neighborhood in 2012, Zimmerman's relatives and defenders insisted that the murder was not racist because Zimmerman was Latino. Zimmerman's brother Robert explicitly stated that Zimmerman was not "some kind of mythological racist monster [because] he is actually a Hispanic non-racist person."[3] All of which strongly suggests that sociologist George Yancey's survey research indicating that Latinos (unlike African Americans) are more disposed to believing that Latinos cannot be racist is also applicable in the more extreme context of physical violence and murder.[4]

Unfortunately, George Zimmerman and Alex Michael Ramos are not isolated examples of Latinos harboring racialized violence. The Southern Poverty Law Center has noticed that there is a disturbing trend of more Latinos joining White supremacist hate groups.[5] These Latinos include people like Christopher Rey Monzon, a twenty-two-year-old Cuban American, associated with the neo-Confederate hate group League of the South. Monzon was arrested weeks after Charlottesville for charging at protesters in a separate Florida demonstration. Nick Fuentes, a nineteen-year-old student who hosts an alt-right podcast called *America First*, also participated in the Charlottesville protests. In an interview with National Public Radio, Juan Cadavid, a Colombian-born Californian who now goes by the name Johnny Benitez, shared how he is an advocate for what he called "white identity politics"—which includes embracing the "14 Words"[6] slogan used by White supremacists: "We must secure the existence of our people and a future for white children."[7] Finally, the January 6, 2021, terrorist attack on the US capitol included Latino members of the White supremacist group Proud Boys (including but not limited to Bryan Betancur, Louis Colon, Nicholas DeCarlo, Gabriel Garcia, and William Pepe). Disturbingly, the Proud Boys' chairman is Cuban American Enrique Tarrio.

PRISONS

When the criminal justice system has been able to see beyond the veil of the "I can't be racist—I'm Latino" defense to anti-Black racial violence and convict Latino White supremacists, it in turn places them in prison institutions that themselves breed White supremacy and reinforce the anti-Blackness of Latino inmates. Anti-Defamation League researchers have noted that Latino White nationalists in California's large prison-gang systems have aligned themselves with White supremacist gangs. One prison gang known as the Nazi Low Riders (NLR) is made up of California Youth Authority inmates who serve as foot soldiers for the Aryan Brotherhood. The NLR gang is willing to accept Latinos with the proviso that "you must have at least half white blood, but no black blood."[8] NLR is also present in other states like Arizona, Colorado, Florida, and Illinois.

Prisons often operate with explicit norms of racial segregation, despite US Supreme Court case law that racially segregated prisons compromise an inmate's Equal Protection racial equality rights.[9] Institutionally, creating such racialized prison spaces to control prison violence is not supposed to be tolerated unless absolutely needed for proper prison administration. However, preserving prison security is considered by the Supreme Court to be a compelling state interest that can justify racial segregation. This, in effect, permits many prisons to continue to structure and maintain racially segregated spaces.[10]

Absent official membership in White prison gangs, Latino-specific gangs still position themselves in opposition to African American prison gangs. This is underscored by repeated instances of prison riots rooted in Latino versus African American gang violence. In 2009, a California prison riot occurred when Latino prison gangs started fighting African American gangs in hand-to-hand combat.[11] This incident left more than two hundred prisoners injured and fifty-five hospitalized. Yet, when questioned about the violence, a prison official revealed that another riot among "Hispanic and black prisoners" had occurred earlier that same year. Similarly, in 2007, an eight-hundred-inmate California prison riot occurred "when a black and a Hispanic prisoner began fighting, prompting other prisoners to join divided along racial lines."[12] Another California prison experienced a weeklong race riot in 2006 that resulted in the deaths of prisoners.[13]

Latino prisoners who are not gang members when they enter the prison system are quickly indoctrinated into the "convict code" rules on Latino inmates not associating with African American inmates.[14] Jesse Vasquez, who spent eighteen years in California state prisons, explains how California prisons taught him racism at the age of eighteen. "My first lesson in racial discrimination happened at the maximum-security prison at Calipatria, Calif. An older Mexican dude with the signature handlebar mustache told me in a Hollywood whisper, 'Hey, homie, we don't associate with llantas (tires) around here. The animales (animals) have their own rules. We follow ours. Don't talk to them too much because someone might feel disrespected, and you're going to get dealt with.'"[15] Getting dealt with meant—"I'd get beat up or stabbed for . . . interactions with the black guys: The phone on their side of the day room and their concrete tables on the yard were off limits. No eating, lingering or trading with them. And definitely no arguing: If a black guy so much as raised his voice, I was supposed to punch him in the mouth even if it started a riot."[16] As another Latino prison gang member details, there is a "zero tolerance towards blacks" inasmuch as the Latino gangs forbade them "to drink from water fountains or use telephones blacks have used, to touch blacks, or to accept drugs or cigarettes from blacks."[17]

The Latino prison gang vigilance toward prizing segregation from African Americans then mutually reinforces the Latino
street-gang focus on keeping African Americans out of so-called
Latino spaces regardless of their lack of affiliation with Black
gangs. This is because incarcerated Latino gang members dictate
the rules of racial segregation, the level of violence for mainte-
nance of the segregation, and the gang initiation rituals designating street anti-Black violence as the ticket for admission into
the Latino gang.[18] In California specifically, interethnic violence
centers on the targeting of African American residents by Latino
street gangs operating with the explicitly stated goal of eradicating
African Americans from "Latino" spaces. This is clearly demonstrated by the evidence brought forth in a number of criminal
cases and the police and FBI investigations that precipitated them.
They begin with Latino gang initiations that require unprovoked
physical attacks on random Black people.

In 2017, California resident Louis Vasquez was sentenced to
twenty-one years to life in prison for the attempted murder of two
Black men who were strangers to him, because he was directed
to attack two random Black people by a gang.[19] Vasquez followed
the gang directive by first attacking a shopping center employee
in the Los Angeles County community of Covina who was collecting shopping carts in front of the mall. The employee was
an eighteen-year-old African American teenager whom Vasquez
stabbed in the shoulder with a kitchen knife and yelled racial slurs
at during the attack. After attacking the teenager, Vazquez then
proceeded to target an African American man who was walking
toward the CVS pharmacy in the strip mall. A surveillance video
captured how Vasquez chased the CVS customer and stabbed him
in the shoulder and knee area.

Several years before, the west San Fernando Valley area of Los
Angeles witnessed very similar Latino gang-initiated violence. Anthony Gonzales and Francisco Vasquez were two men that were
driven to the west San Fernando Valley by Latino gang members
for the purpose of harming Black passersby.[20] After being dropped

off, both men opened fire on two randomly selected African American men as they yelled racial slurs at them. Neither of the victims were gang members or persons that had provoked the violence. Both Vasquez and Gonzales were convicted of a racial hate crime and attempted murder of the African American men.

Other Latino-gang anti-Black violence has been larger scale and much more systematic. Federal prosecutors have successfully proven outright conspiracies. In 2019, seven members of the Los Angeles Hazard Grande (Big Hazard) Latino street gang pled guilty to firebombing the Ramona Gardens public housing complex in East Los Angeles with the specific intent of driving Black residents out of the Boyle Heights neighborhood.[21] The Hazard Grande gang was affiliated with the Mexican Mafia prison gang, which ordered the firebombings as part of their mutual commitment to eradicating Black people from the predominantly Latino Ramona Gardens complex. At the time of the 2014 firebombing, African Americans comprised only 4 percent of the nearly eighteen hundred people living in Ramona Gardens.

Weeks of planning culminated in the targeting of African American households on a Mother's Day evening while Black families and children were sleeping. While wearing masks and wielding hammers, gang members smashed the windows of Black families' apartments in order to toss in ignited Molotov cocktails (glass bottles filled with gasoline). Prior to the attack, the gang members monitored the Black residents and warned them that they were living in Hazard Grande territory and would be at risk as long as they stayed there.

While the number of Black families living in Ramona Gardens was very small, their presence was still a marked contrast to their near absence over the two previous decades, precipitated in 1992 as Black families fled when the Hazard Grande gang detonated explosive devices in the apartments of two Black families. At that time only seven Black families lived in the complex, but they all evacuated after the Hazard Grande terrorized them. By 2014, the Latino gang viewed even a handful of Black families as an encroachment into their space and warranted another fire-bombing. The gang members were successfully convicted because of the joint investigation of the Federal Bureau of Investigation, the Los Angeles Police Department, the Los Angeles Fire Department, and the Bureau of Alcohol, Tobacco, Firearms and Explosives. Part of what incentivized the federal and state government agencies to expend their joint resources on the investigation and prosecution of the firebombings was the history of Latino gangs terrorizing peaceful Black residents as a campaign of racial exclusion. Several years before the Ramona Gardens attack, a Latino gang caused twenty homicides when it conducted a campaign to push Black residents out of the unincorporated Florence-Firestone neighborhood of Los Angeles.[22]

Back in 2011, another Southern California city, Azusa, was also the center of a twenty-four-count indictment charging fifty-one Latino defendants for conspiring to murder African Americans.[23] Detective Robert Landeros of the Azusa police department noted, "This has been a 20 year conspiracy to violate the civil rights of African Americans in the city."[24] The indictment was the culmination of a three-year criminal investigation of the Varrio Azusa 13 gang, a Latino gang attempting to clear Azusa of African Americans during a two-decade crime spree of harassment and attacks.

Particularly relevant to the issue of interethnic violence is that the attacks were not against rival gang members. Rather, the conspiracy was characterized by its animus against civilian African American homeowners and students whom Azusa 13 wished to push out of the city or prevent from moving there.[25] All fifty-one gang members were convicted of various charges, including a conspiracy to purge Azusa of its Black residents. At the sentencing of the guilty parties, the judge emphatically stated that the gang leader "was a proponent of the racial cleansing of the city of Azusa."[26]

The same charges were lodged in the 2009 criminal indictment against 147 members of the Varrio Hawaiian Gardens Latino gang for engaging in a conspiracy to systematically rid Hawaiian

Gardens of all African Americans.[27] At the time, it was the largest gang sweep in US history.[28] The accused gang leaders were convicted and received lengthy prison sentences for their "conspiracy against African American community members, solely due to their race" after boasting about being racist and referring to themselves as a "hate gang."[29]

The impetus for the large-scale government investigations into Latino-gang anti-Black violence was in large measure triggered by public attention to the murder of Cheryl Green on December 15, 2006, a fourteen-year-old eighth grader. The teen was gunned down in broad daylight as she perched near her scooter, chatting with friends in her Harbor Gateway neighborhood of Los Angeles. In the case of Cheryl Green, members of the Latino 204th Street gang were tried and found guilty of murder and a hate crime.[30] During the trial, federal prosecutors demonstrated that African American residents were terrorized in an effort to force them out of a neighborhood perceived as Latino.[31] Yet as early as 2001, the British Broadcasting Company noted in a news item entitled "Hate in Action" that Latino gangs in Los Angeles had a clear mission of anti-Black ethnic cleansing in their neighborhoods that motivated their involvement in anti-Black hate crimes in the United States.[32]

Hence, the Avenues Latino gang members were convicted for a six-year conspiracy to assault and murder African Americans in Highland Park, just twenty-three miles away from Harbor Green.[33] During the trial, prosecutors demonstrated that the Latino expulsion of African American residents was suggestive of ethnic cleansing. One African American victim in the case was murdered as he looked for a parking space near his Highland Park home, and another African American victim was shot simply for waiting at a bus stop in Highland Park. Debra Wong Yang, the US attorney for the Central District of California stated that the men "were killed by the defendants simply because they were African Americans who chose to live in a particular neighborhood. As this case demonstrates, we will aggressively pursue hate crimes such as this and convict those responsible for such reprehensible acts."[34] In another incident, a woman was knocked off her bicycle and her husband was threatened with a box cutter by one of the Latino attackers, who said, "You N——rs have been here long enough."[35]

Later, a 2007 investigation into the Los Angeles–area Latino anti-Black violence noted that the predominant pattern was one of Latino gang members assaulting Black passersby while either yelling racial expletives, such as "Fuck N——rs. This is T-Flats [Varrio Tortilla Flats gang area]" and "What the fuck are you N——rs doing here? . . . Monkeys," or posting racially exclusionary graffiti by the murder sites, such as "Mayates [N——rs] get out" and "187 N——rs" (referring to California Penal Code 187 for murder).[36] In fact, the Los Angeles County Commission on Human Relations notes that Latino street gangs have been the most violent perpetrators of hate crimes in the region, primarily against African Americans.[37]

The involvement of gangs in Los Angeles has induced many to deny the racial import of the violence.[38] Yet, longitudinal studies of hate crimes in Los Angeles County demonstrate a clear racial aspect. When UCLA urban planner Karen Umemoto conducted a statistical study of Los Angeles County law enforcement data over a five-year period, she uncovered a number of disturbing patterns.[39] First, there was a disproportionate rate of increase in the victimization of African Americans as compared with other groups. The number of African American victims increased by 70 percent, while the number of Asian American and Pacific Islander victims increased 21 percent, the number of White victims increased by 6 percent, and the number of Latino victims decreased by 8.4 percent. In contrast to the victimization trends, there was a slight decline in the number of reported African American perpetrators, while there was an increase with all other groups. Latino perpetrators had the sharpest rise in number with a 59.2 percent increase. Most disturbing, though, was the study's discovery that Latinos were disproportionately the perpetrators of bias crimes against African Americans with no known gang affiliations.

While it is true that general crime statistics very likely undercount the number of incidents where undocumented Latino immigrants are victims of crime, given their reticence to call any attention to their undocumented status by reporting a crime, it is also true that the number of incidents where African Americans are the victims of Latino crime may also suffer an undercount due to the manner in which many criminal databases code Latino offenders as solely "White."[40] Furthermore, hate crime *murders* is not a context where victim reporting is necessary for criminal investigation. And it is within this context that Latinos have been documented as the disproportionate aggressors against African Americans rather than being the victims of African American attacks.

African Americans have been singled out for racial violence in ways that make the issue of racism inescapable. Indeed, the court convictions detailed in this chapter demonstrate that labeling the terrorism as racially motivated is not the mere result of sensation-seeking media outlets that describe it as such but, more importantly, a reflection of the careful presentation of evidence with the exacting criminal law standard of guilt beyond a reasonable doubt.[41]

However, it should be noted that this chapter's examination does not purport to present physical assault as the predominant interaction between African Americans and Latinos, nor as the primary source of violence in communities of color. Indeed, it still continues to be the case that the greatest source of bloodshed in communities of color is intraracial.[42] Nevertheless, even though the interethnic violence may be a statistically small occurrence, it is still a troubling state of affairs that civil rights organizations state merits analysis and a resolution.

THE ROLE OF RESIDENTIAL SEGREGATION

Empirical research suggests that a variety of factors contribute to Latino anti-Black interactions that can vary by region of the country.[43] What is quite noteworthy, though, is the predominance of California, and Los Angeles in particular, as the scene of Latino anti-Black violence. No other multiracial city has reported Los Angeles' levels of Latino anti-Black assaults. How did the Los Angeles metropolitan area come to such a state of affairs, despite the cautionary legacy of the 1992 unrest? To begin to understand the Los Angeles context, it is centrally important to circle back to the issues of residential segregation and racially segmented labor markets discussed in the previous chapters, rather than relying upon the popular but oversimplified notion that Latino-specific dynamics in California are caused by the presence of large numbers of Latino immigrants.

While Latino immigrants have been documented to express negative views of African Americans, and demonstrate a preference for segregation from African Americans, the violence in Los Angeles has been perpetuated in large measure by US-born Latinos.[44] It is US-born Latinos who, in becoming "Americanized," experience themselves as socially undesirable raced subjects. Those who are not wealthy enough or light enough to be permitted the social access of assimilation are seemingly locked into the urban-poverty quagmire of underfinanced schools, inadequate healthcare, and scarce employment opportunities.

At the same time that employers actively seek Latino immigrant labor for low-wage positions, low-skill-labor US Latinos are excluded as a "less malleable" worker population. Indeed, the Americanization process provides English-speaking, US-born Latinos with greater information and assertiveness about worker rights. Moreover, US-born Latinos have a sense of enhanced status as US English-speaking applicants, and this in combination with their repeated exposure to rampant US consumerism, disinclines them to seek the same low-wage jobs as Latino immigrants. This results in a high rate of jobless US-born Latino men on the street searching for status and meaning, which is a context ripe for gang culture violence that exploits the tensions of residential segregation.

Living in segregated proximity to African Americans, who are derided in Latin America as well as the United States, facilitates the notion that US Latino status depends upon a clear separation and removal of African Americans from "Latino spaces." In this way, California Latino gang members are employing "turf defense." Turf defense is the social-psychological dynamic in which a racially homogeneous group seeks to preserve their residential homogeneity.[45] When Latinos are segregated out of White non-Hispanic spaces and fighting for status in limited "colored" spaces, turf defense explodes into interethnic violence, a continuing legacy of White segregation. Indeed, in each of the California locations in which the federal government has investigated and prosecuted Latino gang members for what is tantamount to ethnic cleansing campaigns, African Americans have made up a small percentage of the neighborhood. Rather, the area is statistically dominated by Latinos, where both groups are clearly segregated from White non-Hispanics.[46]

Latinos are generally segregated from African Americans but are even more segregated from White non-Hispanics. However, in some locations Latinos are more segregated from African Americans than they are from White non-Hispanics.[47] Nevertheless, recent trends indicate that Latinos and African Americans are increasingly likely to be neighbors.[48] Being neighbors jointly excluded from White non-Hispanic spaces influences Latino and African American involvement with the criminal justice system. In a study that examined census data and arrest data from New York and California, a correlation was found between racial segregation and Latino and African American violence. Specifically, the study noted that the racial segregation of Latinos and African Americans from White non-Hispanics seemingly contributes to the commission of homicides by Latinos and African Americans.[49] Being excluded from White non-Hispanic spaces and opportunities subjugates Latinos and African Americans in ways that create powder kegs of frustration and displaced searches for community power. As a consequence, the turnover of neighborhoods from majority Black to majority Latino creates its own ethnic tensions that also contribute to interethnic violence.[50]

Even so, the actual rate of segregation is less a factor in turf defense than the social meaning of the space.[51] As Elise Boddie notes, like human beings, geographic spaces can have a racial identity.[52] Racial meanings are accorded to spaces based on social biases about the people who inhabit, frequent, or are associated with particular places. Changes in the demography of residents over time changes the racial identity of spaces. Once those social meanings are developed, residents can then become invested in protecting the racial meaning of a space as vociferously as their own personal identity, because it feels like their racial status is at stake. Excluding others is a device to erect and sustain racial hierarchy. This then helps explain how the historically African American city of Compton in Los Angeles County has also witnessed Latino anti-Black hate crimes against non-gang-affiliated African American residents since its shift to becoming 65 percent Latino and only 33 percent African American as of the 2010 census.[53] As of 2019, Latinos are 68 percent and African Americans only 29 percent of the Compton population.[54]

Boddie calls it "racial territoriality" when people of color are excluded from public spaces that are identified as White and treated as being only for White people. Extending Boddie's useful concept of racial territoriality to the exclusionary actions of people of color themselves helps elucidate the turf defense dynamic observed within interethnic violence among Latinos and African Americans.[55] This is well exemplified by a California Pomona 12th Street gang member who, during his murder trial for participation in the Latino "N——r Killers" campaign, stated that it would be "humiliating" to 12th Street gangsters to allow African Americans to live in their neighborhood.[56]

EVERYDAY VIOLENCE

It would be a mistake, though, to relegate the concern about Latino anti-Black violence only to members of Latino gangs in California and official White supremacist organizations. Some examples of non-gang-affiliated Latino anti-Black violence in California include Arturo Santiago, while riding a North County Transit bus, striking a Black man on his head with a glass bottle while uttering racial slurs.[57] Another incident is that of Latinos Jeremiah Hernandez and William Soto, who were tried for burning an eleven-foot cross outside the house of a Black teenager in San Luis Obispo County, California, while she was home watching television.[58] At the time the crime occurred, Hernandez was thirty-two years old and Soto was twenty years old.

Extensive property damage can also accompany Latino anti-Black racial harassment in California. Latino Mark Anthony Taylor, a student at California State University at Chico (CSU-Chico), was found guilty of causing $175,000 worth of property damage when he battered the door and window of the apartment where two CSU-Chico African American students (Abdul Benjamin and Brandon Sykes) lived, all while yelling: "N——r," "we hate you fucking N——rs," "you fucking N——rs get out of here," and "you fucking N——rs, why are you here?"[59] Mark Anthony Taylor was also incarcerated because his racist conduct that day included physically assaulting Brandon while calling him a "fucking N——r" a number of times and stating that he, Taylor, represented "white pride" and was thus "tired of all the things you blacks are doing around here." Notably, Mark Anthony Taylor was joined by three White non-Hispanic students who endorsed his White supremacist violence by urging him to "get that N——r."

Moreover, a number of examples illustrate the operation of anti-Black violence in quotidian Latino spaces across the country. Luis Alberto Gonzalez, a White Cuban, was walking in Hialeah, Florida (a predominantly Latino city outside Miami), when he saw two Black men (brothers Andy Alexander and Tarvis James) exiting a pizza parlor. Gonzalez decided to yell at them "You fucking N——rs! What are you doing in my town robbing people?!"[60]

Gonzalez then got in his car, and when the brothers simply walked away, Gonzalez was angered because he thought they "appeared arrogant" as they walked past him. Angered by the "arrogance" of two Black men walking the streets of Hialeah, Gonzalez accelerated his car toward the brothers and attempted to run them over. When questioned by the police, Gonzalez admitted that what motivated his actions was his prejudice against Black people.

Yet, initially, Gonzalez claimed that it was Andy and Tarvis who initiated the interaction by robbing him at gunpoint. Only when Gonzalez provided a series of conflicting versions of his robbery story did the police investigate further and conclude from the collective statements of several witnesses that Gonzalez was not the victim of a crime but rather the aggressor of violence against men who posed no threat to him. In short, Gonzalez's anti-Black hostility informed not only his act of violence but also his falsified accusation of a criminal act by his victims.

Other cases from around the country also evidence anti-Black violence from individual Latinos. For example, in Winter Park, Florida, at Full Sail University, Xavier Nunez stabbed a Black student in his Statistics class with a screwdriver while yelling racial slurs.[61] The police arrested Nunez for aggravated battery with a deadly weapon after he told them that he hated Black people. In Illinois, Anthony Morales, a Latino student from Northwestern University, pleaded guilty to joining a classmate in vandalizing the university's chapel, which he had spray-painted with anti-Black racist slurs.[62] In Iowa, Latino Andy Benavidez instigated a fistfight with a Black man he called a racial slur. While committing the aggression, he wore a surgical mask (prior to the COVID-19 pandemic) because he was "allergic to black people" and did not want their germs to infect him.[63] Police charged Benavidez with a hate crime after he admitted that he fought with the victim only because he was Black. In New Mexico, Jose Campos was arrested by police after they found him graffiti-tagging racial slurs outside the home of a Black woman.[64]

LATINO LAW ENFORCEMENT

Even Latino police officers exhibit anti-Blackness when acting upon the stereotypical concept of all Blacks as criminal.[65] This is best encapsulated by the manner in which Latino Texas state trooper Brian T. Encinia escalated a routine traffic stop into an intensely violent encounter. In 2015, Encinia stopped African American motorist Sandra Bland for failing to signal a lane change in Prairie View, Texas, near Houston. When Sandra refused to stop smoking her cigarette during the stop, Encinia ordered her out of the car, threatening to "yank" her out as he drew his Taser and then shouted, "I will light you up." The patrol car's dash camera footage also recorded Sandra being restrained in handcuffs and the sound of her sobbing voice saying she was in pain from having been slammed to the ground. Three days later, Sandra was found in her jail cell dead from hanging, in what was ruled a suicide. Encinia ultimately resigned from the Texas State Troopers and agreed never to work in law enforcement again.

Today, Sandra Bland is remembered for inspiring the #SayHerName campaign against police racial bias and violence. What few have taken notice of is that while Encinia is racially White, he is ethnically Latino.[66] The oversight preserves the image of police racial bias as uniquely a White non-Hispanic problem, which in turn leaves unattended the implications of Latino anti-Blackness. Yet, many Afro-Latinos report that Latino police officers are harsher in their treatment of Latinos than non-Latino police officers are.[67]

Moreover, Latino police officers' attitudes about police violence against Blacks work in lockstep with that of White non-Hispanic police officers'. Specifically, unlike African American police officers, Latino and White non-Hispanic police officers interpret fatal encounters between the police and Blacks as isolated incidents rather than as signs of a broader problem between the police and Blacks.[68] Significantly, as with White non-Hispanic officers, Latino officer attitudes about Blackness result in the unjustified killing of Black people. Such was the case when Minnesota Latino police officer Jeronimo Yanez killed African American Philando Castile during a routine traffic stop for a defective brake light. The encounter was captured by the squad car dash cam and broadcast on Facebook in 2016.[69]

In fact, before the worldwide observance of the 2021 Derek Chauvin trial for killing George Floyd, one of the few convictions of police officer misconduct, was that of a Latino police officer named Raimundo Atesiano. Atesiano was a police chief in Biscayne, Florida, with a policy of directing his officers to pin any unsolved crimes on random Black people. His mandate to his officers was that "if they [Blacks] have burglaries that are open cases that are not solved yet, if you see anybody black walking through our streets and they have somewhat of a record, arrest them so we can pin them for all the burglaries."[70] He also used a designated code to alert officers when a Black person "was seen in the city and needed to be stopped and confronted." Chief Raimundo Atesiano's campaign against Black people was not halted until he was sentenced in 2018 to three years in prison for encouraging wrongful arrests.[71]

Importantly, the speculation that Latino police officers in the United States are merely mimicking White non-Hispanic racial attitudes in order to ingratiate themselves with the White non-Hispanic police hierarchies in which they seek to advance is severely undermined by the comparison to police conduct in Puerto Rico. In the US territory of Puerto Rico, Puerto-Rican Latino officers dominate the police force yet evidence the same racial attitudes about Blackness as Latino officers in White non-Hispanic-dominated police forces. As one Afro-Puerto Rican college student, Nina Figueroa, observes, "The police in Puerto Rico are very racist and also have a lot of social stigmas because they believe that black people come from the hood, come here to steal . . . that we are criminals."[72] Indeed, the police department has been under federally mandated reform since 2013 and is still being monitored for compliance with nondiscrimination and equal protection laws.[73]

Yet, Afro-Latinos in Puerto Rico are repeatedly harassed and monitored closely by the police without probable cause. Nor are Afro-Latino children excluded from police racial aggression. Eleven-year-old special-education student Alma Yariela Cruz argued with two bullies who had taunted her for two years with racial slurs, such as *"negra sucia"* (dirty Black girl), *"negra asquerosa"* (disgusting Black girl), *"negra dientúa"* (big-tooth Black girl), along with racist commentary about her Afro-descended hair. But when the police were called to the school, they filed criminal charges against Alma. This diminutive and slender dark-skinned Afro-Latina child was charged with disturbing the peace and battery, and the Puerto Rico Department of Justice prosecuted the case for over a year amid outrage from social-activist groups before finally withdrawing the claim as unfounded.[74]

As distinct as Puerto Rico is from California and California is from Florida and all the other contexts discussed in this book, what remains constant is the role of Latino Whiteness in anti-Black violence and Latino law enforcement hostility. What the stories of discrimination related in this chapter reveal is that the Latino pursuit of social status is entangled with denigrating Blackness as a device for performing Whiteness. To police the boundaries of Latino White spaces (metaphorically and often literally) from unwanted Black incursions is to effectively embody Whiteness itself, regardless of one's racial appearance. Whether conscious or implicit, the Latino alignment with Whiteness that discriminates against Blackness, all while denying that Latinos are even capable of harboring bias, makes Latinos not only victims of racism themselves but also part of the problem of White supremacy. The next chapter considers what this means for the future of racial equality in the United States.

CHAPTER 6

LATINOS AND THE FUTURE OF RACIAL EQUALITY IN THE UNITED STATES

I n my examination of how discrimination claims of Latino anti-Blackness arise in varied contexts like the workplace, the market for housing sales and rentals, schools, public venues, and the criminal justice system, two central patterns become evident. First, anti-Blackness is much more significant than many commentators care to admit. Second, the ability to identify and address Latino anti-Blackness is hampered by the notion that Latinos can't be prejudiced or racist simply by virtue of being Latino.

In some respects, these dynamics were anticipated by sociologist Eduardo Bonilla-Silva's observation that "the post-civil rights era has brought changes in how racial stratification seems to operate" whereby color gradations "will become more salient factors of stratification" and dark-skinned Latinos will be racially subordinated to light-skinned Latinos in a Latin American manner.[1]

In a related fashion, legal scholars Lani Guinier and Gerald Torres together forecasted that US race relations would evolve to offer light-skinned Latinos a "racial bribe." A "racial bribe is a strategy that invites specific racial or ethnic groups to advance within the existing black-white racial hierarchy by becoming 'white' . . . to secure high status for individual group members within existing hierarchies."[2] Guinier and Torres specifically note that a racial bribe is evident whenever lighter-skinned Latinos are offered a chance to be considered more acceptable to White non-Hispanics than darker-skinned Latinos "so long as they maintain their social distance from Blackness."[3]

However, the racial bribe is not limited to instances in which Latinos consciously reject identifying with Blackness, but instead more broadly encompasses the overarching Latino exaltation of Whiteness. Yet, efforts to raise the concern in public discourse regarding the Latino proclivity for esteeming Whiteness to the detriment of Afro-descendants is frequently met with heated Latino outrage and denial. When articles were posted to the social media news outlets *Huffington Post* and *Latino Rebels* regarding the topic of White Latino privilege, Latino commentators vociferously disclaimed the existence of Latino Whiteness and Latino White privilege.[4]

Undergirding numerous responses was a disturbing resistance to acknowledge how differently Latinos can be racially positioned depending upon their pigment, phenotype, and hair texture. It is a Latino ethnic nationalism that elevates a color-blind notion of Latinidad (a vision of a panethnic Latino community). One blog post that was part of the social media storm was entitled "Who and What the Hell Is a White Hispanic?"[5] The online debates illustrated the way in which the notion of Latino homogeneity allows White Latinos to "enjoy their White privilege unbridled while pretending [Latinos] across the entire color spectrum have the same opportunities and are treated equally" and are never agents in the oppression of Blackness.[6] This social media glimpse into contemporary Latino public discourse on race and identity suggests that without an effective intervention unmediated Latino racial attitudes will continue to hinder US racial equality efforts.

It is for this reason that the tales of Latino anti-Black discrimination recounted in this book are so important, inasmuch as they help disrupt the Latino myth of "racial innocence"[7] and clarify

Latino agency in racism. The stories show how the performance of Latino Whiteness entails subordinating Blackness as embodied by Afro-Latinos, African Americans, and other Afro-descendants in an unstated racial bribe for social status, all while claiming a mantle of Latino racial innocence. This is so even for those Latinos whose White self-identity may conflict with others perceptions of them as non-White, as is often the case with light-skinned Latinos of low socioeconomic status.[8] As sociologist Nicholas Vargas explains, "contested" Latino claims to Whiteness can "seek to legitimate group membership as [W]hite by expressing similar and sometimes even amplified notions of colourblindness than their non-contested white counterparts" with conservative racial views.[9]

Yet, Latino leaders and organizations often advance Latino advocacy projects that ignore Afro-Latino concerns regarding anti-Blackness. This is partly explained by the pressing need to address the many ways the entire multihued collective of Latinos are discriminated against in US society.[10] As critical race theory scholar Laura Gomez notes, the deep societal prejudice against the Latino category itself merits serious study and attention.[11]

Nevertheless, a unified-front advocacy presumption of a homogeneous Latinidad that experiences discrimination in exactly the same way sustains the racial innocence platform. Plainly stated, the reality of anti-Latino societal prejudice can be deployed to block any recognition that Latinos can themselves harbor anti-Black bias. Overlooking the particular inequalities that Afro-Latinos suffer undermines actual group solidarity for effectively advancing social justice.

In fact, when Latinos experience discrimination at the hands of other Latinos, their sense of collective belonging to other Latinos, which sociologists refer to as "linked fate," decreases.[12] Inasmuch as Afro-Latinos report greater rates of discrimination from fellow Latinos as compared to what White-identified Latinos report, Afro-Latinos are more likely to feel less of a linked fate with other Latinos. Indeed, Afro-Latinos indicate sensing more intragroup conflict among Latinos than do White-identified Latinos, who are more likely to believe that relations between Latinos are good.[13] In turn, Afro-Latino dissatisfaction with Latinos as an ethnic collective can hinder the ability to galvanize unified political action.

ELECTORAL POLITICS AND EQUALITY EFFORTS

Electoral politics studies demonstrate that a sense of Latino linked fate is an important influence on Latino political choices.[14] The voting rights context is where Latino anti-Blackness has to be carefully navigated to effectively protect Latino political participation. The process for designing electoral districts provides a perfect illustration.

After the results from a census count of the US population is released every ten years, electoral voting district boundaries are reassessed for balance based on population size. This ensures that regions have equal representation in the number of government representatives they elect. In addition, the Voting Rights Act of 1965 mandates that redistricting plans be free of racial discrimination. Thus, a redistricting plan is required to provide politically cohesive racial groups that are sufficiently large and geographically compact an equal opportunity to participate in the political process by electing a candidate of their choice.

As Latinos and African Americans increasingly live in neighboring areas, voting rights lawyers have determined that working in solidarity across racial groups is crucial for helping ensure the political power of people of color. As the US Supreme Court has repeatedly narrowed the applicability of the Voting Rights Act for challenging racially discriminatory voting districts, racial solidarity has become even more important. This need is embodied in the turn to "unity mapping."

Unity mapping brings together community leaders from various racial and ethnic groups that live in close proximity to each other to craft a consensus plan, which is then jointly presented to redistricting authorities to consider as they decide electoral district boundaries.[15] This entails extensive community hearings to assess the degree to which different groups share concerns and what district configurations would best present these common interests. How disheartening then when these vital pursuits for helping communities of color are themselves subject to racially hostile mindsets that undermine joint collaborations.[16]

During his tenure as president and general counsel of Latino Justice PRLDEF, Juan Cartagena encountered Latino anti-Blackness in his own unity-mapping efforts. During community outreach sessions, Cartagena heard Latino residents state regarding African Americans, "We don't want to be in the same district with them" and "we don't want to be like them."[17] While Cartagena did once manage to surmount anti-Black bias in 2010 to successfully create a unity map for New York City's city council districts, his organization has not been able to do so in other regions.

Similarly, Thomas Saenz, president and general counsel of MALDEF (Mexican American Legal Defense and Education Fund) has also experienced unity-mapping defeats with Latinos in Texas.[18] Janai S. Nelson, now president and director-counsel of the NAACP Legal Defense and Education Fund, asserts that unity mapping entails "really difficult conversations" about racial power sharing in which anti-Black bias is felt even when not stated in a blatant manner, but "you can feel it. You can almost cut it with a knife."[19] Failing to acknowledge Latino anti-Black bias thus hinders the cross-racial cooperation necessary for unity mapping and the important project of making the Latino vote count.

Coming to terms with Latino anti-Black sentiments could also help illuminate, in part, why some Latinos cast votes for candidates who overtly manifest bias against Latinos. As voting-rights expert Terry Smith pointedly observed about Donald Trump's 2016 presidential election, Latinos "gave Trump nearly 30 percent of their vote, a curious tally for an ethnic group that had borne the brunt of Trump's racial ridicule."[20] Some Latinos continued to support Trump across his entire presidential term,

during which he promoted White supremacist ideas and policies.[21] Latino allegiance to such a politician cannot be explained
solely as a matter of Republican Party allegiance when the candidate epitomizes blatant disregard for the equality of Latinos.
Like working-class White non-Hispanics who vote against their
own socioeconomic interest in pursuit of an association with the
privilege of White racial identity, White-identified Latinos can
and have done the same.[22]

In short, ignoring how Latinos have a race as well as an ethnicity disserves the attempt to organize collective Latino political-
and social-justice-reform efforts.[23] It can also misinform how
Latino organizations assess public policies and their interventions.
The US government's consideration about how to structure census taking provides an important example.

CENSUS POLITICS AND CIVIL RIGHTS

For the last few years the Census Bureau has been consider-
ing a proposal to add "Latino" and "Hispanic" to the list of
government-defined races on its decennial population survey
questionnaire.[24] This would be a dramatic change from treating
Latino/Hispanic as an ethnicity to instead treating it as a race.
Since the 1980 census, "Hispanic origin" has been part of a separate ethnicity question rather than being listed as an option in the
"What race are you?" question on the census.[25] Such a two-part
formulation in 2010 enabled Latinos to indicate their ethnic origin as Hispanic and simultaneously indicate their racial identity as
White, Black, Asian, American Indian, or Native Hawaiian. Despite the fact that the 2020 Decennial Census Program decided to
continue to use the existing format of two separate questions, the
Census Bureau remains interested in supporting a change to the
single question format in the future, and a number of Latino organizations endorse that proposed change despite the alarm raised
by Afro-Latino activists about its potential adverse impact on civil
rights measures.[26]

Latino census-box checking affects how civil rights laws are implemented. The racial and ethnic classifications that the Census Bureau uses were devised in 1977 for the specific purpose of facilitating the application of civil rights laws. By comparing the census count of individuals by race to the statistical presence of each racial group in workplaces, housing purchases and rentals, and access to mortgages, racial disparities can be uncovered and then investigated for discriminatory practices. Collapsing Latino/Hispanic ethnic identity into the list of racial categories with Black in particular risks obscuring the number of Afro-Latinos and the monitoring of socioeconomic status differences of Latinos that exist across race.

Yet, national Latino organizations are so focused on promoting Latino unity, however well intentioned, that they can be shortsighted about the distinctive needs of Afro-Latinos. This is part of what demographer Michael Rodriguez-Muñiz calls "population politics."[27] For example, the National Association of Latino Elected and Appointed Officials (NALEO) Educational Fund, the Mexican American Legal Defense and Education Fund, and the National Council of La Raza all publicly endorsed the Census Bureau recommendation to treat Hispanic as a homogeneous racial category, with the assertion that there would be very little loss in necessary data, since Afro-Latinos could always elect to check both the "Hispanic" race box and the "Black" race box to indicate their Afro-Latino identity.[28]

What such a perspective underappreciates is how Latino anti-Black bias will surely inhibit the Census Bureau's count of Afro-Latinos in ways that the experiments with test questions cannot readily appreciate. When "Hispanic" is juxtaposed as a racial category distinct from others, Latinos perceive the other categories as pertaining only to non-Hispanics. This helps explain why prior to the 2020 Census, Puerto Ricans in Puerto Rico differed in their use of the "Some Other Race" (SOR) box compared to Puerto Ricans living in the mainland United States. The Census

Bureau views the use of the SOR box as a respondent's lack of identification with the established racial boxes. Notably, Latinos in the United States use the SOR box more than any other group, writing in responses such as "Mexican," "Hispanic," or "Latin American." Thirty-seven percent of Latinos did so on the 2010 census, as did 42 percent on the 2000 census.[29] Yet, only 11 percent of Puerto Ricans in Puerto Rico itself selected "Some Other Race" or "Two or More Races" on the 2010 census, as compared with the 30.8 percent of mainland Puerto Ricans that selected "Some Other Race" or "Two or More Races."[30] On the island of Puerto Rico, Puerto Ricans can view the racial categories as pertaining to themselves and not exclusively to US mainland racial groups. In contrast, stateside Puerto Ricans' census-box checking occurs in a context of comparison to US racial groups of African Americans and White non-Hispanics. Such comparisons thereby implicate Latino racial attitudes.

To be sure, the Latino affinity for Whiteness discussed in chapter 1 operates in tandem with a Latino cultural flight from Blackness. Both hinder the Census Bureau count of Afro-Latinos. Juxtaposing Hispanic as a "race" distinct from others would further aggravate the undercount. Inasmuch as Latinos historically prefer to view Blackness as always situated outside their national identities, the Black category would be deemed as uniquely African American in contrast to Hispanic as a "race."[31] For instance, the distancing of Blackness in Puerto Rico enables Puerto Ricans to view Blackness as imbued primarily in their Dominican neighbors, while Dominicans instead view Blackness as imbued primarily in their Haitian neighbors.[32] A similar racial distancing happens in other Latin American countries where Blackness is presumed to be contained in geographically limited spaces rather than being a fundamental part of the nation state.[33] For these Latinos, Latino Blackness is never within but instead displaced elsewhere. For US-based Latinos, "real" Blackness is imbued only in African Americans and English-speaking Afro-Caribbeans and Africans.

Again, Blackness is always somewhere else. Even in Miami's large
Caribbean population, Blackness is often exclusively associated
with African Americans, such that Afro-Cubans consistently report not feeling welcomed by fellow White Cuban residents.[34]

The Latino disassociation from Blackness on census forms has
only been reinforced by the Census Bureau decision to have the
2020 race question for the very first time list possible ethnic origins
for each racial category.[35] Notably excluded from the Black origin
options was Latino ethnicity. Thus, in the choice of Black ethnic origins, only "African American, Jamaican, Haitian, Nigerian,
Ethiopian, Somali, etc." were listed as examples. The Census 2020
list thereby situated Blackness as something separate and apart
from Latino ethnicity, yielding only 1.9 percent of Latinos who
indicated their race as solely Black.[36] In contrast, when Latinos
are instead asked whether they are Afro-Latino, Afro-Caribbean,
or of other African descent in Latin America, the percentage of
Latinos claiming Blackness rises to 24 percent.[37] The 2020 census
formulation of the Black race question instead discouraged the
recognition of Latino Blackness, in ways that some census data
experts had predicted it would.[38]

An additional hindrance to being able to collect census data
that accurately detects the socioeconomic differences between
Afro-Latinos and other Latinos is the disinclination light-skinned
Latinos have for acknowledging their greater access to societal
preferences because of their White appearances. This dynamic
was especially on display in the 2020 census results. During the
months the 2020 census was being administered, the nation was
sheltering in place from COVID-19 and transfixed by the mul-
titude of George Floyd–inspired #BlackLivesMatter protests on
their screens. For Latinos, this moment was also accompanied by
the amplification of Afro-Latino voices naming Latino Whiteness
as part of anti-Blackness. Many White-presenting Latinos expressed discomfort at being implicated within racism, as reflected
in one Latina's observation: "I just don't usually go for white be-

cause although my people's colonizers were, I definitely am not."[39] Or, as some Latino Twitter users tweeted: "I'm not white, I'm latino. I've never had white privilege or been look [sic] at as so,"[40] and "White privilege is a myth. I'm Latino and even I know white privilege is a myth."[41] That Latino iteration of "White fragility" surfaced in a significant way in the 2020 census responses.[42] The number of Latinos who identified as White alone decreased by 52.9 percent.[43]

Even more telling, is the landslide shift from White-identified Latinos selecting only the White racial category, as they had done in prior censuses, to large numbers instead selecting White in combination with other racial categories. For instance, Mexican American Julissa Arce had always selected the White box in response to the race question, presumably based upon her outward appearance, but on the 2020 census, she instead added additional categories such as American Indian, Chinese, and "Some Other Race."[44] Indeed, the percentage of Latino White-only response checking declined from 53 percent to 20.3 percent, at the same time that the percentage of Latino multiple-race response checking increased from 6 percent to 32.7 percent.[45] The same pattern also occurred on the island of Puerto Rico, with the percentage of Latino White-only response checking declining from 75.8 percent to 17.1 percent, at the same time that the percentage of Latino multiple-race response checking increased from 3.3 percent to 49.8 percent.[46] By electing to group themselves within the amorphous census category of "two or more races," White Latinos in Puerto Rico and across the United States hindered the ability to make comparisons that reveal the existence of racial disparities amongst Latinos. For instance, this hamstrings the legal system's ability to sanction an employer who systematically rejects qualified Afro-Latino applicants while simultaneously hiring White Latinos. Without racially specific Latino census data to compare to the business's hiring pattern, such an employer's racism is swept away with the defense "I do hire Latinos." But

Whiteness and Blackness make a real difference in the lives of
Latinos, and we need census data that helps to measure that for
social justice intervention.

Moreover, the Census Bureau exacerbated the obfuscation of
intra-Latino racial disparities with its 2020 innovation of listing
ethnic origins for the White racial category that noticeably excluded Latinos, just as the Black racial category ethnic-origins list
did. The White racial category instead invited respondents to identify their origins in the White category by listing German, Irish,
English, Italian, Lebanese, and Egyptian examples. Furthermore,
as with prior census tabulations, if a Latino respondent checked
the White racial category and nevertheless inserted a Latino ethnic origin in the "Some Other Race" write-in space, the Census
Bureau counted that as an indication of a Latino checking "Two or
More Races" to express a multiracial identity. Put together, these
two Census Bureau choices in 2020 resulted in Latino White-only
racial category checking declining by fourteen million people, at
the same time that the number of Latinos tabulated as White in
combination with some other race increased by fifteen million.[47]
With one small administrative sleight of hand, the 2020 census
transformed White Latinos into "multiracial" Latinos whose
White privilege can no longer be readily quantified.

Further altering the census form to collapse Hispanic ethnicity into the census's racial categories rather than having it remain
a separate ethnicity question will likely escalate the White Latino
population disinclination to acknowledge the significance of
their Whiteness. The ethnicity into race alteration proposal also
shields Latinos from confronting their own possible Blackness.
In contrast, retaining two separate questions enables all Latinos
to demarcate their Hispanic origin as an ethnicity with the first
question and then reflect on their racial origins with the second
question specifically on race. This way forces the confrontation
with the census racial question for a cognitive dissonance that is
quite useful. This is borne out by the Afro-Latino narratives re-
lating how the census race question brings out from the shadows

family discussions of Blackness and race.[48] Yet none of these insights are visible and relevant to policy making as long as Latino leaders continue to ignore the existence of Blackness and racism within their communities. The same cautionary concern applies to grassroots activists and Latino communities.

LATINO-AFRICAN AMERICAN RACIAL COALITION BUILDING

Even though productive coalitions between Latino and African American communities have been formed regarding concrete political issues of concern, they continue to be fragile and not broadly embraced by many Latinos. For example, attempts to mobilize Latinos regarding racialized violence perpetrated by police officers have been complicated by the need to navigate White-identified Latino views of "African Americans as automatically warranting police officers' fear or suspicion" and critiques of African American behavior as "too aggressive or feisty toward the police."[49] Even with the massive onslaught of support for #BlackLivesMatter in the wake of George Floyd's brutal death in 2020, there were Latinos who were captured on film yelling racial slurs while chasing away African American men on the street, whom they automatically presumed were present to loot their neighborhood.[50] Indeed, some Latinos are seemingly "obsessed with demonizing Black Lives Matter."[51] In fact, Latinos who align themselves with African Americans in their politics risk being assaulted by other Latinos using the derogatory Spanish term "*mayatero*" (n——r lover) and viewed as being disassociated from authentic Latino politics.[52] Latino commentators asserting that "until our global Latine community understands that Black Lives Matter, we are no better than the white supremacists that hate us" court great Latino outrage in response.[53] Notably, Afro-Latinos stand out in their strong support for #BlackLivesMatter when questioned in surveys.[54]

Against this backdrop of exclusionary impulses are notable examples of Latino–African American coalition building that have surged often out of moments of social crisis. In the 1960s, the

Young Lords alliance with the Black Panthers provided an example of Chicago African American and Latino communities coming together to pursue programs of direct action to bring their neighborhoods such services as day care, free breakfasts, and vocational training.[55] Within New York City, the Young Lords Party also participated in Black Power movements and African American civil rights.[56] In Winston-Salem, North Carolina churches and nonprofit agencies productively fostered Latino–African American alliances, after White non-Hispanic residents began to demonize the Latino US presence in the wake of post-9/11 immigrant surveillance and a weakened economy.[57]

Within electoral politics, African American–Latino cooperation is exemplified by the example of the 1983 Chicago mayoral campaign of Harold Washington, the first Black candidate for mayor.[58] Latino communities in Chicago voted in huge numbers for Washington. Of the forty-eight thousand votes that separated Washington from his Republican rival, close to twenty-eight thousand of them were cast from Latino communities.

Interethnic community-based advocacy organizations and worker-based coalitions are also spaces for partnership.[59] In Los Angeles, the Community Coalition was founded in 1989 as an African American and Latino organization with the goal of transforming beleaguered South Los Angeles neighborhoods through public safety campaigns, gang reduction efforts, and many other programs.[60] Across the country, the Black Alliance for Just Immigration (BAJI) provides an example of Black-Latino cooperation in response to the growing societal anti-immigrant animus.[61] BAJI is an education and advocacy group comprising African Americans and Black immigrants from Africa, Latin America, and the Caribbean that together oppose repressive immigration bills. BAJI also brings together all these communities to dialogue about the myths and stereotypes, as well as the cultural, social, and political issues that divide those groups. Moreover, BAJI provides the African American community with a progressive analysis and framework on immigration that links the interests of African Americans with those of immigrants of color. BAJI's analysis emphasizes the impact of racism and economic globalization on African American and immigrant communities as a basis for forging alliances across these communities.

Similarly, Encuentro Diaspora Afro in Boston was founded in response to the growing racial tensions from increased Latino immigration to the city.[62] The organization acts as an Afro-Latino culture ambassador to African American community advocacy and political events and also designs community seminars and programs to improve cross-ethnic relations. Notably, participants have been quick to identify Boston's intense residential racial segregation as a key factor in racial hostilities.

What this small sampling of Latino–African American coalition efforts indicates is that there are venues for addressing interethnic conflict.[63] Indeed, as noted historian Paul Ortiz reminds us, "an African American and Latinx history of the United States teaches us that the self-activity of the most oppressed is the key to liberty."[64] Why then are these efforts alternatively described as the "failed promise of black-Latino/a solidarity?"[65]

THE FUTURE OF RACIAL EQUALITY

The stories gathered in this book suggest that efforts toward interethnic coalition building for social justice will not be broad-based, sustaining, and fully transformational until Latino anti-Blackness is recognized and addressed. Indeed, experienced labor organizers note that "Latino leaders are past due in questioning [how Latino networks can] operate under an 'anti-blackness' narrative and pigmentocratic framework that affords privileges to light-skinned individuals."[66] In addition to Latino civil rights leaders, other actors who strongly influence the advance of racial equality are the lawyers and judges who enforce our nation's antidiscrimination laws. The stories of discrimination within this book are proffered with the hope that they will elucidate the complicated terrain of Latino acts of discrimination and the role of anti-Blackness in its manifestation.

Some readers may question why the sampling of stories in this book should matter. They may be of the view that the stories are limited in number and representative of each person's individual experience only at a finite point in time. Such a view loses sight of the fact that social movements are built with individual stories. Take for example the feminist movement. Long before institutions found value in surveying women about their perspectives, the feminist movement crafted policy platforms from individual stories of women that had been articulated in consciousness-raising sessions, rather than dismissing them as isolated instances of harm.[67] The excavated voices lifted up in this book illuminate a pattern of Latino anti-Blackness across time, geographic spaces, and contexts. It is time to listen to those marginalized voices and have them matter.

For legal actors, the book's interrogation of the "Latinos can't be prejudiced" defense to racism is especially clarifying for the enforcement of antidiscrimination laws. Educating both lawyers and judges about how Latinos are not only victims of discrimination but also part of the problem of societal discrimination will fortify the ability of law to redress discrimination in an increasingly diverse society. This intervention is also needed for the public at large that serve as jurors in cases of discrimination. Veteran antidiscrimination law attorney Chris Kleppin says that when he works on Latino anti-Black bias cases he has found that, just like judges, there are also jurors who "really don't get it and find all of this to be just nonsense. I've also seen people shake their heads and volunteer and say, I don't understand this. *And so it's all about education.*"[68]

For proper enforcement of antidiscrimination law, any judicial presumption that Latinos cannot harbor racial bias against one another is a danger. Therefore, it is critically important for lawyers to explicitly educate the judiciary in their court filings, and juries as well, with expert presentations about the particulars of Latino anti-Black bias.[69] In fact, EEOC supervising trial attorney Kimberly Cruz says that all civil rights lawyers have to be prepared to educate the judges they interact with.[70]

One case in particular is an ideal model of how, when legal actors are educated about Latino anti-Black bias, antidiscrimination law is more appropriately enforced. Civil rights attorney Judith Berkan effectively did so by including the expert testimony of Palmira Ríos, an Afro–Puerto Rican sociologist and former commissioner and president of the Puerto Rican Civil Rights Commission. Ríos's testimony as a qualified expert on race discrimination in Puerto Rico was instrumental in illuminating how the Sears Roebuck branch in Puerto Rico operated under a racial hierarchy when Victor Rivera Sanchez, an Afro–Puerto Rican, worked there.[71]

When Victor applied for a job at the Sears retail location in Mayaguez, Puerto Rico, his aspiration was to obtain a commissioned sales position. However, upon his arrival at the store he was immediately directed to the warehouse. What Victor discovered was that the warehouse was *the* Sears Mayaguez location for its Black employees. With three hundred employees storewide, only seventeen were Black and primarily relegated to the warehouse. The warehouse of Black workers was referred to as "the tribe," directly conjuring the vision of an African tribe far removed from the light-skinned and Whiter employees on the sales floor. Latino supervisors and coworkers continually verbally assaulted those Black employees with a litany of racially derogatory Spanish terms for Blackness, such as "*Negro, Negrito, Moreno, Africano,*" and the term "*Bembon*" (a stupid person with a presumably African large, thick lower lip).

In the twelve years that Victor worked there, the warehouse was vigilantly maintained as a so-called African tribe, not only by directing Black applicants there but also by assiduously preventing

Black employees from being transferred out to any other department. Applicant skin shades were monitored with the requirement
of application photographs for all employee files. Darker-skinned
employees were diverted to what were deemed Black-appropriate
positions. One exclusionary tactic was to uniquely demand previous sales experience from Black applicants, contrary to written
sales job descriptions that omitted any requirement of previous
sales experience. In turn, White applicants with no sales experience were chosen for those sales jobs instead.

Victor endured years of applying for transfers and promotions
that were always denied. A hiring context devoid of uniform criteria essentially authorized the Latino supervisors to make selections
not based on merit but instead upon their own biases. Complaints
Victor made to his Latino supervisor and Latina director of human relations about the anti-Black, racially hostile work environment all went unheeded as unworthy of investigation. The final
insult that prompted Victor to file a legal claim was when he was
rejected yet again for a sales position that was instead given to a
White employee who had not even applied for the job. The White
employee landed the position through the racially exclusive network of supervisors that chose to transfer him.

Ríos's expert witness report explained how common racism is
in the Puerto Rican labor market, and she provided context for the
indicators of anti-Black bias exhibited at Sears Mayaguez itself. As
a result, the judge assigned to the case, Jaime Pieras Jr., had clarity
about how racism operated at Sears Mayaguez, despite the judge
himself being White and a member of Puerto Rico's social elite as
a federal judge appointed by Ronald Reagan. When Sears claimed
that the case should be dismissed because Victor was properly denied transfers to positions for which he lacked experience (despite
the fact that supervisors had erratically imposed experience re-
quirements for those positions), Judge Pieras Jr. rejected the request for dismissal outright. Thereafter, Victor was able to reach
a settlement agreement with Sears Roebuck de Puerto Rico to

resolve his dispute thanks to the work that his lawyer did in educating the judge about Latino anti-Blackness.

In short, educating legal actors about Latino anti-Black bias enhances the enforcement of antidiscrimination law. It is my hope that this book's unmasking of Latino anti-Black bias can aid not only legal actors but all who are joined in the pursuit for racial equality. Let Latino racial innocence be cancelled.

ON BEING AN AFRO-LATINA INTERROGATING LATINO ANTI-BLACKNESS

The search for stories of Latino acts of racial discrimination cannot be done with a simple Google search, because most law cases do not garner the high level of media attention to activate a search engine's cataloging. Nor will a single query into electronic case law databases suffice. This is because the legal research service databases of Westlaw and Lexis do not neatly categorize cases by the racial and ethnic identity of all the parties. For that reason, the hunt for cases necessitated numerous exhaustive searches for judicial mentions of racial and ethnic party identities, with every possible iteration of Latino identity since the 1964 enactment of the Civil Rights Act. The detailed list of all search queries and data files is publicly available in an online Methodology Appendix.[1]

Given the possibility of missing a relevant case in this large-scale search due to human error, I included cases across a broad span of time (1964–2021) to track the consistent racial patterns and concerns of those cases that could be found. Furthermore, to gather data about cases that victims never file because they are overwhelmed and beleaguered, I also conducted qualitative interviews with civil rights leaders, attorneys, educators, and self-identified Afro-Latino respondents whom I contacted via Afro-Latino identity-based organizations. Finally, I located additional accounts of discrimination in national and local news electronic databases.

What drove me to persist with the painstaking hunt for the narratives of discrimination when so many Latino scholars and commentators instead suggest that Latino anti-Blackness does not merit deep exploration? My family history as an Afro-Latina would not permit otherwise. This is because embodying Blackness within a Latino family can so deeply ground one in the materiality of Latino bias that fantasies of Latino color-blind unity are unable to interfere with a questioning of Latino racial attitudes.

Inasmuch as this book has centered itself on excavating the narratives of Afro-Latinos and African Americans who have experienced Latino anti-Black bias, it is only fair for me to share my own race story as well. This is because no amount of Latino "we are a racially harmonious rainbow people" rhetoric can ever change that I am the daughter of an Afro–Puerto Rican mother *almost given away because of her Blackness*. Thus, like every story about race, its beginnings go back generations. But for me, the 1940s is the key marker for my own racial inheritance (as well as my great-great-grandparents' stories of their lives in slavery).

In the 1940s my maternal grandmother, Lucrecia, was a country girl, or what her fellow Puerto Ricans called a *jíbara*, from a mountain village in Puerto Rico.[2] Her African ancestry appeared slightly in her *trigueña* (light-wheat-colored) skin tone but was not very apparent in her facial features or hair texture. Her older sisters were similarly light skinned and favored their fair-complected mother more than their darker-skinned father. For this reason, Lucrecia and her sisters considered themselves a race apart from those who appeared more unambiguously Afro-descended. Any tinge of color in the family was attributed to the long-ago legacy of Taíno Indians on the island. It was immaterial to the family that Taíno Indians were documented to have been exterminated by Spanish conquerors by the mid-sixteenth century.[3]

When my grandmother, Lucrecia, fell in love with and united herself with carpenter and guitarist Juan, her family was not pleased. While he himself was a mixed-race grandchild of a former slave and son of an Afro–Puerto Rican mother and White Spaniard, his appearance was what Lucrecia's family labeled Black, and thus unacceptable. Puerto Rican identity may claim to celebrate racial mixture, but some of us are thought to look more mixed than others. Dark-skin deviations from the idealization of light skin with European features and straight hair are ejected from the Puerto Rican portrait of racial mixture. Lucrecia's family was no exception from this Puerto Rican (and Latin American) anti-Black conception of racial mixture.[4]

Infidelity eventually caused further strain on their union, and Lucrecia's older sisters encouraged her to leave Juan and migrate to New York. Hoping to teach Juan a lesson and have him mend his ways, Lucrecia secretly boarded a ship from Puerto Rico to New York in the early 1940s with her two-year-old daughter. She was unknowingly three months pregnant with a second child and entertained the romantic notion that Juan would chase her to New York and commit himself to being faithful. Feeling abandoned and hurt himself, Juan never did follow her to New York City. Lucrecia did not inform him of the birth of his second child until she was approximately eight years old.

Lucrecia's second child, Nina (my mother), was born in the 1940s, and much to the dismay of Lucrecia's family, to them the child was dark. Too dark. Too dark to count as racially mixed and certainly too dark to pass as a "White" Puerto Rican. Baby Nina did not pass the "look behind the ears" Caribbean test to seek out the future darkness of infants.[5] Even more problematic, Nina's skin tone (approximating that of the 1940s African American singer and actress Lena Horne—the Beyoncé of her time) would complicate the family's image as disassociated from Blackness. The campaign to send baby Nina away began in earnest. Lucrecia's family lobbied to have baby Nina placed for adoption with an African American family. Any African American family would do, as long as baby Nina was removed from the household. Only as an adult researcher would I later learn from a colleague how much the family impulse paralleled the dynamic in Puerto Rico of returning foster children like damaged goods when they became "too dark."[6] At the same time, the family's animus toward the Afro–Puerto Rican father that baby Nina favored did not extend to her older sister, Mónica. Mónica was lighter in complexion with long straight hair. Mónica's African ancestry did not announce itself so loudly in her appearance, and she was immediately accepted by the family. Their physical comparison between the two sisters was a constant obsession, with Nina being called *monito* (little monkey) and *negrita bembe* (little Black African-like girl), while Mónica was simply called *la nena* (the little girl).

Lucrecia ultimately refused to succumb to the family pressure to give baby Nina away, but she never let Nina forget it. It is uncertain whether Lucrecia refused to give Nina away because she still entertained the hope that her partner would swoop in from Puerto Rico for a reunification or whether it was rooted in a semblance of maternal affection. What is irrefutable is that Lucrecia viewed Nina's darker skin tone and African tresses as problematic. Her kinky curls—*pelo malo* (bad hair) was a source of consternation that compelled Lucrecia to continually shave baby Nina's hair in the hope that it would grow out straighter. Any infraction of Lucrecia's rules of discipline were greeted with both a beating and an expression of regret for not having given her away to an African American family at birth, along with the threat to place Nina in a foster home.

This was a marked contrast to the indulgence accorded her older sister, Mónica, who had slightly lighter skin and, more importantly, straighter *pelo lindo* (pretty hair). Even milk in the home was rationed across a color line. Lucrecia's mother, my great-grandmother, would allocate the milk in the home to Mónica and give Nina water instead. Birthday party celebrations were reserved for Mónica alone. Unlike for Mónica, light-colored nail polish was forbidden for Nina lest her hands look even darker. The racialized distinctions between the two girls continued their entire lives.

The pain of family rejection based on her apparent African ancestry was so profound for my mother that she shared her stories with me very early on. My own childhood experiences with differential treatment based on how mixed or Black I looked on any given day or context only reinforced my understanding of the relevance of anti-Black sentiment within celebrations of idealized notions of mixture. My appearance reflects the mixture of my mother Nina's Afro–Puerto Rican physical traits and those of my father's White-skinned background. While slightly lighter in skin shade than my mother, the brownness of my skin would never cause anyone to view me as White. Many have told me that I am a doppelganger for their various relatives in India. However, the comparison to relatives in India often disappears depending on what my hair decides to do that day. On a low humidity day with enough hair care products to make my hair lay down and be wrestled into a curl-hiding bun, I look more Indian. If I let it out and allow the curls to reign supreme, my African ancestry is more apparent to others.

How much of my perspective on the meaning of race might have diverged had my hair been different? I wonder. My *abuelita* (grandmother) Lucrecia was never happier than when my hair was greased down into two long braids down my back, and I looked to her to be an indigenous "Taína." But her absolute preference was for me to have my hair blow-dried straight, regardless of how short in duration the look would last (one day in humid weather, or maybe a week with the aid of large rollers, dry air, and a nightly "dubi" scalp wrapping of the hair for maximum stretch). However, the Hair Wars began in earnest when I cut off my hair in an act of adolescent rebellion. My grandmother was mystified as to why I would choose to have my curls spring out on display, resembling my mother's Afro. In my grandmother's eyes, my mother was unfortunately afflicted with overtly "bad hair," but why in the world would I choose to emulate that style when I had the "benefit" of being better situated to beat my hair into submission with a "more attractive" simulation of Whiteness. Every visit to her apartment on the Lower East Side of Manhattan was greeted with some version of "*Ay ese pelo*" (Oh, that hair) or "*¿Porque no haces algo con ese pelo?*" (Why don't you do something with that hair?).

Wearing my hair in a short, curly mop also worked to seemingly eject me from my presumed membership in the Latino imaginary. Encountering Latino merchants and other Latino service providers, I was constantly greeted with a surprised "Oh, you speak Spanish" and "Where did you learn to speak Spanish?" My hair now barred the door to automatic entrée to Latino kinship. I had to earn my way back into Latinaness by constantly speaking Spanish loudly and referencing my Latina culture. Like in Latin America, the imagined Latino community had and has a decided vision of mixture that does not encompass tightly coiled hair with brown skin. The anti-Black slurs I heard used in the Latino community with respect to African Americans only reinforced my early impressions that Blackness was problematic, despite our assertions of Latino pride in being a mixture of races. It became evident to me that cultural *mestizaje* pride (race-mixture pride) aside, not all parts of the mixture were equally welcomed or celebrated.

When I became older and took on the role of translating government forms into Spanish for my grandmother, our disputes about race escalated into the Census Conflict. In the 1980s she was fine with responding yes to the question of whether her ethnicity was of Hispanic origin. After I translated the census question, she told me to check the Hispanic-origin ethnicity box "Yes." But when it came to the separate question regarding racial ancestry, she became agitated and wanted us to just skip the question. Being an argumentative teenager with control over the English-language form, I insisted that she engage with the category options of White, Black, Native American, Asian, or other. Screaming matches ensued as she demanded that I insert "*Boricua*" (Puerto Rican) as a race into the "Some Other Race" slot, and I insisted that Puerto Rican is not a race unto itself. If we were so proud of being racially mixed Puerto Ricans, why not list all parts of the mixture on the "Some Other Race" line? That was unacceptable to her.

By the time the census forms were modified in 2000 to permit multiple-box-checking responses to the racial category question, she was living in a nursing home unable to communicate in any language about government forms. Yet, everything about her lifelong aversion to attributing her light brown skin to African ancestry and her preference for deflecting from race within the unenumerated racial mixture of Puerto Rican identity tells me that she would have been uninterested in the ability to check multiple racial boxes, let alone the "Black" box. My *abuelita* has long since passed away. However, I hope that the insights contained in this book can contribute to the social justice effort of interrupting Latino anti-Black bias among other Latinos who are reticent about checking a "Black" box or dealing with Blackness in any form. *Ojalá y Aché!*[17]

ACKNOWLEDGMENTS

Thanks to Gayatri Patnaik, the best editor I have ever worked with.

Immeasurable gratitude to my mother and all the interviewees who so kindly shared their candid reflections on what were often very painful memories. This book would not have been the same without your insights.

I also owe thanks to each person who generously read and commented on earlier versions of various book chapters: William (Sandy) Darity Jr., Laura Gomez, Bruce Green, Hilda Llorens, Ana Ramos-Zayas, Bernd Reiter, Susan Scafidi, Lourdes Torres, and Rodman Williams. Much appreciation as well to my census data gurus: Howard Hogan, Nicholas Jones, Mark Hugo Lopez, and Jeffrey Passel.

I was also greatly benefitted by the opportunity to present chapters before the Fordham University Law School Scholarship Workshop and its 10/10 series, the Afro-Descendant Working Group Colloquia, the UCLA Advanced Critical Race Theory Workshop Seminar, the Cafecito Network of Latina Lawyers, the New York City Commission on Human Rights, the US Attorney's Office in Los Angeles, the Hispanic Lobbyists Association, the Association of Black Sociologists, and the National Conference of Black Political Scientists.

And last but never ever least are the Fordham University Law School librarians and the legion of research assistants who help me each and every day—thank you for all you do.

Any shortcomings are, lamentably, entirely my own.

NOTES

CHAPTER 1: WHAT IS LATINO ANTI-BLACKNESS?
1. Vilson, "My Skin Is Black, My Name Is Latino. That Shouldn't Surprise You."
2. Fanon, *Black Skin, White Masks.*
3. Quarshie and Slack, "Census: US Sees Unprecedented Multiracial Growth, Decline in the White Population for First Time in History."
4. Vespa, Medina, and Armstrong, *Demographic Turning Points for the United States.*
5. Jung and Costa Vargas, *Antiblackness*; Costa Vargas, *The Denial of Antiblackness.*
6. "Hispanic Population to Reach 111 Million by 2060"; Population by Hispanic or Latino Origin: 2010 and 2020.
7. Gosin, "The Death of 'La Reina de la Salsa': Celia Cruz and the Mythification of the Black Woman."
8. Godreau, "Folkloric 'Others': *Blanqueamiento* and the Celebration of Blackness as an Exception in Puerto Rico."
9. Lao-Montes, "Afro-Latin@ Difference and the Politics of Decolonization."
10. Román and Flores, introduction to *The Afro-Latin@ Reader*, 1.
11. The various terms for referring to Latinos is discussed at the end of this chapter.
12. Goldberg, *Racist Culture.*
13. Quesada, "The Violent History of Latin America Is ALL About Promoting Whiteness."
14. Okamoto and Mora, "Panethnicity."
15. Gotanda, "A Critique of 'Our Constitution Is Color-Blind.'"
16. Wilkerson, *Caste.*
17. Eberhardt, *Biased.*
18. Poets Medrano, *Regando esencias [The Scent of Waiting]*; Perdomo, *Where a Nickel Costs a Dime.* Novelists Acevedo, *The Poet X*; Llanos-Figueroa, *Daughters of the Stone*; Díaz, *The Brief Wondrous Life of Oscar Wao*; Serrano, *Gunmetal Black.* Memoirists Díaz, *Ordinary Girls*; Redd, "Something Latino Was Up with Us"; Thomas, *Down These Mean Streets.*
19. García-Peña, "Dismantling Anti-Blackness Together"; Petra Rivera-Rideau, "Expanding the Dialogues: Afro-Latinx Feminisms"; Jaime, "How Latinx

People Can Fight Anti-Black Racism in Our Own Culture"; López, "It's Time for Non-Black Latinx People to Talk About Anti-Blackness in Our Own Communities"; Julie Torres, "Black Latinx Activists on Anti-Blackness"; Pérez, "As Non-Black POC, We Need to Address Anti-Blackness."

20. Holder and Aja, *Afro-Latinos in the U.S. Economy.*
21. "Afro-Latinos in 2017: A Demographic and Socio-Economic Snapshot"; Logan, *How Race Counts for Hispanic Americans*; López and Gonzalez-Barrera, "Afro-Latino: A Deeply Rooted Identity Among U.S. Hispanics"; Monforti and Sanchez, "The Politics of Perception."
22. Vargas, "Latinos and Criminal Justice, Policing, and Drug Policy Reform."
23. Quiros and Dawson, "The Color Paradigm."
24. LaVeist-Ramos et al., "Are Black Hispanics Black or Hispanic?"
25. Gravlee, Dressler, and Bernard, "Skin Color, Social Classification, and Blood Pressure in Southeastern Puerto Rico."
26. López et al., "What's Your 'Street Race'?"
27. Roth, "Racial Mismatch."
28. López, "Killing Two Birds with One Stone?"; Nolasco, "Doing Latinidad While Black."
29. Hernández, *Racial Subordination in Latin America*, 2.
30. Hernández, "Roots of Anger."
31. Ashla, reader response, *Los Angeles Times.*
32. Adriana E. Padilla, reader response, *Los Angeles Times.*
33. Telles, Sawyer, and Rivera-Salgado, *Just Neighbors?*
34. Roth and Kim, "Relocating Prejudice."
35. Roth and Kim, "Relocating Prejudice; Massagali, "What Do Boston-Area Residents Think of One Another?," 144–64.
36. Smith, "Market Rivals or Class Allies?"; Marrow, *New Destination Dreaming*, 120–34.
37. Hernández, "'Too Black to Be Latino/a'," 154; Prud'homme, "Race Relations Browns vs. Blacks"; Morales, "Brown Like Me?"
38. *Black Latinas Know Collective* (blog); *Radio Caña Negra* podcast; Latinx Racial Equity Project.
39. Crenshaw et al., *Critical Race Theory*, defining critical race theory as the scholarly examination of the relationship among race, racism, and power to reveal practices of systemic and structural subordination facilitated and permitted by legal discourse and legal institutions.
40. Spivak, "Subaltern Studies: Deconstructing Historiography."
41. Hernández, *Racial Subordination in Latin America*, 73.
42. SlaveVoyages Trans-Atlantic Slave Trade Database, http://www.slavevoyages .org/estimates/bE6pXgi9. Accessed Oct. 27, 2021.
43. Telles, *Pigmentocracies*, 3.
44. Sawyer, *Racial Politics in Post-Revolutionary Cuba*; Cle_land, *The Power of Race in Cuba.*
45. Telles, *Pigmentocracies.*
46. Reiter and Simmons, *Afro-Descendants, Identity, and the Struggle for Development in the Americas.*
47. Hall, "A Descriptive Analysis of Skin Color Bias in Puerto Rico," 177–78.

48. Torres, "La gran familia Puertorriqueña 'ej preta de Beldá'" (The Great Puerto Rican Family Is Really Black), 285, 297.

49. Valentín and Minet, "Las 889 páginas de telegram entre Rosselló Nevares y sus allegados."

50. Dulitzky, "A Region in Denial."

51. Miller and Garran, *Racism in the United States*, 289.

52. Valdes, "Race, Ethnicity, and Hispanismo in a Triangular Perspective," 326.

53. De Carvalho-Neto, "Folklore of the Black Struggle in Latin America."

54. Hordge-Freeman, *The Color of Love*; Hordge-Freeman and Veras, "Out of the Shadows, into the Dark," 146–60.

55. Adames, Chavez-Dueñas, and Organista, "Skin Color Matters in Latino/a Communities"; Derlan et al., "Longitudinal Relations Among Mexican-Origin Mothers' Cultural Characteristics, Cultural Socialization, and 5-Year-Old Children's Ethnic–Racial Identification."

56. Hordge-Freeman and Veras, "Out of the Shadows, into the Dark."

57. Bonilla-Silva, "Reflections About Race by a *Negrito Acomplejao*."

58. Cruz-Janzen, "Latinegras," 170.

59. Cruz-Janzen, "Latinegras," 179.

60. Comas-Díaz, "LatiNegra," 168.

61. Comas-Díaz, "LatiNegra," 176.

62. Llorens, "Identity Practices."

63. Comas-Díaz, "LatiNegra," 177.

64. Jorge, "The Black Puerto Rican Woman in Contemporary American Society," 138.

65. Candelario, *Black Behind the Ears*.

66. Calzada, Kim, and O'Gara, "Skin Color as a Predictor of Mental Health in Young Latinx Children."

67. Quiñones Rivera, "From Triguenita to Afro Puerto Rican."

68. Feliciano, Lee, and Robnett, "Racial Boundaries Among Latinos."

69. Jorge, "The Black Puerto Rican Woman," 139.

70. Morales, "Parental Messages Concerning Latino/Black Interracial Dating."

71. McClain et al., "Racial Distancing in a Southern City"; Torres-Saillant, "Problematic Paradigms"; Valdes, "Race, Ethnicity, and Hispanismo in a Triangular Perspective," 307.

72. Candelario, *Black Behind the Ears*.

73. Candelario, *Black Behind the Ears*, 339.

74. Howard, "Afro-Latinos and the Black-Hispanic Identity."

75. Dulitzky, *A Region in Denial*, 39.

76. Mindiola et al., *Black-Brown Relations and Stereotypes*, 20–29, 37–38.

77. Yancey, *Who Is White?*, 65.

78. Krupnikov and Piston, "The Political Consequences of Latino Prejudice Against Blacks."

79. Mindiola, *Black-Brown Relations and Stereotypes*, 35.

80. Mindiola, *Black-Brown Relations and Stereotypes*, 44–45.

81. Marcus L. Britton, "Close Together but Worlds Apart?"

82. Charles, *Won't You Be My Neighbor?*, 161.

83. Mindiola, *Black-Brown Relations and Stereotypes*, 46.

84. McClain et al. "Racial Distancing in a Southern City."

85. Wilkinson, *Partners or Rivals?*, 64.
86. Charles, "Neighborhood Racial-Composition Preferences," 379.
87. Yancey, *Who Is White?*, 70–71; Lindo, "Miembros de las diversas razas prefieren a los suyos."
88. National Conference of Christians and Jews, *Taking America's Pulse*.
89. Piatt, *Black and Brown in America*, 52–57.
90. Barreto, Gonzalez, and Sánchez, "Rainbow Coalition in the Golden State?"
91. Bobo and Hutchings, "Perceptions of Racial Group Competition."
92. Gomez-Aguinaga et al., "Importance of State and Local Variation in Black-Brown Attitudes," 214–25.
93. Bobo and Hutchings, "Perceptions of Racial Group Competition," 964.
94. Sampson and Raudenbush, "Seeing Disorder," 319, 332–33, 336.
95. Darity, Hamilton, and Dietrich, "Passing on Blackness"; Loveman and Muniz, "How Puerto Rico Became White."
96. US Census Bureau, "Hispanic or Latino Origin by Race."
97. Darity and Boza, "Choosing Race," 4–5; Darity et al., "Bleach in the Rainbow."
98. Darity et al., "Bleach in the Rainbow."
99. Cohn, "Millions of Americans Changed Their Racial or Ethnic Identity from One Census to the Next."
100. DiFulco, "Can You Tell a Mexican from a Puerto Rican?," 86.
101. Pessar, *A Visa for a Dream*, 44.
102. Howard, *Coloring the Nation*, 114–15.
103. Nieves, "The Representation of Latin@s in the Media"; Fletcher, "The Blond, Blue-Eyed Face of Spanish TV"; Goin, "Marginal Latinidad."
104. Calderón, *My Time to Speak*, 59.
105. Flores, "Race Discrimination Within the Latino Community."
106. Flores, "Race Discrimination Within the Latino Community," 30–31.
107. Pew Research Center, *Majority of Latinos Say Skin Color Impacts Opportunity in America and Shapes Daily Life*, 21; *National Survey of Latinos Report*, 74.
108. US Census Bureau, "Population by Hispanic or Latino Origin: 2010 and 2020, Table 3"; US Census Bureau, "The Hispanic Population in the United States: 2019."
109. Del Castillo, *The Treaty of Guadalupe Hidalgo*; McDonald, *The Mexican War*.
110. Foley, *Quest for Equality*.
111. Haney López, "Protest, Repression, and Race."
112. Salazar, "Chicanos Would Find Identity Before Coalition with Blacks," 239, 241.
113. Salazar, "Negro Drive Worries Mexican-Americans," 113.
114. Salazar, "Negro Drive Worries Mexican-Americans."
115. Hernández, "Afro-Mexicans and the Chicano Movement," 1537.
116. Murguia and Forman, "Shades of Whiteness."
117. Barbaro, "Ethnic Resentment," 77, 89–91.
118. Barbaro, "Ethnic Resentment," 91.
119. Barbaro, "Ethnic Resentment," 90.
120. Hutchinson, "Urban Tension."
121. Lee and Suro, "Latino-Black Rivalry Grows."
122. Martínez, "African-Americans, Latinos, and the Construction of Race."

123. Kasindorf and Puente, "Hispanics and Blacks Find Their Futures Entangled."
124. Kasindorf and Puente, "Hispanics and Blacks Find Their Futures Entangled."
125. Archibold, "Racial Hate Feeds a Gang War's Senseless Killing."
126. Rivera, "Poly High Violence Just Made News, But Parents Say It's a Decades-Old Problem."
127. Chideya and Del Barco, "Racial Tension at Los Angeles High School."
128. "Brawl Erupts at Carson High School Between 30 Black, Latino Students"; "Lunchtime Brawl Involving 40 People Breaks Out at LA High School After Tensions Flared Between Black and Hispanic Students at Prom"; "Riots Break Out Between Black, Latino Students at Victorville School"; Buchanan, "Tensions Mounting Between Blacks and Latinos Nationwide."
129. Lee and Suro, "Latino-Black Rivalry Grows."
130. Lee and Suro, "Latino-Black Rivalry Grows."
131. Guidry, "Reaching the People Across the Street."
132. De Genova and Ramos-Zayas, *Latino Crossings*, 187–89; McClain et al., *Racial Distancing in a Southern City*; Swarns, "Bridging a Racial Rift That Isn't Black and White."
133. Heard, "Racial Strife Runs Deep at High School."
134. LeDuff, "At a Slaughterhouse, Some Things Never Die."
135. Marrow, *New Destination Dreaming*, 118.
136. Schleef and Cavalcanti, *Latinos in Dixie*, 54, 88.
137. Jones, "Blacks May Be Second Class, But They Can't Make Them Leave," 73.
138. Dunn and Stepick, "Blacks in Miami," 41.
139. Dunn and Stepick, "Blacks in Miami," 45.
140. Stack and Warren, "The Reform Tradition and Ethnic Politics," 174.
141. Grenier and Castro, "Blacks and Cubans in Miami," 137, 151.
142. Peery, "Witnessing History," 305, 306–8.
143. Logan, *How Race Counts for Hispanic Americans*, 7.
144. Logan, *How Race Counts for Hispanic Americans*, 8.
145. Betancur, "Framing the Discussion of African-American-Latino Relations," 159–72.
146. Opie, *Upsetting the Apple Cart*.
147. De Genova and Ramos-Zayas, *Latino Crossings*, 40.
148. Lee, *Building a Latino Civil Rights Movement*.
149. Jorge, "The Black Puerto Rican Woman in Contemporary American Society," 134, 139.
150. Cruz, "Interminority Relations in Urban Settings," 84, 90.
151. Cruz, "Interminority Relations in Urban Settings," 91.
152. Barbaro, "Ethnic Resentment," 83.
153. Lee and Diaz, "'I Was the One Percenter,'" 64.
154. Cruz, "Interminority Relations in Urban Settings," 91; Melendez, *We Took the Streets*.
155. Ramos-Zayas, *National Performances*.
156. Itzigsohn et al., "Immigrant Incorporation and Racial Identity," 50, 69.
157. Monforti and Sanchez, "The Politics of Perception," 261–62; "National Survey of Latinos," 74.
158. Freeman, "A Note on the Influence of African Heritage on Segregation," 137, 141.

159. Itzigsohn and Dore-Cabral, "Competing Identities?," 225, 240.
160. Russell, "Perth Amboy Gang Tensions Worry Parents."
161. Ortiz, *Never Again a World Without Us.*
162. Mora, Perez, and Vargas, "Who Identifies as 'Latinx'?"
163. Noe-Bustamante, Mora, and Lopez, "About One-in-Four U.S. Hispanics Have Heard of Latinx, but Just 3% Use It."
164. Salinas and Lozano, "Mapping and Recontexualizing the Evolution of the Term 'Latinx.'"
165. Ramos, *Finding Latinx.*

CHAPTER 2: *"NO JUEGUES CON NIÑOS DE COLOR EXTRAÑO"*

1. Blades, "Plástico."
2. Hernández, *Racial Subordination in Latin America*, 109–11, 128.
3. Sued Badillo and Lopez Cantos, *Puerto Rico Negro*; Morales Carrión, *Auge y decadencia de la trata negrera en Puerto Rico (1820–1860)*; Kinsbruner, *Not of Pure Blood*, 32.
4. Duany, "Making Indians out of Blacks," 31–32.
5. Santiago-Valles, "Policing the Crisis in the Whitest of All the Antilles," 43–44.
6. Betances, "The Prejudice of Having No Prejudice in Puerto Rico, Part II," 22, 33.
7. Llorens, Garcia-Quijano, and Godreau, "Racismo en Puerto Rico"; Santiago-Valles, "Policing the Crisis in the Whitest of All the Antilles," 43–44; Muñoz Vásquez and Alegría Ortega, *Discrimen por razón de raza y los sistemas de seguridad y justicia.*
8. Puerto Rico Civil Rights Act, 1 P.R. Laws Ann. §§ 13–19 (1943); P.R. Const. Art. II, § 1 (1952); 29 P.R. Laws Ann. § 146 (codifying as amended 1959 P.R. Laws 100).
9. 48 U.S.C. § 734.
10. 42 U.S.C. §§ 2000a et seq.
11. *Bermudez Zenon*, 790 F. Supp. 41, 43.
12. Dinzey-Flores, *Locked In, Locked Out*, 4.
13. US Census Bureau, QuickFacts, "Miami City, Florida."
14. US Census Bureau, "Race and Ethnicity in the United States: 2010 Census and 2020 Census."
15. Booth, "Miami."
16. Aja et al., *The Color of Wealth in Miami.*
17. Sawyer, "Racial Politics in Multiethnic America."
18. *Laroche*, 62 F. Supp.2d 1375. Complaint at 1.
19. Labaton, "Denny's Restaurants to Pay $54 Million in Race Bias Suits."
20. Grillo, *Black Cuban, Black American.*
21. Greenbaum, *More Than Black*, 310.
22. *In re* Trujillo, 2002 WL 1491999.
23. *In re* Pryor, 1994 WL 910076.
24. *In re* Andrews, 2003 WL 23529549.
25. US Census Bureau, "Carlsbad, New Mexico Population: Census 2010 and 2000."
26. US Census Bureau, "Carlsbad, New Mexico Population: Census 2010 and 2000"; US Census Bureau, QuickFacts: "Carlsbad City, New Mexico."

27. *Pirtle*, 2003 WL 27385258.
28. *Pirtle*, 2003 WL 27385258. Complaint at 16.
29. *Pirtle*, 2003 WL 27385258. Complaint at 7.
30. Haywood, "'Latino Spaces Have Always Been the Most Violent,'" 759.
31. Haywood, "'Latino Spaces Have Always Been the Most Violent,'" 774.
32. Garcia-Louis and Cortes, "Rejecting Black and Rejected Back."
33. Garcia-Louis and Cortes, "Rejecting Black and Rejected Back," 11.
34. Smith and Jones, "Intraracial Harassment on Campus."
35. Telzer and Vazquez Garcia, "Skin Color and Self-Perception of Immigrant and U.S.-Born Latinas."
36. Haywood, "'Latino Spaces Have Always Been the Most Violent,'" 777–80.
37. Literte, "Competition, Conflict, and Coalition."
38. Office for Civil Rights, "Section 101 Privacy Act and Freedom of Information Act," 5.
39. Office for Civil Rights, "Pending Cases Under Investigation at Elementary-Secondary and Post-Secondary Schools as of May 28, 2021."
40. Dache, Haywood, and Mislán, "A Badge of Honor Not Shame."
41. Straus, "Unequal Pieces of a Shrinking Pie"; Williams and Garza, "A Case Study in Change and Conflict."
42. Hardie and Tyson, "Other People's Racism."
43. Straus, "Unequal Pieces of a Shrinking Pie," 507.
44. Ericksen and Casuso, "Race Fights Break Out at Samohi."
45. Stovall, interview with author, 2–19.
46. "6 Students Arrested After Fight at Streamwood H.S."
47. Hodge, "Hard Lessons."
48. Hodge, "Hard Lessons."
49. Ayala, "Racismo institucional en las escuelas: Una condena para lxs niñxs negrxs; Torres Gotay, "Justicia desiste del caso contra estudiante de educación especial."
50. Cruz-Janzen, "Y tu abuela a'onde esta?"
51. *Fennell*, 963 F. Supp. 2d 623.
52. Recio, "Black and Ugly."
53. Sinnette, Arthur Alfonso Schomburg, 13.
54. Valdés, *Diasporic Blackness*.
55. Cortés, interview with author, 48–64.
56. Stovall, interview with author, 86–90.
57. Vilson, interview with author, 99–120.
58. Montoya, interview with author, 132–62.
59. "Providence, 2019–20 Report Card: Overview," accessed June 24, 2021. Afro-Latino numbers are not specified in the data in which the remaining student population is reported as 9 percent White, 5 percent Asian, 4 percent multiracial, and 1 percent Native American.
60. Teach for America fellow, Rhode Island, interview with author; "Providence, 2019–20 Report Card: Civil Rights Data Collection for 2017–2018," accessed June 24, 2021, showing disproportionate suspensions and school arrests for students of color compared to White students.
61. Generation Teach, "Why We Exist and What We Do," accessed July 20, 2021.

62. Teaching fellow, Generation Teach Rhode Island Program, interview with author, 22–30.
63. Teaching fellow, Generation Teach Rhode Island Program, interview with author, 140–52.
64. Epstein, Blake, and Gonzalez, *Girlhood Interrupted*.
65. Stovall, interview with author, 76–82.
66. Jackson et al., "Betrayed: Chicago Schools Fail to Protect Students from Sexual Abuse and Assault, Leaving Lasting Damage"; Schuler, *Annual Report—Fiscal Year 2019*.
67. City of Chicago School District 299, teacher demographics, accessed July 20, 2021.
68. Cruz-Janzen, "Latinegras," 171.

CHAPTER 3: WORKING IN THE USA
1. *Olumuyiwa*, 1999 WL 529553.
2. *Ajayi*, 336 F.3d 520; *Dunn*, 288 F. Supp. 3d 749; *EEOC v. New Koosharem Corp*, No. 2:13-cv-2761 (W.D. Tenn.); *Gallentine*, 919 F. Supp. 2d 787; *Young*, 2009 WL 3352148; *EEOC v. E&D Services, Inc.*, No. SA-08-CA -0714-NSN (W.D. Tex.); *EEOC v. Lockheed Martin*, Civil No. 05-00479 SPK (D. Haw.); *Cruz*, No. 3-21709 (S.D. Fla. Mia. Div.); Reform Bd. of Trustees, 1999 WL 258488, at *1; *Hines*, 2010 WL 2599321; *Roberts*, 2003 WL 1194102, at *1; *Ferguson*, No. 2017-026195-CA-01 (Fla. Cir. Ct.); *Bradshaw*, No. 2016-020723-CA-01 (Fla. Cir. Ct.); *Green*, No. 2015-024883-CA-01 (Fla. Cir. Ct.); *Turner*, 49 Misc.3d 1220(A); *Boyce*, 958 N.Y.S.2d 306; *Bowen*, 49 S.W. 3d 902; *In re* Johnson, 1998 WL 104771.
3. *Cruz*, No. 3-21709 (S.D. Fla. Mia. Div.).
4. Berrey, Nelson, and Nielsen, *Rights on Trial*; Nielsen and Nelson, "Rights Realized?"
5. Clermont and Schwab, "Employment Discrimination Plaintiffs in Federal Court," 127.
6. Clermont and Schwab, "Employment Discrimination Plaintiffs in Federal Court."
7. Hornby, "Summary Judgment Without Illusions," 273, 279–80.
8. Johnson v. Pride Indus., 2018 WL 6624691, dismissal of case pending appeal; *Osei-Buckle*, 1998 WL 552126, at *1; *Patino*, 1997 WL 416949, at *1; *Farias*, 925 F.2d 866, 879; *Atencia*, 2020 WL 3893582; *Shelby*, 2019 WL 1958001; *Smiley*, 2010 WL 10669508; *Cortez*, No. 03-1251 BB/LFG (D. New Mexico); *Isaac*, 2002 WL 31086118, at *1; *Allen*, 2001 WL 1249054, at *1; *Hogan*, 102 F. Supp. 2d 1180; *Russell*, 46 F. Supp. 2d 1330; *Harper*, 1999 WL 147698, at *1; *Vincent*, 3 F. Supp. 2d 1405; *Bernard*, 1996 WL 457284; *Mathura*, 1996 WL 157496; *Foster*, 2016 WL 4098676; *Johnson*, 2009 WL 867131; *Donjoie*, No. 2018-036551-CA-01 (Fla. Cir. Ct.); *Beard*, 2013 WL 5947951; *Walcott*, 2013 WL 593488; *McCleary*, 2019 WL 7205918; *Hicks*, 2003 WL 21788903; *McCrimmon*, 2003 WL 1862156; *Quintana*, 1989 WL 645048; *In re* Green, 2020 WL 2303164; *In re* Garcia, 2018 WL 6625532; *In re* Hernandez, 2007 WL 9254612.
9. Giuliano, Levine, and Leonard, "Manager Race and the Race of New Hires."
10. *Arrocha*, No. CV021868, 2004 WL 594981.

11. Fanon, *Peau noir, masques blancs (Black Skin, White Masks)*.
12. *Castaneda*, 430 U.S. 482.
13. Collins, *Black Feminist Thought*; Crenshaw, "Demarginalizing the Intersection of Race and Sex."
14. *Young*, 2009 WL 3352148.
15. "Remedies for Employment Discrimination." Punitive damages may also be awarded to punish an employer who has committed an especially malicious or reckless act of discrimination. There are limits on the amount of compensatory and punitive damages a person can recover depending on the size of the employer.
16. *Bartholomew*, No. 3:11CV02219 (D.P.R.).
17. *Webb*, 992 F. Supp. 1382.
18. *Sprott*, 1998 WL 472061, at *1.
19. Manager of learning and organizational development, email to author.
20. Joshi and Kline, "Lack of Jury Diversity"; Democracy and Government Reform Team, *Examining the Demographic Compositions of U.S. Circuit and District Courts*; Bannon and Adelstein, "State Supreme Court Diversity—February 2020 Update."
21. Mendez, interview with author.
22. Mindiola, Flores Niemann, and Néstor, *Black-Brown: Relations and Stereotypes*, 31–35.
23. *Portugues-Santa*, 614 F. Supp. 2d 221.
24. *Vance*, 570 U.S. 421; *De Los Santos Rojas*, 85 F. Supp. 3d 615.
25. "Section 15: Race and Color Discrimination."
26. *EEOC v. Koper*, U.S. Dist. Ct. of P.R. Case No. 09–1563.
27. Johnson v. Pride Indus., (No. 19–50173) 2018 WL 6624691. Dismissal of case pending appeal.
28. US Census Bureau, "QuickFacts: El Paso County, Texas."
29. *Ash*, 546 U.S. 454, 456.
30. West, *Race Matters*.
31. Stack, "Black Workers' Suit Accuses Job Agency of Favoring Hispanic Applicants."
32. *Hunt*, 2018 Fair Emp. Prac. Case (BNA) 59,091.
33. Stack, "Black Workers' Suit Accuses Job Agency of Favoring Hispanic Applicants."
34. *EEOC v. Rodriguez*, 1994 WL 714003.
35. Haslip-Viera, *White Latino Privilege*.
36. *EEOC v. Rodriguez*, at *10.
37. Morales, "The Utility of Shared Ethnicity on Job Quality Among Latino Workers"; Elliot and Smith, "Ethnic Matching of Supervisors to Subordinate Work Groups."
38. *Farias*, 925 F.2d 866, 879.
39. Newman, *No Shame in My Game*; Smith, *Mexican New York*.
40. Fuentes-Mayorga, "Sorting Black and Brown Latino Service Workers in Gentrifying New York Neighborhoods."
41. Hersch, "Profiling the New Immigrant Worker."
42. Murguia and Telles, "Phenotype and Schooling Among Mexican Americans," 276–89.

43. Hersch, "The Persistence of Skin Color Discrimination for Immigrants"; Hersch, "Colorism Against Legal Immigrants to the United States."
44. Rosenblum et al., "Looking Through the Shades."
45. Melendez, Rodriguez, and Barry Figueroa, *Hispanics in the Labor Force*.
46. Hill, *Black Labor and the American Legal System*, 182–83, 254; Royster, *Race and the Invisible Hand*, 29–33; Higginbotham, "Employment for Professional Black Women in the Twentieth Century."
47. *Felix*, 27 Emp. Prac. Dec. P 32,241, 22,2768 n. 6.
48. Denton and Massey, "Racial Identity Among Caribbean Hispanics"; Padilla, "'But You're Not a Dirty Mexican'"; Uhlmann et al., "Subgroup Prejudice Based on Skin Color Among Hispanics in the United States and Latin America."
49. Tafoya, "Shades of Belonging."
50. Valcarel, "Growing Up Black in Puerto Rico."
51. Hernández, "Afro-Latin@s and the Latino Workplace."
52. Cruz-Janzen, "Y tu abuela a'onde esta?"; Quiñones Rivera, "From Trigueñita to Afro-Puerto Rican."
53. Belluck, "John H. Pratt, 84, Federal Judge Who Helped Define Civil Rights."
54. Crenshaw, "Demarginalizing the Intersection of Race and Sex," 139.
55. Banks, "Colorism."
56. *Falero Santiago*, 10 F. Supp. 2d 93.
57. White, "The Irrational Turn in Employment Discrimination Law."
58. *Ash*, 126 S. Ct. 1195.
59. Orozco and Tareque, *2020 State of Latino Entrepreneurship Report*.
60. *Minorities in Business*.
61. Kramer Mills et al., *Latino-Owned Businesses*.
62. Orozco and Tareque, *2020 State of Latino Entrepreneurship Report*.
63. Noe-Bustamante, Lopez, and Krogstad, "U.S. Hispanic Population Surpassed 60 Million in 2019, but Growth Has Slowed."
64. Orozco and Tareque, *2020 State of Latino Entrepreneurship Report*.
65. Morales, "The Utility of Shared Ethnicity," 439–65; Aguilera, "The Impact of Social Capital on the Earnings of Puerto Rican Migrants."
66. Elliot and Smith, "Ethnic Matching of Supervisors," 258–76.
67. Rushing and Winfield, "Bridging the Border Between Work and Family."

CHAPTER 4: *"OYE NEGRO, YOU CAN'T LIVE HERE"*

1. Quinta, interview with author.
2. Fair Housing Act, 42 U.S.C. § 3603(b) (1968).
3. 42 U.S.C. § 1982 (1866).
4. Reosti, "'We Go Totally Subjective,'" 625.
5. Limón et al., *State of Hispanic Homeownership Report*, 4; "Homeownership Rate in the U.S. 1990–2020."
6. *Martinez*, No. CV 05-7608-JTL, 2007 WL 8435675, at *1.
7. Lacayo, "Latinos Need to Stay in Their Place"; "Hate Crimes on the Rise in Orange County: Report"; Fry and Queally, "Hate Crimes Targeting Jews and Latinos Increased in California in 2018, Report Says"; Carroll, "'They Just Don't Fit In.'"

8. US Census Bureau, "2010 Census of Population: General Population Characteristics, Illinois."
9. López, "Cosa de Blancos."
10. Clealand, "Undoing the Invisibility of Blackness in Miami."
11. Aja, *Miami's Forgotten Cubans*, 28.
12. Nicholas, "Racial and Ethnic Discrimination in Rental Housing."
13. Greenbaum, *More Than Black*; Prohías and Casal, *The Cuban Minority in the US.*
14. Grillo, *Black Cuban, Black American.*
15. Aja, *Miami's Forgotten Cubans*, 47–49.
16. Grillo, *Black Cuban, Black American.*
17. Gosin, *The Racial Politics of Division*, 6.
18. Hay, "I've Been Black in Two Countries," 46.
19. "Current Hispanic or Latino Population Demographics in Miami, Florida 2020, 2019 by Gender and Age."
20. Mirabal, *Suspect Freedoms*, 189.
21. Hoffnung-Garskof, *Racial Migrations.*
22. Delgado, "Puerto Rican."
23. Maciag, "Residential Segregation Data for U.S. Metro Areas."
24. Keys v. Garcia, HUDALJ 05–89–0457–1.
25. Machicote, "Dear Latines."
26. US Census Bureau, "1990 Census of Population: General Population Characteristics, Illinois."
27. Gabriel and Painter, "Mobility, Residential Location, and the American Dream."
28. Limón et al., *2019 State of Hispanic Homeownership Report*, 9; "NAHREP Releases New State of Hispanic Homeownership Report."
29. US Census Bureau, "2000 Census of Population: General Population Characteristics, New York."
30. US Census Bureau, "1990 Census of Population: General Population Characteristics, New York."
31. Tulsen, 1999 WL 521272, at *1.
32. Rochester, *The Black Tax.*
33. García, "The Birth of the MS13 in New York"; "MS-13 on Long Island."
34. US Census Bureau, "2000 Census of Population: General Population Characteristics, Iowa."
35. *Echols*, 1998 WL 21060, at *1.
36. *United States v. Barberis*, 887 F. Supp. 110.
37. *Frazier*, 27 F.3d 828.
38. US Census Bureau, "1990 Census of Population: General Population Characteristics, New York."
39. Paquette, "Book Details Klan Role in Smithtown's Past"; Glaberson, "15 Hate Groups in Region, Monitoring Organization Says."
40. *Frazier*, 27 F.3d at 831.
41. Scott, interview with author, 74–80.
42. Hendley, interview with author, 89–119.
43. LaRaia, interview with author, 51–56.
44. Dinzey-Flores, *Locked In, Locked Out*, 6–7, 134.

45. Fair Housing Act of 1968, 42 U.S.C. § 3604 (2019), prohibiting discrimination in the sale, rental, or related services is prohibited against any person on the basis of race, color, or national origin.
46. Larkin, "The Forty-Year 'First Step,'" 1617.
47. Massey and Denton, *American Apartheid*, 151.
48. Massey and Bitterman, "Explaining the Paradox of Puerto Rican Segregation," 326; Gans, "Second Generation Decline," 1–20.
49. South, Crowder, and Chavez, "Migration and Spatial Assimilation Among US Latinos: Classical Versus Segmented Trajectories," 514.
50. Iceland and Nelson, "Hispanic Segregation in Metropolitan America," 752; Sacks, "The Puerto Rican Effect on Hispanic Residential Segregation," 98.
51. Uzogara, "Who Desires In-Group Neighbors?"
52. Lofland, *A World of Strangers*.
53. Britton, "Close Together but Worlds Apart?"

CHAPTER 5: PHYSICAL VIOLENCE
1. Johnson, "5 Things About Alex Michael Ramos."
2. Clemente, "Not in Our Name: A Puerto Rican White Supremacist in Charlottesville."
3. Hing, "The Curious Case of George Zimmerman's Race."
4. Yancey, "'Blacks Cannot Be Racist.'"
5. Resto-Montero, "With the Rise of the Alt-Right, Latino White Supremacy May Not Be a Contradiction in Terms."
6. "14 Words: General Hate Symbols, Hate Slogans/Slang Terms."
7. Resto-Montero, "With the Rise of the Alt-Right, Latino White Supremacy May Not Be a Contradiction in Terms."
8. Resto-Montero, "With the Rise of the Alt-Right, Latino White Supremacy May Not Be a Contradiction in Terms."
9. Johnson v. California, 543 U.S. 499.
10. Spiegel, "Prison Race Rights."
11. Moore, "Hundreds Hurt in California Prison Riot."
12. Tanner, "Hispanics Battle Blacks in Major Calif. Prison Riot."
13. Ripston and Butler, "Legality of Segregating Prisoners by Race."
14. Raphael, "California Prisons Struggle to Adapt to Desegregation."
15. Vasquez, "One Prison Taught Me Racism. Another Taught Me Acceptance."
16. Vasquez, "One Prison Taught Me Racism. Another Taught Me Acceptance."
17. Quinones, "Race, Real Estate, and the Mexican Mafia."
18. Quinones, "Race, Real Estate, and the Mexican Mafia."
19. *In re* Louis Vasquez on Habeas Corpus, Case No. C087261 (Cal. 3rd App. Dist. June 4, 2018); Gonzales, "La Puente Man Sentenced to Decades in Prison for Stabbing 2 Men in Covina."
20. Holland, "2 Convicted of Racial Hate Crime in San Fernando Valley Shootings."
21. "Final Gang Defendant in Federal Hate Crimes Indictment Pleads Guilty in Firebombing of African-American Residences," press release no. 19–067.
22. Rubin, "Gang Member Gets Prison for Firebombing Black Families in Boyle Heights."
23. U.S. v. Rios et al., Docket No. 2:11-cr-00492 (C.D. Cal. June 1, 2011).

24. Ng, "Latino Gang Charged with Racial Cleansing Attacks in California Town."

25. Hutchinson, "Will Latino Gang Arrests Deepen Black-Brown Divide?"

26. Quinones, "Azusa 13 Street Gang Leader, Son Sentenced to Prison."

27. U.S. v. Flores et al., Docket No. 2:09-cr-00445 (C.D. Cal. May 6, 2009).

28. "Massive Racketeering Case Targets Hawaiian Gardens Gang Involved in Murder of Sheriff's Deputy, Attacks on African-Americans and Widespread Drug Trafficking."

29. Cunningham and Kimball, "Gangs, Guns, Drugs and Money"; Glover and Winton, "Dozens Arrested in Crackdown of Latino Gang Accuse of Targeting Blacks."

30. People v. Alcarez et al., No. NA072796 (LA County Superior Court Jan. 1, 2007).

31. Spano, "Blacks Were Targeted, Witness Insists."

32. Marrero, "El odio en acción."

33. U.S. v. Cazares et al., 788 F.3d 956 (9th Cir. 2015); US Department of Justice, Gang Members Convicted of Federal Hate Crimes for Murders, Assaults of African Americans.

34. US Department of Justice, Gang Members Convicted of Federal Hate Crimes for Murders, Assaults of African Americans.

35. Murr, "A Gang War with a Twist."

36. Rafael, *The Mexican Mafia*, 216.

37. Quinones, "Last Suspect in Cheryl Green Hate-Crime Murder Gets 238 Years."

38. Hipp and Tita, "Ethnically Transforming Neighborhoods and Violent Crime Among and Between African-Americans and Latinos."

39. Umemoto and Mikami, "A Profile of Race-Bias Hate Crime in Los Angeles County."

40. Davis and Erez, "Immigrant Populations as Victims," 1.

41. Cuevas, "Race and the L.A. Human."

42. Steffensmeier et al., "Reassessing Trends in Black Violent Crime, 1980–2008."

43. Márquez, *Black-Brown Solidarity*, 12; Telles, Sawyer, and Rivera-Salgado, *Just Neighbors?*, 1–28.

44. Meinero, "La Vida Loca Nationwide: Prosecuting Sureño Gangs Beyond Los Angeles."

45. Lyons, "Defending Turf: Racial Demographics and Hate Crime Against Blacks and Whites."

46. 2010 Census data reports the racial demographic statistics for each of the following California neighborhoods. Azusa: 3% African American, 67.57% Hispanic, 19.3% White persons not Hispanic; Hawaiian Gardens: 3.83% African American, 77.24% Hispanic, 7.32% White persons not Hispanic; Highland Park: 2.13% African American, 71.69% Hispanic, 13.16% White persons not Hispanic; Harbor Gateway: 9.63% African American, 48.48% Hispanic, 28.66% White persons not Hispanic. "Racial/Ethnic Composition, Cities and Communities, Los Angeles County: By Percentages, 2010 Census."

47. Logan, *How Race Counts for Hispanic Americans*; Parisi et al., "Multi-Scale Residential Segregation," using an "Index of Dissimilarity."

48. Telles et al., *Just Neighbors?*, 1.
49. Feldmeyer, "The Effects of Racial/Ethnic Segregation on Latino and Black Homicide."
50. Vigil, "Ethnic Succession and Ethnic Conflict."
51. Lefebvre, *The Production of Space.*
52. Boddie, "Racial Territoriality."
53. "Two California Men Indicted in Federal Hate Crime Case Stemming from New Year's Eve Attack on African-American Youths."
54. US Census Bureau, QuickFacts Table, "Compton City, California."
55. Bell, *Hate Thy Neighbor.*
56. Rafael, *The Mexican Mafia.*
57. Shroder, "Suspect Arrested in Carlsbad Hate Crime."
58. *Hernandez et al.*, Case No. B236093, California 2nd App. Dist.; "4 Face Arson, Hate Crime Trial for Cross Burning."
59. Taylor, 2006 WL 2239659.
60. *Gonzalez*, Case No. 3D13–1474 (Fla. 3rd Dist. Ct. of App.) (denying appeal from lower court conviction).
61. *State of Florida v. Nunez*, Case No. 2013-CF-002454-A-O (Fla. Orange Cnty.); "Full Sail Student Stabbed in Class with Screwdriver, Deputies Say."
62. Moran, "Hate Crime Charges Dropped Against Northwestern Chapel Vandals."
63. Glueck, "Iowa City Man Charged with Hate Crime for Assaulting Black Man."
64. Unger, "Hate Crime Strikes Rio Rancho."
65. Baumgartner, Epp, and Shoub, *Suspect Citizens.*
66. Dart and Laughland, "Sandra Bland."
67. Vargas, "Latinos and Criminal Justice, Policing, and Drug Policy Reform," question 25.
68. López and Krogstad, "How Hispanic Police Officers View Their Jobs."
69. "Philando Castile Death."
70. Hauser, "Florida Police Chief Gets 3 Years for Plot to Frame Black People for Crimes."
71. U.S. v. Atesiano, No. 1:18-cr-20479, 2018 WL 5831092.
72. Alford, "'They Believe We're Criminals.'"
73. Cratty, "Agreement Announced to Reform Puerto Rico's Police Force."
74. Torres Gotay, "Justicia desiste del caso contra estudiante de educación especial."

CHAPTER 6: LATINOS AND THE FUTURE OF RACIAL EQUALITY
IN THE UNITED STATES

1. Bonilla-Silva, "We Are All Americans!"
2. Guinier and Torres, *The Miner's Canary*, 225.
3. Guinier and Torres, *The Miner's Canary.*
4. Haslip-Viera, ed., *White Latino Privilege.*
5. Saenz, "Who and What the Hell Is a White Hispanic?"
6. García, "White Privilege and the Effacement of Blackness," 79.
7. Hernández, *Racial Subordination in Latin America*, 2.
8. Vargas, "Latina/o Whitening?"

9. Vargas, "Off White."
10. Ramirez and Peterson, *Ignored Racism*; Morales, *Latinx*.
11. Gómez, *Inventing Latinos*.
12. Sanchez and Rodriguez Espinosa, "Does the Race of the Discrimination Agent in Latinos' Discrimination Experiences Influence Latino Group Identity?"; Carey et al., "The Determinants and Political Consequences of Latinos' Perceived Intra-Group Competition."
13. Howard, "Afro-Latinos and the Black-Hispanic Identity."
14. McConnaughy et al., "A Latino on the Ballot."
15. Li and Rudensky, "Rethinking the Redistricting Toolbox."
16. Sanchez, "Latino Group Consciousness and Perceptions of Commonality with African Americans"; Kaufmann, "Cracks in the Rainbow."
17. Cartagena, interview with author, 120.
18. Saenz, interview with author, 132.
19. Nelson, interview with author, 54.
20. Smith, *Whitelash*, 1.
21. Valdes, "The Fight for Latino Voters for the G.O.P."
22. Krupnikov and Piston, "The Political Consequences of Latino Prejudice Against Blacks"; Haywood, "Anti-Black Latino Racism in an Era of Trump-ismo," 957.
23. Beltrán, *The Trouble with Unity*.
24. Hernández, "Latino Antiblack Bias and the Census Categorization of Latinos," 283; Gómez, *Inventing Latinos*.
25. Cohn, "Census History: Counting Hispanics."
26. Reyes, "Afro-Latinos Seek Recognition and Accurate Census Count."
27. Rodríguez-Muñiz, *Figures of the Future*, xviii.
28. "The Census Bureau's Proposed 'Combined Question' Approach Offers Promise for Collecting More Accurate Data on Hispanic Origin and Race, but Some Questions Remain."
29. Parker, "Multiracial in America: Proud, Diverse and Growing in Numbers."
30. Hogan, "Reporting of Race Among Hispanics"; Allen, "Investigating the Cultural Conception of Race in Puerto Rico."
31. Hernández, "'Too Black to Be Latino/a': Blackness and Blacks as Foreigners in Latino Studies."
32. Duany, *The Puerto Rican Nation on the Move*.
33. Minority Rights Group, *No Longer Invisible*.
34. Gosin, "'A Bitter Diversion.'"
35. Marks and Rios-Vargas, "Improvements to the 2020 Census Race and Hispanic Origin Question Designs, Data Processing, and Coding Procedures."
36. U.S. Census Bureau, "Hispanic or Latino Origin by Race: 2010 and 2020."
37. López and Gonzalez-Barrera, "Afro-Latino."
38. López and Hogan, "What's Your Street Race?"
39. Contreras and Reyes, "The Multiracial Identity Revolution Among U.S. Latinos."
40. 1andOnlyAlpha, Twitter post.
41. Giron, Twitter post.
42. DiAngelo, *White Fragility*.
43. U.S. Census Bureau, "Hispanic or Latino Origin by Race: 2010 and 2020."

44. Wang, "The 2nd-Largest Racial Group in the U.S. Is 'Some Other Race.'"
45. US Census Bureau, "Hispanic or Latino Origin by Race: 2010 and 2020" (percentages based on the total Hispanic populations for 2010 and 2020 respectively).
46. US Census Bureau, "Race and Ethnicity in the United States: 2010 Census and 2020 Census" (percentages based on the total Hispanic populations for 2010 and 2020 respectively).
47. US Census, "2020 Census: Redistricting File (Public Law 94-171) Dataset" (tabulated from census dataset).
48. Hoy, "Negotiating Among Invisibilities."
49. Rosado, "Puerto Ricans, Dominicans, and the Emotional Politics of Race and Blackness in the U.S.," 115.
50. Eustachewich, "Dominicans in Inwood Blasted on Social Media for Chasing Away Black Men"; Amezcua, "A History of Anti-Blackness Permeates the Grid of Chicago's Southwest Side."
51. Padgett, "Why Are So Many Latinos Obsessed with Demonizing Black Lives Matter? It's Complicated."
52. Márquez, *Black-Brown Solidarity*, 157.
53. Machicote, "Dear Latines."
54. Hordge-Freeman and Loblack, "'Cops Only See Brown Skin, They Could Care Less Where It Originated.'"
55. Fox, *Hispanic Nation*.
56. Fernández, *The Young Lords*.
57. Jones, *The Browning of the New South*.
58. Guinier and Torres, *The Miner's Canary*.
59. Gordon and Lenhardt, "Rethinking Work and Citizenship"; Millet, "Case Study of Black-Brown Bridging."
60. Community Coalition.
61. Grant-Thomas, Sarfati, and Staats, "Natural Allies or Irreconcilable Foes?"
62. Millet, "Case Study of Black-Brown Bridging," 30–35; "Encuentro Diaspora Afro."
63. Pastor et al., "Bridges Puentes."
64. Paul Ortiz, *An African American and Latinx History of the United States*, 204.
65. Foley, *Quest for Equality*.
66. Aja, Bustillo, and Wallace, "Countering 'Anti-Blackness' Through 'Black-Brown' Alliances and Inter-Group Coalitions,'" 77–78.
67. Siegel, "A Short History of Sexual Harassment," 1, 8.
68. Kleppin, interview with author, 172–79.
69. Hernández, "Latino Inter-Ethnic Employment Discrimination and the 'Diversity Defense.'"
70. Cruz, interview with author, 141.
71. *Victor Rivera Sanchez*, No. 02–1161.

EPILOGUE: ON BEING AN AFRO-LATINA INTERROGATING
LATINO ANTI-BLACKNESS

1. The detailed list of all queries and datafiles searched can be viewed on the following research website link: www.ProfessorTKH.com, *Racial Innocence* Book Methodology Appendix page.

2. I have used pseudonyms for all the personal names used in the epilogue in order to protect the privacy of my family and friends. The epilogue includes an excerpt previously published in my work *Multiracials and Civil Rights: Mixed-Race Stories of Discrimination* and is reprinted by permission of the publisher.
3. Haslip-Viera, *Taíno Revival.*
4. Hernández, *Racial Subordination in Latin America.*
5. Candelario, *Black Behind the Ears.*
6. Hall and Whipple, "The Complexion Connection."
7. *Ojalá* is the Spanish term for "God willing" or "Let's hope so." *Aché* is the Santeria religious term for grace and blessing.

BIBLIOGRAPHY

LAWS, REGULATIONS, AND GOVERNMENT DOCUMENTS

"City of Chicago School District 299." Teacher demographics, Illinois Report Card 2019–2020 website, Illinois State Board of Education. https://www .illinoisreportcard.com/district.aspx?districtid=15016299025&source =teachers&source2=teacherdemographics.

Civil Rights Act of 1866, 42 U.S.C. § 1982 (1866).

Cunningham, Jason F., and Sharon R. Kimball. "Gangs, Guns, Drugs and Money." *United States Attorneys' Bulletin: Gang Prosecutions* 62, no. 12 (2014): 12–17.

Fair Housing Act of 1968, 42 U.S.C. § 3604 (2019).

Fair Housing Act, 42 U.S.C. § 3603(b) (1968).

"Final Gang Defendant in Federal Hate Crimes Indictment Pleads Guilty in Firebombing of African-American Residences." Press release no. 19–067, US Department of Justice, US Attorney's Office of the Central District of California, Apr. 9, 2019. https://www.justice.gov/usao-cdca/pr/final-gang -defendant-federal-hate-crimes-indictment-pleads-guilty-firebombing -african.

Marks, Rachel, and Merarys Rios-Vargas. "Improvements to the 2020 Census Race and Hispanic Origin Question Designs, Data Processing, and Coding Procedures." US Census Bureau, Random Samplings Blog, Aug. 3, 2021. https://www.census.gov/newsroom/blogs/random-samplings/2021/08 /improvements-to-2020-census-race-hispanic-origin-question-designs.html.

"Massive Racketeering Case Targets Hawaiian Gardens Gang Involved in Murder of Sheriff's Deputy, Attacks on African-Americans and Widespread Drug Trafficking." Press release, US Attorney's Office, Central District of California, May 21, 2009. https://www.fbi.gov/losangeles/press-releases/2009 /la052109.htm.

Meinero, Seth Adam. "La Vida Loca Nationwide: Prosecuting Sureño Gangs Beyond Los Angeles." *United States Attorneys' Bulletin: Gang Prosecutions* 62, no. 12 (2014): 26–35.

Minorities in Business. Washington, DC: US Small Business Administration, 1999. www.sba.gov/advo/stats/min.pdf.

Office for Civil Rights. "Pending Cases Currently Under Investigation at Elementary-Secondary and Post-Secondary Schools." Washington, DC: US

Department of Education, July 2, 2021. https://www2.ed.gov/about/offices/list/ocr/docs/investigations/open-investigations/tvi.html.

Office for Civil Rights. "Section 101: Privacy Act and Freedom of Information Act." In *Case Processing Manual (CPM)*. Washington, DC: US Department of Education, 2020. https://www2.ed.gov/about/offices/list/ocr/docs/ocrcpm.pdf.

Organic Act of Puerto Rico, Pub. L. No. 64–368, § 9, 39 Stat. 951, 954 (1917) (codified as amended at 48 U.S.C. § 734).

"Providence, 2019–20 Report Card: Civil Rights Data Collection (CRDC) for 2017–2018." Rhode Island Department of Education. https://reportcard.ride.ri.gov/201920/DistrictCRDC?DistCode=28.

"Providence, 2019–20 Report Card: Overview." Rhode Island Department of Education. https://reportcard.ride.ri.gov/201920/DistrictSnapshot?DistCode=28.

Puerto Rico Civil Rights Act, 1 P.R. Laws Ann. §§ 13–19 (1943); P.R. Const. art. II, § 1 (1952); 29 P.R. Laws Ann. § 146 (codifying as amended 1959 P.R. Laws 100).

"Remedies for Employment Discrimination." US Equal Employment Opportunity Commission. https://www.eeoc.gov/remedies-employment-discrimination, accessed July 20, 2021.

Schuler, Nicholas. *Annual Report—Fiscal Year 2019*. Chicago: Office of the Inspector General, Chicago Board of Education, 2020. https://www.scribd.com/document/441923974/Chicago-2019-Report#download&from_embed.

"Section 15: Race and Color Discrimination." In *Equal Employment Opportunity Commission (EEOC) Compliance Manual*. Washington, DC: US Equal Employment Opportunity Commission, 2006. https://www.eeoc.gov/laws/guidance/section-15-race-and-color-discrimination.

Title II of the 1964 Civil Rights Act, 42 U.S.C. §§ 2000a et seq.

"Two California Men Indicted in Federal Hate Crime Case Stemming from New Year's Eve Attack on African-American Youths." Press release no. 13. US Department of Justice, Office of Public Affairs, Feb. 8, 2013. https://www.justice.gov/opa/pr/two-california-men-indicted-federal-hate-crime-case-stemming-new-year-s-eve-attack-african.

US Census Bureau. "1990 Census of Population: General Population Characteristics, Illinois." Washington, DC: 1992. https://www2.census.gov/library/publications/decennial/1990/cp-1/cp-1-15.pdf.

US Census Bureau. "1990 Census of Population: General Population Characteristics, New York." Washington, DC: 1992. https://www2.census.gov/library/publications/decennial/1990/cp-1/cp-1-34-1.pdf.

US Census Bureau. "2000 Census of Population: General Population Characteristics, Iowa." Washington, DC: 2000. https://factfinder.census.gov.

US Census Bureau. "2000 Census of Population: General Population Characteristics, New York." Washington, DC: 2000. https://factfinder.census.gov.

US Census Bureau. "2010 Census of Population: General Population Characteristics, Illinois." Washington, DC: 2010. https://factfinder.census.gov.

US Census Bureau. "2013–2017 American Community Survey 5-Year Estimates." Washington, DC: 2018. https://www.census.gov/programs-surveys/acs/technical-documentation/table-and-geography-changes/2017/5-year.html.

US Census Bureau. "2018 American Community Survey Table of Hispanic or
    Latino Origin Population by Race." https://data.census.gov/cedsci/table?q
    =hispanic%20origin%20by%20race&hidePreview=false&tid=ACSDT1Y
    2018.B03002&vintage=2018.
US Census Bureau. "2019 American Community Survey Table of Hispanic or
    Latino Origin by Race." https://data.census.gov/cedsci/table?q=hispanic%
    20origin%20by%20race&tid=ACSDT1Y2019.B03002&hidePreview=true.
US Census Bureau. "2020 Census: Redistricting File (Public Law 94-171) Data-
    set." Census.gov, Aug. 12, 2021. https://www.census.gov/data/datasets/2020
    /dec/2020-census-redistricting-summary-file-dataset.html.
US Census Bureau. "Hispanic or Latino Origin by Race: 2010 and 2020," 2020
    Census Redistricting Data (Public Law 94-171) Summary File Table 4. https://
    www2.census.gov/programs-surveys/decennial/2020/data/redistricting
    -supplementary-tables/redistricting-supplementary-table-04.pdf. Accessed
    Aug. 13, 2021.
US Census Bureau. "The Hispanic Population in the United States: 2019," Data
    Table 26. Census.gov, Oct. 8, 2021. https://www.census.gov/data/tables
    /2019/demo/hispanic-origin/2019-cps.html.
US Census Bureau. "Hispanic Population to Reach 111 Million by 2060." Cen-
    sus.gov, Oct. 8, 2021, https://www.census.gov/library/visualizations/2018
    /comm/hispanic-projected-pop.html.
US Census Bureau. "Race and Ethnicity in the United States: 2010 Census and
    2020 Census." Census.gov, Aug. 12, 2021. https://www.census.gov/library
    /visualizations/interactive/race-and-ethnicity-in-the-united-state-2010
    -and-2020-census.html.
US Census Bureau. "QuickFacts: Carlsbad City, New Mexico." https://www
    .census.gov/quickfacts/fact/table/carlsbadcitynewmexico/PST045219.
    Accessed July 23, 2021.
US Census Bureau. "QuickFacts: El Paso County, Texas." https://www.census
    .gov/quickfacts/elpasocountytexas. Accessed July 29, 2021. US Census Bu-
    reau. "QuickFacts: Miami City, Florida." https://www.census.gov/quickfacts
    /fact/table/miamicityflorida/PST045219. Accessed July 22, 2019.
US Department of Justice, 2006 Press Release, U.S. Dep't. of Just. Cent. Dist. of
    Cal. Att'y Gen., Gang Members Convicted of Federal Hate Crimes for Mur-
    ders, Assaults of African Americans. (2006) (regarding U.S. v. Martinez, CR
    04–415(b) (D. Ca. Aug. 1, 2006). www.usdoj.gov/usao/cac/pr2006/102.html.
Vespa, Jonathan, Lauren Medina, and David M. Armstrong. "Demographic
    Turning Points for the United States: Population Projections for 2020 to
    2060." US Census Bureau, Feb. 2020. https://www.census.gov/content/dam
    /Census/library/publications/2020/demo/p25-1144.pdf.

LEGAL CASES

Ajayi v. Aramark Bus. Servs., 336 F.3d 520 (7th Cir. 2003).
Allen v. Bake-Line Prods., Inc., No. 98 C 1119, 2001 WL 1249054 (N.D. Ill.
    Oct. 17, 2001).
Arrocha v. CUNY, 2004 WL 594981 (E.D.N.Y. Feb. 9, 2004).
Ash v. Tyson Foods, 546 U.S. 454, 456 (2006).
Ash v. Tyson Foods, Inc., 126 S. Ct. 1195 (2006).

Atencia v. Maricopa Cty. Sheriff's Off., No. CV-19-05855, 2020 WL 3893582 (D. Ariz. July 10, 2020).

Bartholomew v. Martin Brower Co. LLC et al., No. 3:11CV02219 (D.P.R. Oct. 4, 2012).

Beard v. JBT Aerotech Serv., No. 01-12-00155, 2013 WL 5947951 (Tex. App. Nov. 5, 2013).

Bermudez Zenon v. Rest. Compostela, Inc., 790 F. Supp. 41 (D.P.R. Apr. 24, 1992).

Bernard v. N.Y. City Health & Hosps. Corp., No. 93 CIV.8593, 1996 WL 457284 (S.D.N.Y. Aug. 14, 1996).

Bowen v. El Paso Electric Co., 49 S.W. 3d 902 (Tex. App. 2001).

Boyce v. Spitzer, 958 N.Y.S.2d 306 (N.Y. Sup. Ct. 2010).

Bradshaw v. Vivex Biomedical, No. 2016-020723-CA-01 (Fla. Cir. Ct. Aug 10, 2016).

Castaneda v. Partida 430 U.S. 482 (1977).

Cortez v. Wal-Mart Stores, Inc., No. 03-1251 BB/LFG (D. New Mexico Jan. 14, 2005), 157.

Cruz v. Rinker Materials of Fla., No. 3-21709 (S.D. Fla. Mia. Div, Dec. 5, 2003).

De Los Santos Rojas v. Hosp. Español De Auxilio Mutuo de Puerto Rico, Inc., 85 F. Supp. 3d 615 (D.P.R. 2015).

Donjoie v. Whitestone Gulf, No. 2018-036551-CA-01 (Fla. Cir. Ct. Oct. 29, 2018).

Dunn v. Hunting Energy Serv., 288 F. Supp. 3d 749 (S.D. Tex. 2017).

EEOC v. E&D Services, Inc., No. SA-08-CA-0714-NSN (W.D. Tex. Aug. 2009).

EEOC v. Koper Furniture, Inc., U.S. Dist. Ct. of P.R. Case No. 09-1563 (2009).

EEOC v. Lockheed Martin, Civil No. 05-00479 SPK (D. Haw. settled Jan. 2, 2008).

EEOC v. New Koosharem Corp., No. 2:13-cv-2761 (W.D. Tenn., Dec. 5, 2014).

EEOC v. Rodriguez, 1994 WL 714003 (E.D. Cal., Nov. 16, 1994).

Falero Santiago v. Stryker, 10 F. Supp. 2d 93 (D.P.R. 1998).

Farias v. Bexar Cnty. Bd. of Trs. for Mental Health Mental Retardation Serv., 925 F.2d 866 (5th Cir. 1991).

Felix v. Marquez, 27 Emp. Prac. Dec. P 32,241, 22,2768 n. 6 (D.D.C. 1981).

Fennell v. Marion Independent School District, 963 F. Supp. 2d 623 (W.D. Tex. 2013).

Ferguson v. Sage Parts Plus, No. 2017-026195-CA-01 (Fla. Cir. Ct. Nov. 10, 2017).

Foster v. BAE Sys. Inc., No. A141373, 2016 WL 4098676 (Cal. Ct. App. July 29, 2016).

Frazier v. Rominger, 27 F.3d 828 (2d Cir. 1994).

Gallentine v. Housing Auth. of City of Port Arthur, Tex., 919 F. Supp. 2d 787 (E.D. Tex. 2013).

Gonzalez v. the State of Florida, Case No. 3D13-1474, Fla. 3rd Dist. Ct. of App (May 2, 2014).

Green v. Best Western Int'l, No. 2015-024883-CA-01 (Fla. Cir. Ct. Oct 26, 2015).

Harper v. Hunter Coll., No. 95 CIV. 10388, 1999 WL 147698 (S.D.N.Y. Mar. 15, 1999).

Hernandez et al. v. San Luis Obispo Superior Court, Case No. B236093, California 2nd App. Dist. (Sept. 23, 2011).

Hicks v. Treasure Serv./Metro Dade Transit, DOAH No. 02-1410, 2003 WL 21788903 (Fla. Div. Admin. Hearings Aug. 1, 2003).

Hines v. City of Los Angeles, No. B215896, 2010 WL 2599321 (Cal. Ct. App. June 30, 2010).

Hogan v. Henderson, 102 F. Supp. 2d 1180 (D. Ariz. 2000).

Hunt v. Pers. Staffing Grp., LLC, 2018 Fair Emp. Prac. Case (BNA) 59,091.

In re Andrews v. JPK Enter. et. al, CCHR No. 03-P-107, 2003 WL 23529549 (Chi. Comm'n Hum. Rel. Dec. 1, 2003).

In re Garcia, IHRC No. 2013CF2356, 2018 WL 6625532 (Ill. Hum. Rts. Comm'n Nov. 21, 2018).

In re Green, IHRC No. 2018CA1970, 2020 WL 2303164 (Ill. Hum. Rts. Comm'n Apr. 29, 2020).

In re Hernandez, CCHR No. 05-E-14, 2007 WL 9254612 (Chi. Comm'n Hum. Rel. Nov. 28, 2007).

In re Johnson, IHRC No. 1996CF1009, 1998 WL 104771 (Ill. Hum. Rts. Comm'n Jan. 13, 1998).

In re Louis Vasquez on Habeas Corpus, Case No. C087261 (Cal. 3rd App. Dist. June 4, 2018).

In re Pryor v. Echevarria, CCHR No. 93-PA-62/63, 1994 WL 910076 (Chi. Comm'n Hum. Rel. Oct. 19, 1994).

In re Trujillo, CCHR No. 01-PA-52, 2002 WL 1491999 (Chi. Comm'n Hum. Rel., May 15, 2002).

In re Louis Vasquez on Habeas Corpus, Case No. C087261 (Cal. 3rd App. Dist. June 4, 2018).

In the Matter of the Accusation of the Dep't of Fair Emp. and Hous. v. Mark Anthony Taylor, Fair Emp. and Hous. Comm'n of the State of Cal., Case Dec. No. 06-05, 2006 WL 2239659 (June 6, 2006).

Isaac v. Sch. Bd. of Miami-Dade Cnty., No. 00-0890-CIV, 2002 WL 31086118 (S.D. Fla. Sept. 3, 2002).

Johnson v. California, 543 U.S. 499 (2005).

Johnson v. Morales, No. B204818, 2009 WL 867131 (Cal. Ct. App. Apr. 2, 2009).

Johnson v. Pride Indus., No. 19-501173, 2018 WL 6624691 (5th Cir. 2019).

Laroche v. Denny's, Inc., 62 F. Supp.2d 1375 (S.D. Fla. 1999).

Martinez v. Cal. Inv. XII, No. CV 05-7608-JTL, 2007 WL 8435675 (C.D. Cal. Dec. 12, 2007).

Mathura v. Council for Hum. Servs. Home Care Servs., Inc., No. 95CIV4191, 1996 WL 157496 (S.D.N.Y. Apr. 2, 1996).

McCleary v. Cole, DOAH No. 201916366, 2019 WL 7205918 (Fla. Div. Admin. Hearings Nov. 26, 2019).

McCrimmon v. DaimlerChrysler Corp., DOAH No. 02-3575, 2003 WL 1862156 (Fla. Div. Admin. Hearings Apr. 9, 2003).

Olumuyiwa v. Harvard Prot. Corp., No. 98-CV-5110, 1999 WL 529553 (E.D.N.Y. July 21, 1999).

Osei-Buckle v. Laidlaw Transit, Inc., No. CV-96-00753-DDP, 1998 WL 552126 (9th Cir. Aug. 27, 1998).

Patino v. Rucker, No. 96-7531, 1997 WL 416949 (2d Cir. July 25, 1997).

People v. Alcarez, et al., Docket No. NA072796 (Los Angeles County Superior Court Jan. 1, 2007).

Pirtle v. Allsup's Convenience Store, Inc., 2003 WL 27385258 (D.N.M. Apr. 2, 2003).

Portugues-Santa v. B. Fernandez Hermanos, Inc., 614 F. Supp. 2d 221 (D.P.R. 2009).

Quintana v. Hillsborough Cty, DOAH No. 88–5125, 1989 WL 645048 (Fla. Div. Admin. Hearings Feb. 7, 1989).

Reform Bd. of Trustees, No. 97 C 1172, 1999 WL 258488 (N.D. Ill. Apr. 13, 1999).

Rivera Sanchez v. Sears Roebuck de Puerto Rico, No. 02–1161 (D.P.R. Feb. 25, 2003).

Roberts v. CBS Broad. Inc., No. BC 227280, 2003 WL 1194102 (Cal. Ct. App. Mar. 17, 2003).

Russell v. Am. Eagle Airlines, 46 F. Supp. 2d 1330 (S.D. Fla. 1999).

Sec'y of the U.S. Dep't of Hous. and Urb. Dev. (for Andre Echols) v. Frank V. Quijas, HUDALJ 07-97-0691, 1998 WL 21060 (Jan. 16, 1998).

The Sec'y of the U.S. Dep't of Hous. and Urb. Dev. on behalf of Elias Tulsen and Patricia Tulsen v. Thomas Clemente and Andrew Clemente, HUDALJ No. 02-96-0060-8, 1999 WL 521272 (July 14, 1999).

The Sec'y of the U.S. Dep't of Hous. and Urb. Dev. on behalf of Mitchell Keys v. Garcia, HUDALJ 05-89-0457-1, 1990 WL 547179 (Mar. 20, 1990).

Shelby v. Kwik Kar/Guide Star, No. 3:18-CV-0532, 2019 WL 1958001 (N.D. Tex. May 2, 2019).

Smiley v. San Antonio Indep. Sch. Dist., No. 5:09-CA-00029-FB, 2010 WL 10669508 (W.D. Tex. 2010).

Sprott v. Franco, No. 94 Civ. 3818, 1998 WL 472061 (S.D.N.Y. Aug. 7, 1998).

State of Florida v. Xavier Antonio Nunez, Case No. 2013-CF-002454-A-O, Fla. Orange Cnty. 9th Cir. (Mar. 27, 2013).

Turner v. Manhattan Bowery Mgmt., 49 Misc. 3d 1220(A) (N.Y. Sup. Ct. 2015).

U.S. v. Atesiano, No. 1:18-cr-20479, 2018 WL 5831092 (S.D. Fla. Nov. 7, 2018).

U.S. v. Cazares, et al., 788 F.3d 956 (9th Cir. 2015).

U.S. v. Flores et al., Docket No. 2:09-cr-00445 (C.D. Cal. May 6, 2009).

U.S. v. Martinez, CR 04-415(b) (D. Ca. Aug. 1, 2006).

U.S. v. Rios et al., Docket No. 2:11-cr-00492 (C.D. Cal. June 1, 2011).

U.S. v. Barberis, 887 F. Supp. 110 (D. Md. 1995).

Vance v. Ball State Univ., 570 U.S. 421 (2013).

Vincent v. Wells Fargo Guard Servs., Inc. of Fla., 3 F. Supp. 2d 1405 (S.D. Fla. 1998).

Walcott v. Texas S. Univ., No. 01-12-0035, 2013 WL 593488 (Tex. App. Feb. 13, 2013).

Webb v. R&B Holding Co., 992 F. Supp. 1382 (S.D. Fla. 1998).

Young v. Columbia Sussex Corp., No. CV-08-01325, 2009 WL 3352148 (D. Ariz. Oct. 16, 2009).

INTERVIEWS

Berkan, Judith (Berkan/Mendez Law Firm). Apr. 6, 2020. Zoom audio transcript.

Cartagena, Juan (president and general counsel, LatinoJustice PRLDEF). Apr. 1, 2020. Zoom audio transcript.

Cortés, Noemí (program director, Surge Institute Academy). June 30, 2021. Zoom audio transcript.

Cruz, Kimberly A. (supervisory trial attorney, US Equal Employment Opportunity Commission, New York District Office). June 24, 2021. Zoom audio transcript.

Hendley, Amber (fair housing testing coordinator, Roosevelt University in Chicago). July 20, 2020. Zoom audio transcript.

Kleppin, Chris. (Kleppin Law Firm). June 18, 2020. Zoom audio transcript.

LaRaia, Catherine (clinical fellow, Suffolk Law School Housing Discrimination Testing Program). Aug. 4, 2020. Zoom audio transcript.

Manager of learning and organizational development. Email to author. July 29, 2004.

Mendez, Luz Minerva. June 9, 2021. Telephone interview.

Montoya, Roberto (instructor of education, University of Colorado Denver School of Education). July 6, 2021. Zoom audio transcript.

Nelson, Janai S. (associate director-counsel, now president and director-counsel, NAACP Legal Defense and Educational Fund). Apr. 9, 2020. Zoom audio transcript.

Quinta (pseudonym). Dec. 6, 2019. Telephone interview.

Roller, Shamus (executive director, National Housing Law Project). July 28, 2020. Zoom audio transcript.

Saenz, Thomas (president and general counsel, MALDEF). Apr. 10, 2020. Zoom audio transcript.

Scott, Kate (director, Equal Rights Center). Aug. 12, 2020. Zoom audio transcript.

Stovall, David (professor of Black studies and educational policy studies, University of Illinois at Chicago). June 30, 2021. Zoom audio transcript.

Teaching fellow at Teach for America, Rhode Island school. Mar. 21, 2021. Telephone interview.

Teaching fellow at Generation Teach Rhode Island Program. Apr. 2, 2021. Zoom audio transcript.

Vilson, Jose Luis (director, EduColor). July 20, 2021. Zoom audio transcript.

SECONDARY SOURCES

1andOnlyAlpha. Twitter Post, June 30, 2021, 12:07 AM. [Twitter account suspended].

"4 Face Arson, Hate Crime Trial for Cross Burning." Fox News, Sept. 13, 2011. https://www.foxnews.com/us/4-face-arson-hate-crime-trial-for-cross-burning.amp.

"6 Students Arrested after Fight at Streamwood H.S." CBS Chicago, May 13, 2014. https://chicago.cbslocal.com/2014/05/13/6-students-arrested-after-fight-at-streamwood-h-s.

"14 Words: General Hate Symbols, Hate Slogans/Slang Terms." Anti-Defamation League. https://www.adl.org/education/references/hate-symbols/14-words.

Acevedo, Elizabeth. The Poet X. New York: Quill Tree Books, 2018.

Adames, Hector Y., Nayeli Y. Chavez-Dueñas, and Kurt C. Organista. "Skin Color Matters in Latino/a Communities: Identifying, Understanding, and Addressing Mestizaje Racial Ideologies in Clinical Practice." Professional Psychology: Research and Practice 47, no. 1 (2016): 46–55.

"Afro-Latinos in 2017: A Demographic and Socio-Economic Snapshot." Unidos US, Feb. 2019, http://publications.unidosus.org/bitstream/handle/123456789/1926/AfroLatino_22219_v2.pdf?sequence=4&isAllowed=y.

Aguilera, Michael Bernabé. "The Impact of Social Capital on the Earnings of Puerto Rican Migrants." *Sociological Quarterly* 46, no. 4 (Autumn 2005): 569–92.

Aja, Alan A. *Miami's Forgotten Cubans: Race, Racialization, and the Miami Afro-Cuban Experience.* New York: Palgrave Macmillan, 2016.

Aja, Alan A., Gretchen Beesing, Daniel Bustillo, Danielle Clealand, Mark Paul, Khaing Zaw, Anne E. Price, William Darity Jr., and Darrick Hamilton. *The Color of Wealth in Miami.* Ohio State University, Duke University, and the Insight Center for Community Economic Development, 2019. https://socialequity.duke.edu/portfolio-item/the-color-of-wealth-in-miami.

Aja, Alan A., Daniel Bustillo, and Antwuan Wallace. "Countering 'Anti-Blackness' Through 'Black-Brown' Alliances and Inter-Group Coalitions: Policy Proposals to 'Break the Silence.'" *Journal of Intergroup Relations* 35, no. 2 (2014): 58–87.

Alford, Natasha S. "'They Believe We're Criminals': Black Puerto Ricans Say They're a Police Target." *Guardian*, Oct. 9, 2019. https://www.theguardian.com/world/2019/oct/09/they-believe-were-criminals-black-puerto-ricans-say-theyre-a-police-target.

Allen, Reuben. "Investigating the Cultural Conception of Race in Puerto Rico: Residents' Thoughts on the U.S. Census, Discrimination, and Interventionist Policies." *Latin American and Caribbean Ethnic Studies* 12, no. 3 (2017): 201–26.

Amezcua, Mike. "A History of Anti-Blackness Permeates the Grid of Chicago's Southwest Side." *The Abusable Past* (*Radical History Review* digital venue), June 10, 2020. https://www.radicalhistoryreview.org/abusablepast/a-history-of-anti-blackness-permeates-the-grid-of-chicagos-southwest-side.

Archibold, Randal C. "Racial Hate Feeds a Gang War's Senseless Killing." *New York Times*, Jan. 17, 2007.

Ashla, Mario. Reader response to opinion editorial "Roots of Anger: Longtime Prejudices, Not Economic Rivalry, Fuel Latino-Black Tensions" by Tanya Katerí Hernández. *Los Angeles Times*, Jan. 11, 2007. https://www.latimes.com/archives/la-xpm-2007-jan-11-le-thursday11-story.html.

Ayala, Edmy. "Racismo institucional en las escuelas: Una condena para lxs niñxs negrxs." *Revista* étnica 2 (2019).

Banks, Taunya Lovell. "Colorism: A Darker Shade of Pale." *UCLA Law Review* 47, no. 6 (2000): 1705–46.

Bannon, Alicia, and Janna Adelstein. "State Supreme Court Diversity—February 2020 Update." Brennan Center for Justice, NYU Law, Feb. 20, 2020. https://www.brennancenter.org/our-work/research-reports/state-supreme-court-diversity-february-2020-update.

Barbaro, Fred. "Ethnic Resentment." In *Black/Brown/White Relations: Race Relations in the 1970s*, ed. Charles V. Willie, 77–94. New Brunswick, NJ: Transaction, 1977.

Barreto, Matt A., Benjamin F. Gonzalez, and Gabriel R. Sanchez. "Rainbow Coalition in the Golden State? Exposing Myths, Uncovering New Realities in Latino Attitudes Toward Blacks." In *Black and Brown in Los Angeles: Beyond Conflict and Coalition*, ed. Josh Kun and Laura Pulido, 203–32. Berkeley: University of California Press, 2014.

Baumgartner, Frank R., Derek A. Epp, and Kelsey Shoub. *Suspect Citizens: What 20 Million Traffic Stops Tell Us About Policing and Race*. New York: Cambridge University Press, 2018.

Bell, Jeannine. *Hate Thy Neighbor: Move-In Violence and the Persistence of Racial Segregation in American Housing*. New York: New York University Press, 2013.

Belluck, Pam. "John H. Pratt, 84, Federal Judge Who Helped Define Civil Rights." *New York Times*, Aug. 14, 1995.

Beltrán, Cristina. *The Trouble with Unity: Latino Politics and the Creation of Identity*. Oxford: Oxford University Press, 2010.

Berrey, Ellen, Robert L. Nelson, and Laura Beth Nielsen. *Rights on Trial: How Workplace Discrimination Law Perpetuates Inequality*. Chicago: University of Chicago Press, 2017.

Betances, Samuel. "The Prejudice of Having No Prejudice in Puerto Rico, Part II." *The Rican: A Journal of Contemporary Puerto Rican Thought* 3 (1973): 22–37.

Betancur, John J. "Framing the Discussion of African American-Latino Relations: A Review and Analysis." In *Neither Enemies nor Friends: Latinos, Blacks, Afro-Latinos*, ed. Anani Dzidzienyo and Suzanne Oboler, 159–72. Houndmills, UK: Palgrave Macmillan, 2005.

Black Alliance for Just Immigration (website). https://baji.org.

Black Latinas Know Collective (blog). Accessed July 17, 2021. https://www.black latinasknow.org/the-blog.

Blades, Rubén. "Plástico," with Willie Colón. Fania Records, 1978. https://www .letras.mus.br/ruben-blades/417302/.

Bobo, Lawrence, and Vincent L. Hutchings, "Perceptions of Racial Group Competition: Extending Blumer's Theory of Group Position to a Multiracial Social Context," *American Sociological Review* 61, no. 6 (1996): 951–72.

Boddie, Elise C. "Racial Territoriality." *UCLA Law Review* 58, no. 2 (2010): 401–63.

Bonilla-Silva, Eduardo. "Reflections About Race by a *Negrito Acomplejao*." In *The Afro-Latin@ Reader: History and Culture in the United States*, ed. Miriam Jiménez Román and Juan Flores, 445–52. Durham, NC: Duke University Press, 2010.

———. "We Are All Americans!: The Latin Americanization of Racial Stratification in the USA." *Race and Society* 5, no. 1 (2002): 3–16.

Booth, Cathy. "Miami: The Capital of Latin America." *Time*, Dec. 2, 1993. http://content.time.com/time/subscriber/article/0,33009,979733,00.html.

"Brawl Erupts at Carson High School Between 30 Black, Latino Students." KPCC News, Mar. 7, 2012. https://www.scpr.org/news/2012/03/07/31551 /racial-brawl-erupts-carson-high-school-between-30-.

Britton, Marcus L. "Close Together but Worlds Apart? Residential Integration and Interethnic Friendship in Houston." *City and Community* 10, no. 2 (2011): 182–204.

Buchanan, Susy. "Tensions Mounting Between Blacks and Latinos Nationwide." *Southern Poverty Law Center Intelligence Report*, July 27, 2005. https://www .splcenter.org/fighting-hate/intelligence-report/2005/tensions-mounting -between-Blacks-and-latinos-nationwide.

Calderón Ilia. *My Time to Speak: Reclaiming Ancestry and Confronting Race*. New York: Atria Books, 2020.

Calzada, Esther J., Yeonwoo Kim, and Jaimie L. O'Gara. "Skin Color as a Predictor of Mental Health in Young Latinx Children." *Social Science and Medicine* 238 (2019).

Candelario, Ginetta E. B. *Black Behind the Ears: Dominican Racial Identity from Museums to Beauty Shops*. Durham, NC: Duke University Press, 2007.

Carey, Tony E., Jr., Tetsuya Matsubayashi, Regina Branton, and Valerie Martinez-Ebers. "The Determinants and Political Consequences of Latinos' Perceived Intra-Group Competition." *Politics, Groups, and Identities* 1, no. 3 (2013): 311–28.

"Carlsbad, New Mexico Population: Census 2010 and 2000 Interactive Map, Demographics, Statistics, QuickFacts." CensusViewer. http://censusviewer .com/city/NM/Carlsbad. Accessed July 23, 2021.

Carroll, Rory. "'They Just Don't Fit In': UCLA Study Links Racism and Segregation in Orange County." *Guardian*, Sept. 19, 2016. https://www.the guardian.com/us-news/2016/sep/19/ucla-study-racism-segregation-orange -county.

"The Census Bureau's Proposed 'Combined Question' Approach Offers Promise for Collecting More Accurate Data on Hispanic Origin and Race, but Some Questions Remain." NALEO Educational Fund, 2017. https:// d3n8a8pro7vhmx.cloudfront.net/naleo/pages/190/attachments/original /1497288838/Hispanic_Origin_and_Race_Brief_fin_05–17.pdf?1497288838.

Charles, Camille Zubrinsky. "Neighborhood Racial-Composition Preferences: Evidence from a Multiethnic Metropolis." *Social Problems* 47, no. 3 (2000): 379–407.

———. *Won't You Be My Neighbor? Race, Class, and Residence in Los Angeles*. New York: Russell Sage Foundation, 2006.

Chideya, Farai, and Mandalit del Barco. "Racial Tension at Los Angeles High School," NPR, May 16, 2005. https://www.npr.org/templates/story/story .php?storyId=4653328.

Clealand, Danielle Pilar. *The Power of Race in Cuba: Racial Ideology and Black Consciousness During the Revolution*. Oxford: Oxford University Press, 2017.

———. "Undoing the Invisibility of Blackness in Miami." *Black Latinas Know Collective* (blog), Dec. 22, 2019. https://www.blacklatinasknow.org/post/undoing -the-invisibility-of-blackness-in-miami.

Clemente, Rosa. "Not in Our Name: A Puerto Rican White Supremacist in Charlottesville." Aug. 17, 2017. https://rosaclemente.net/not-name-puerto -rican-white-supremacist-charlottesville.

Clermont, Kevin M., and Stewart J. Schwab. "Employment Discrimination Plaintiffs in Federal Court: From Bad to Worse?," *Harvard Law and Policy Review* 3, no. 1 (2009): 103–32.

Cohn, D'Vera. "Census History: Counting Hispanics." Pew Research Center, Mar. 3, 2010. https://www.pewsocialtrends.org/2010/03/03/census-history -counting-hispanics-2.

———. "Millions of Americans Changed Their Racial or Ethnic Identity from One Census to the Next." Pew Research Center, May 5, 2014. https://www. pewresearch.org/fact-tank/2014/05/05/millions-of-americans-changed-their -racial-or-ethnic-identity-from-one-census-to-the-next.

Collins, Patricia Hill. *Black Feminist Thought: Knowledge, Consciousness, and the Politics of Empowerment.* 2nd ed. New York: Routledge, 2000.

Comas-Díaz, Lillian. "LatiNegra: Mental Health Issues of African Latinas." In *The Multiracial Experience: Racial Borders as the New Frontier*, ed. Maria P. P. Root, 167–90. New York: Sage, 1996.

Community Coalition–Los Angeles (website). http://cocosouthla.org.

Contreras, Russell, and Yacob Reyes. "The Multiracial Identity Revolution Among U.S. Latinos." *Axios*, Aug. 19, 2021. https://www.axios.com/multiracial-identity-us-latinos-black-indigenous-75f68985-3376-4b23-912d-8aeac4e57786.html.

Costa Vargas, João H. *The Denial of Antiblackness: Multiracial Redemption and Black Suffering.* Minneapolis: University of Minnesota Press, 2018.

Cratty, Carol. "Agreement Announced to Reform Puerto Rico's Police Force." CNN, July 17, 2013. https://www.cnn.com/2013/07/17/justice/puerto-rico-civil-rights/index.html.

Crenshaw, Kimberlé. "Demarginalizing the Intersection of Race and Sex: A Black Feminist Critique of Antidiscrimination Doctrine, Feminist Theory and Antiracist Politics." *University of Chicago Legal Forum* 1989, no. 1 (1989): 139–67.

Crenshaw, Kimberlé, Neil Gotanda, Gary Peller, and Kendall Thomas, eds. *Critical Race Theory: The Key Writings That Formed the Movement.* New York: New Press, 1996.

Cruz-Janzen, Marta I. "Latinegras: Desired Women—Undesirable Mothers, Daughters, Sisters, and Wives." *Frontiers: A Journal of Women Studies* 22, no. 3 (2001): 168–83.

Cruz-Janzen, Marta I. "Y tu abuela a'onde está?" *SAGE Race Relations Abstracts* 26, no. 2 (2001): 7–24.

Cruz, José E. "Interminority Relations in Urban Settings: Lessons from the Black-Puerto Rican Experience." In *Black and Multiracial Politics in America*, ed. Yvette M. Alex-Assensoh and Lawrence J. Hanks, 84–112. New York: New York University Press, 2000.

"Current Hispanic or Latino Population Demographics in Miami, Florida 2020, 2019 by Gender and Age." Suburban Stats, 2020. https://suburbanstats.org/race/florida/miami/how-many-hispanic-or-latino-people-live-in-miami-florida.

Cuevas, Ofelia Ortiz. "Race and the L.A. Human: Race Relations and Violence in Globalized Los Angeles." In *Black and Brown in Los Angeles: Beyond Conflict and Coalition*, ed. Josh Kun and Laura Pulido, 233–52. Berkeley: University of California Press, 2014.

Dache, Amalia, Jasmine Marie Haywood, and Christina Mislán. "A Badge of Honor Not Shame: An AfroLatina Theory of Black-Imiento for U.S Higher Education Research." *Journal of Negro Education* 88, no. 2 (2019): 130–45.

Darity, William A., Jr., and Tanya Golash Boza. "Choosing Race: Evidence from the Latino National Political Survey (LNPS)." Princeton University, Apr. 2004. https://paa2004.princeton.edu/papers/41644.

Darity, William A., Jr., Jason Dietrich, and Darrick Hamilton. "Bleach in the Rainbow: Latino Ethnicity and Preference for Whiteness." *Transforming Anthropology* 13, no. 2 (2005): 103–9.

Darity, William A., Jr., Darrick Hamilton, and Jason Dietrich. "Passing on
    Blackness: Latinos, Race and Earnings in the USA." *Applied Economics Letters*
    9, no. 13 (2002): 847–53.
Dart, Tom, and Oliver Laughland. "Sandra Bland: Texas Officials Deny Dashcam
    Footage of Arrest Was Doctored." *Guardian*, July 22, 2015. https://www
    .theguardian.com/us-news/2015/jul/22/sandra-bland-texas-dashcam-footage
    -doctored.
Davis, Robert C., and Edna Erez. "Immigrant Populations as Victims: Toward a
    Multicultural Criminal Justice System." *National Institute of Justice Research in
    Brief* (1998): 1–7.
De Carvalho-Neto, Paulo. "Folklore of the Black Struggle in Latin America."
    Latin American Perspective 5, no. 2 (1978): 53–88.
De Genova, Nicholas, and Ana Y. Ramos-Zayas. *Latino Crossings: Mexicans, Puerto
    Ricans, and the Politics of Race and Citizenship.* New York: Routledge, 2003.
Del Castillo, Richard Griswold, *The Treaty of Guadalupe Hidalgo: A Legacy of Con-
    flict.* Norman: University of Oklahoma Press, 1990.
Delgado, Pura. "Puerto Rican: If You're a Shade Darker, You Face Discrimina-
    tion." *Orlando Sentinel*, May 4, 2017. https://www.orlandosentinel.com
    /os-ed-colored-puerto-rican-has-endured-racial-slurs-myword-20170504
    -story.html.
Democracy and Government Reform Team. *Examining the Demographic Composi-
    tions of U.S. Circuit and District Courts.*" Center for American Progress, Feb.
    13, 2020. https://www.americanprogress.org/issues/courts/reports/2020/02
    /13/480112/examining-demographic-compositions-u-s-circuit-district
    -courts.
Denton, Nancy A., and Douglas S. Massey. "Racial Identity Among Caribbean
    Hispanics: The Effect of Double Minority Status on Residential Segrega-
    tion." *American Sociological Review* 54, no. 5 (1989): 790–808.
Derlan, Chelsea L., Adriana J. Umaña-Taylor, Kimberly A. Updegraff, and Lau-
    dan B. Jahromi. "Longitudinal Relations Among Mexican-Origin Mothers'
    Cultural Characteristics, Cultural Socialization, and 5-Year-Old Children's
    Ethnic-Racial Identification." *Developmental Psychology* 53, no. 11 (2017):
    2078–91.
DiAngelo, Robin J. *White Fragility: Why It's So Hard for White People to Talk About
    Racism.* Boston: Beacon Press, 2020.
Díaz, Jaquira. *Ordinary Girls: A Memoir.* New York: Algonquin, 2019.
Díaz, Junot. *The Brief Wondrous Life of Oscar Wao.* New York: Riverhead Books,
    2007.
DiFulco, Denise. "Can You Tell a Mexican from a Puerto Rican?" *Latina* 8, no. 1
    (2003): 86–88.
Dinzey-Flores, Zaire Zenit. *Locked In, Locked Out: Gated Communities in a Puerto
    Rican City.* Philadelphia: University of Pennsylvania Press, 2013.
Duany, Jorge. "Making Indians Out of Blacks: The Revitalization of Taíno
    Identity in Contemporary Puerto Rico." In *Taíno Revival: Critical Perspectives
    on Puerto Rican Identity and Cultural Politics*, ed. Gabriel Haslip-Viera, 31–55.
    New York: Centro de Estudios Puertorriqueños, 1999.
———. *The Puerto Rican Nation on the Move: Identities on the Island and the United
    States.* Chapel Hill: University of North Carolina Press, 2002.

Dulitzky, Ariel E. "A Region in Denial: Racial Discrimination and Racism in Latin America." In *Neither Enemies nor Friends: Latinos, Blacks, Afro-Latinos,* ed. Anani Dzidzienyo and Suzanne Oboler, 39–59. Houndmills, UK: Palgrave Macmillan, 2005.

Dunn, Marvin, and Alex Stepick III, "Blacks in Miami." In *Miami Now! Immigration, Ethnicity, and Social Change,* ed. Guillermo J. Grenier and Alex Stepick III, 41. Gainesville: University Press of Florida, 1992.

Eberhardt, Jennifer L. *Biased: Uncovering the Hidden Prejudice That Shapes What We See, Think, and Do.* New York: Viking, 2019.

Elliot, James R., and Ryan A. Smith. "Ethnic Matching of Supervisors to Subordinate Work Groups: Findings on 'Bottom-Up' Ascription and Social Closure." *Social Problems* 48, no. 2 (2001): 258–76.

Encuentro Diaspora Afro. "Encuentro Diaspora Afro @encuentrodiasporaafro." Facebook. https://www.facebook.com/encuentrodiasporaafro. Accessed July 22, 2021.

Epstein, Rebecca, Jamilia J. Blake, and Thalia Gonzalez. *Girlhood Interrupted: The Erasure of Black Girls' Childhood.* Georgetown Law Center on Poverty and Inequality, 2017. https://www.law.georgetown.edu/poverty-inequality-center /wp-content/uploads/sites/14/2017/08/girlhood-interrupted.pdf.

Ericksen, Olin, and Jorge Casuso. "Race Fights Break Out at Samohi." *Santa Monica Lookout,* Apr. 15, 2005. https://www.surfsantamonica.com/ssm_site /the_lookout/news/News-2005/April-2005/04_15_05_Race_Fights_Break _Out_at_Samohi.htm.

Eustachewich, Lia. "Dominicans in Inwood Blasted on Social Media for Chasing Away Black Men," *New York Post,* June 3, 2020. https://nypost.com/2020 /06/03/dominicans-in-inwood-blasted-for-chasing-away-black-men.

Fanon, Frantz. *Black Skin, White Masks.* Translated by Charles Lamm Markman. New York: Grove Press, 1967.

———. *Peau noire, masques blancs* [Black Skin, White Masks]. Paris: Éditions du Seuil, 1952.

Feldmeyer, Ben. "The Effects of Racial/Ethnic Segregation on Latino and Black Homicide." *Sociological Quarterly* 51, no. 4 (2010): 600–623.

Feliciano, Cynthia, Rennie Lee, and Belinda Robnett. "Racial Boundaries Among Latinos: Evidence from Internet Daters' Racial Preferences." *Social Problems* 58, no. 2 (2011): 189–212.

Fernández, Johanna. *The Young Lords: A Radical History.* Chapel Hill: University of North Carolina Press, 2020.

Fletcher, Michael A. "The Blond, Blue-Eyed Face of Spanish TV." *Washington Post,* Aug. 3, 2000.

Flores, Carlos. "Race Discrimination Within the Latino Community." *Diálogo* 5, no. 1 (2001): 30–31.

Foley, Neil. *Quest for Equality: The Failed Promise of Black-Brown Solidarity.* Cambridge, MA: Harvard University Press, 2010.

Fox, Geoffrey. *Hispanic Nation: Culture, Politics, and the Constructing of Identity.* Secaucus, NJ: Carol, 1996.

Freeman, Lance. "A Note on the Influence of African Heritage on Segregation: The Case of Dominicans." *Urban Affairs Review* 35, no. 1 (1999): 137–46.

Fry, Hannah, and James Queally. "Hate Crimes Targeting Jews and Latinos Increased in California in 2018, Report Says." *Los Angeles Times,* July 3, 2019. https://www.latimes.com/local/lanow/la-me-ln-jewish-latino-hate-crime -report-20190703-story.html.

Fuentes-Mayorga, Norma. "Sorting Black and Brown Latino Service Workers in Gentrifying New York Neighborhoods." *Latino Studies* 9 (2011): 106–25.

"Full Sail Student Stabbed in Class with Screwdriver, Deputies Say." Click Orlando.com, Feb. 21, 2013. https://www.clickorlando.com/news/full-sail -student-stabbed-in-class-with-screwdriver-deputies-say-.

Gabriel Haslip-Viera, ed. *Taíno Revival: Critical Perspectives on Puerto Rican Identity and Cultural Politics.* Princeton, NJ: Markus Wiener, 2001.

Gabriel, Stuart A., and Gary Painter. "Mobility, Residential Location, and the American Dream." *Real Estate Economics* 36, no. 3 (2008): 499–531.

Gans, Herbert. "Second-Generation Decline: Scenarios for the Economic and Ethnic Futures of Post-1965 American Immigrants." *Ethnic and Racial Studies* 15 (1992): 173–92.

García-Louis, Claudia, and Krista L. Cortes. "Rejecting Black and Rejected Back: AfroLatinx College Students' Experiences with Anti-AfroLatinidad." *Journal of Latinos and Education* (2020): 1–16.

García, Carlos. "The Birth of the MS13 in New York." InSight Crime, Mar. 9, 2018. https://www.insightcrime.org/news/analysis/birth-ms13-new-york.

García, William. "White Privilege and the Effacement of Blackness: Puerto Rico and Its Diaspora in the Early 21st Century." In *White Latino Privilege: Caribbean Latino Perspectives in the Second Decade of the 21st Century,* ed. Gabriel Haslip-Viera, 73–89. New York: Latino Studies Press, 2018.

García-Peña, Lorgia. "Dismantling Anti-Blackness Together." NACLA, June 8, 2020. https://nacla.org/news/2020/06/09/dismantling-anti-blackness -together.

Generation Teach (website). https://www.generationteach.org/why.

Giron, Jonathan. Twitter post. Sept. 21, 2021, 10:17 PM. https://twitter.com /JonathanGiron70/status/1440500465385410563.

Giuliano, Laura, David I. Levine, and Jonathan Leonard. "Manager Race and the Race of New Hires." *Journal of Labor Economics* 27, no. 4 (2009): 589–631.

Glaberson, William. "15 Hate Groups in Region, Monitoring Organization Says." *New York Times,* Mar. 22, 1998. https://www.nytimes.com/1998/03/22 /nyregion/15-hate-groups-in-region-monitoring-organization-says.html.

Glover, Scott, and Richard Winton. "Dozens Arrested in Crackdown on Latino Gang Accused of Targeting Blacks." *Los Angeles Times,* May 22, 2009. https:// www.latimes.com/archives/la-xpm-2009-may-22-me-gang-sweep22-story .html.

Glueck, Kevin. "Iowa City Man Charged with Hate Crime for Assaulting Black Man." CBS2/FOX28, Mar. 14, 2016. https://cbs2iowa.com/news/connects -against-crime/iowa-city-man-charged-with-hate-crime-for-assaulting -black-man.

Godreau, Isar P. "Folkloric 'Others': *Blanqueamiento* and the Celebration of Blackness as an Exception in Puerto Rico." In *Globalization and Race: Transformations in the Cultural Production of Blackness,* ed. Kamari Maxine Clarke and Deborah A. Thomas, 171–88. Durham, NC: Duke University Press, 2006.

Goin, Keara K. "Marginal Latinidad: Afro-Latinas and US Film." *Latino Studies* 14, no. 3 (2016): 344–63.

Goldberg, David Theo. *Racist Culture: Philosophy and the Politics of Meaning.* Malden, MA: Blackwell, 1993.

Gomez-Aguinaga, Barbara, Gabriel R. Sanchez, and Matt Barreto. "Importance of State and Local Variation in Black-Brown Attitudes: How Latinos View Blacks and How Blacks Affect Their Views." *Journal of Race, Ethnicity, and Politics* 6, no. 1 (2021): 214–52. https://doi.org/10.1017/rep.2019.33.

Gómez, Laura E. *Inventing Latinos: A New American Story of Racism.* New York: New Press, 2020.

Gonzales, Ruby. "La Puente Man Sentenced to Decades in Prison for Stabbing 2 Men in Covina." *San Gabriel Valley Tribune*, Dec. 5, 2017. https://www.sgv tribune.com/2017/12/05/la-puente-man-sentenced-to-decades-in-prison -for-stabbing-2-men-in-covina.

Gordon, Jennifer, and Robin A. Lenhardt. "Rethinking Work and Citizenship." *UCLA Law Review* 55, no. 5 (2003): 1161–238.

Gosin, Monika. "'A Bitter Diversion': Afro-Cuban Immigrants, Race, and Everyday-Life Resistance." *Latino Studies* 15, no. 1 (2017): 4–28.

———. "The Death of 'La Reina de la Salsa': Celia Cruz and the Mythification of the Black Woman." In *Afro-Latin@s in Movement: Critical Approaches to Blackness and Transnationalism in the Americas,* ed. Petra R. Rivera-Rideau, Jennifer A. Jones, and Tianna S. Paschel, 85–107. New York: Palgrave Macmillan, 2016.

———. *The Racial Politics of Division: Interethnic Struggles for Legitimacy in Multicultural Miami.* Ithaca, NY: Cornell University Press, 2019.

Gotanda, Neil. "A Critique of 'Our Constitution Is Color-Blind.'" *Stanford Law Review* 44, no. 1 (1991): 1–68.

Grant-Thomas, Andrew, Yusuf Sarfati, and Cheryl Staats. "Natural Allies or Irreconcilable Foes? Reflections on African American/Immigrant Relations." *Poverty and Race Research Action Council* 19, no. 2 (2010): 1–12.

Gravlee, Clarence C., William W. Dressler, and H. Russell Bernard. "Skin Color, Social Classification, and Blood Pressure in Southeastern Puerto Rico." *American Journal of Public Health* 95, no. 12 (2005): 2191–97.

Greenbaum, Susan D. *More Than Black: Afro-Cubans in Tampa.* Gainesville: University Press of Florida, 2002.

Grenier, Guillermo J., and Max Castro. "Blacks and Cubans in Miami: The Negative Consequences of the Cuban Enclave on Ethnic Relations." In *Governing American Cities: Inter-Ethnic Coalitions, Competition, and Conflict,* ed. Michael Jones-Correa, 137–57. New York: Russell Sage Foundation, 2001.

Grillo, Evelio. *Black Cuban, Black American: A Memoir.* Houston: Arte Público Press, 2000.

Guidry, Francis W. "Reaching the People Across the Street: An African American Church Reaches Out to Its Hispanic Neighbors." PhD diss., Drew University Theological School, 1997.

Guinier, Lani, and Gerald Torres. *The Miner's Canary: Enlisting Race, Resisting Power, Transforming Democracy.* Cambridge, MA: Harvard University Press, 2002.

Hall, Ronald E. "A Descriptive Analysis of Skin Color Bias in Puerto Rico: Ecological Applications to Practice." *Journal of Sociology and Social Welfare* 27, no. 4 (2000): 171–83.

Hall, Ronald E., and Ellen E. Whipple. "The Complexion Connection: Ideal Light Skin as Vehicle of Adoption Process Discrimination vis-à-vis Social Work Practitioners." *Journal of Human Behavior in the Social Environment* 27, no. 7 (2017): 669–77. https://doi.org/10.1080/10911359.2017.1321511.

Haney López, Ian. "Protest, Repression, and Race: Legal Violence and the Chicano Movement." *University of Pennsylvania Law Review* 150 (2001): 205–44.

Hardie, Jessica Halliday, and Karolyn Tyson. "Other People's Racism: Race, Rednecks, and Riots in a Southern High School." *Sociology of Education* 86, no. 1 (2013): 83–102.

Haslip-Viera, Gabriel, ed. *White Latino Privilege: Caribbean Latino Perspectives in the Second Decade of the 21st Century.* New York: Latino Studies Press, 2018.

"Hate Crimes on the Rise in Orange County: Report." NBC Los Angeles, Sept. 25, 2018. https://www.nbclosangeles.com/news/local/Hate-Crimes-on-the-Rise-in-Orange-County-Report-494325841.html.

Hauser, Christine. "Florida Police Chief Gets 3 Years for Plot to Frame Black People for Crimes." *New York Times*, Nov. 28, 2018. https://www.nytimes.com/2018/11/28/us/florida-police-chief-frame-black-people.html.

Hay, Michelle. *"I've Been Black in Two Countries": Black Cuban Views on Race in the U.S.* El Paso, TX: LFB Scholarly Publishing, 2009.

Haywood, Jasmine M. "Anti-Black Latino Racism in an Era of Trumpismo." *International Journal of Qualitative Studies in Education* 30, no. 10 (2017): 957–64.

———. "'Latino Spaces Have Always Been the Most Violent': Afro-Latino Collegians' Perceptions of Colorism and Latino Intragroup Marginalization." *International Journal of Qualitative Studies in Education* 30, no. 8 (2017): 759–82.

Heard, Jacquelyn. "Racial Strife Runs Deep at High School: Black and Hispanic Staff, Students Clash at Farragut." *Chicago Tribune*, Nov. 17, 1992.

Hernández, Tanya Katerí. "Afro-Latin@s and the Latino Workplace." In *The Afro-Latin@ Reader: History and Culture in the United States*, ed. Miriam Jiménez Román and Juan Flores, 520–26. Durham, NC: Duke University Press, 2010.

———. "Afro-Mexicans and the Chicano Movement: The Unknown Story." Review of *Racism on Trial: The Chicano Fight for Justice* by Ian F. Haney López. *California Law Review* 92, no. 5 (2004): 1537–51.

———. "Latino Antiblack Bias and the Census Categorization of Latinos: Race, Ethnicity, or Other?" In *Antiblackness*, ed. Moon-Kie Jung and João H. Costa Vargas, 283–96. Durham, NC: Duke University Press, 2021.

———. "Latino Inter-Ethnic Employment Discrimination and the Diversity Defense." *Harvard Civil Rights—Civil Liberties Law Review* 42, no. 2 (2007): 259–316.

———. *Multiracials and Civil Rights: Mixed-Race Stories of Discrimination.* New York: NYU Press, 2018.

———. *Racial Subordination in Latin America: The Role of the State, Customary Law, and the New Civil Rights Response.* Cambridge: Cambridge University Press, 2013.

———. "Roots of Anger: Longtime Prejudices, Not Economic Rivalry, Fuel Latino-Black Tensions." *Los Angeles Times*, Jan. 7, 2007.

———. "'Too Black to Be Latino/a': Blackness and Blacks as Foreigners in Latino Studies." *Latino Studies* 1 (2003): 152–59.

Hersch, Joni. "Colorism Against Legal Immigrants to the United States." *American Behavioral Scientist* 62, no. 14 (2018): 2117–32.

———. "The Persistence of Skin Color Discrimination for Immigrants." *Social Science Research* 40, no. 5 (2011): 1337–49.

———. "Profiling the New Immigrant Worker: The Effects of Skin Color and Height." *Journal of Labor Economics* 26, no. 2 (2008): 345–86.

Higginbotham, Elizabeth. "Employment for Professional Black Women in the Twentieth Century." In *Ingredients for Women's Employment Policy*, ed. Christine Bose and Glenna Spitze, 73–91. Albany, NY: SUNY Press, 1987.

Hill, Herbert. *Black Labor and the American Legal System: Race, Work, and the Law.* Madison: University of Wisconsin Press, 1985.

Hing, Julianne. "The Curious Case of George Zimmerman's Race." *ColorLines*, July 22, 2013. https://www.colorlines.com/articles/curious-case-george-zimmermans-race.

Hipp, John R., and George E. Tita. "Ethnically Transforming Neighborhoods and Violent Crime Among and Between African-Americans and Latinos: A Study of South Los Angeles." Department of Criminology, Law and Society, University of California, 2010. https://faculty.sites.uci.edu/johnhipp/files/2018/06/Haynes-Final-Report2377_Ethnically-Transforming-Neighborhoods.pdf.

Hodge, Damon. "Hard Lessons." *Las Vegas Weekly*, Mar. 7, 2008. https://lasvegasweekly.com/news/archive/2008/mar/07/hard-lessons.

Hoffnung-Garskof, Jesse. *Racial Migrations: New York City and the Revolutionary Politics of the Spanish Caribbean.* Princeton, NJ: Princeton University Press, 2019.

Hogan, Howard. "Reporting of Race Among Hispanics: Analysis of ACS Data." In *The Frontiers of Applied Demography*, ed. David A. Swanson, 169–91. Cham, Switzerland: Springer International, 2016.

Holder, Michelle, and Alan A. Aja. *Afro-Latinos in the U.S. Economy.* Lanham, MD: Lexington Books, 2021.

Holland, Gale. "2 Convicted of Racial Hate Crime in San Fernando Valley Shootings." *Los Angeles Times*, Sept. 30, 2011. https://latimesblogs.latimes.com/lanow/2011/09/hate-crime-convictions-in-san-fernando-valley-shootings.html.

"Homeownership Rate in the U.S. 1990–2020." Statista Research Department, Feb. 17, 2021. https://www.statista.com/statistics/184902/homeownership-rate-in-the-us-since-2003/#:~:text=The%20homeownership%20rate%20in%20the,are%20occupied%20by%20the%20owners.

Hordge-Freeman, Elizabeth. *The Color of Love: Racial Features, Stigma, and Socialization in Black Brazilian Families.* Austin: University of Texas Press, 2015.

Hordge-Freeman, Elizabeth, and Angelica Loblack. "'Cops Only See the Brown Skin, They Could Care Less Where It Originated': Afro-Latinx Perceptions of the #BlackLivesMatter Movement." *Sociological Perspectives* 64, no. 4 (2021): 518–35.

Hordge-Freeman, Elizabeth, and Edlin Veras. "Out of the Shadows, into the Dark: Ethnoracial Dissonance and Identity Formation Among Afro-Latinxs." *Sociology of Race and Ethnicity* 6, no. 2 (2019): 146–60.

Hornby, D. Brock. "Summary Judgment Without Illusions." *Green Bag* 2, no. 13 (2010): 273–88.

Howard, David. *Coloring the Nation: Race and Ethnicity in the Dominican Republic.* Oxford, UK: Signal Books, 2001.

Howard, Tiffany. "Afro-Latinos and the Black-Hispanic Identity: Evaluating the Potential for Group Conflict and Cohesion." *National Political Science Review* 19, no. 1 (2018): 29–50.

Hoy, Vielka Cecilia. "Negotiating Among Invisibilities: Tales of Afro-Latinidades in the United States." In *The Afro-Latin@ Reader: History and Culture in the United States*, ed. Miriam Jiménez Román and Juan Flores, 426–30. Durham, NC: Duke University Press, 2010.

Hutchinson, Earl Ofari. "Urban Tension: Latinos' New Clout Threatening to Blacks." *Los Angeles Daily News*, Jan. 26, 2003.

———. "Will Latino Gang Arrests Deepen Black-Brown Divide?" *TheGrio*, June 8, 2011. http://thegrio.com/2011/06/08/will-latino-gang-arrests-deepen -Black-brown-divide.

Iceland, John, and Kyle Anne Nelson. "Hispanic Segregation in Metropolitan America: Exploring the Multiple Forms of Spatial Assimilation." *American Sociological Review* 73, no. 5 (2008): 741–65.

Itzigsohn, José, and Carlos Dore-Cabral. "Competing Identities? Race, Ethnicity and Panethnicity Among Dominicans in the United States," *Sociological Forum* 15, no. 2 (2000): 225–47.

Itzigsohn, José, Silvia Giorguli, and Obed Vazquez. "Immigrant Incorporation and Racial Identity: Racial Self-Identification Among Dominican Immigrants." *Ethnic and Racial Studies* 28, no. 1 (2005): 50–78.

Jackson, David, Jennifer Smith Richards, Gary Marx, and Juan Perez Jr. "Betrayed: Chicago Schools Fail to Protect Students from Sexual Abuse and Assault, Leaving Lasting Damage." *Chicago Tribune*, July 27, 2018. http://graphics .chicagotribune.com/chicago-public-schools-sexual-abuse/gaddy.

Jaime, Angie. "How Latinx People Can Fight Anti-Black Racism in Our Own Culture." *Teen Vogue*, June 1, 2020. https://www.teenvogue.com/story/how -latinx-people-can-fight-anti-black-racism-in-our-own-culture.

Johnson, Craig. "5 Things About Alex Michael Ramos: Georgia Man Tied to Charlottesville Violence." *Patch*, Aug. 30, 2017. https://patch.com/georgia/marietta/5 -things-alex-michael-ramos-georgia-man-tied-charlottesville-violence.

Jones, Jennifer A. *The Browning of the New South*. Chicago: University of Chicago Press, 2019.

Jones, Jennifer A. "Blacks May Be Second Class, But They Can't Make Them Leave: Mexican Racial Formation and Immigrant Status in Winston-Salem." *Latino Studies* 10, no. 1 (2012): 60–80.

Jorge, Angela. "The Black Puerto Rican Woman in Contemporary American Society." In *The Puerto Rican Woman*, ed. Edna Acosta-Belen, 134–41. New York: Praeger, 1979.

Joshi, Ashish S., and Christina T. Kline. "Lack of Jury Diversity: A National Problem with Individual Consequences." American Bar Association, Sept. 1, 2015. https://www.americanbar.org/groups/litigation/committees/diversity -inclusion/articles/2015/lack-of-jury-diversity-national-problem-individual -consequences.

Jung, Moon-Kie, and Costa Vargas João Helion. *Antiblackness*. Durham, NC: Duke University Press, 2021.

Kasindorf, Martin, and Maria Puente. "Hispanics and Blacks Find Their Futures Entangled." *USA Today*, Sept. 10, 1999.

Kaufmann, Karen M. "Cracks in the Rainbow: Group Commonality as a Basis for Latino and African-American Political Coalitions." *Political Research Quarterly* 56, no. 2 (2003): 199–210.

Kinsbruner, Jay. *Not of Pure Blood: The Free People of Color and Racial Prejudice in Nineteenth-Century Puerto Rico*. Durham, NC: Duke University Press, 1996.

Kramer Mills, Claire, Jessica Battisto, Scott Lieberman, Marlene Orozco, Iliana Perez, and Nancy S. Lee. *Latino-Owned Businesses: Shining a Light on National Trends*. Palo Alto, CA: Stanford Graduate School of Business, 2018. https:// www.gsb.stanford.edu/sites/gsb/files/publication-pdf/slei-report-2018-latino -owned-businesses-shinging-light-national-trends.pdf.

Krupnikov, Yanna, and Spencer Piston. "The Political Consequences of Latino Prejudice Against Blacks." *Public Opinion Quarterly* 80, no. 2 (2016): 480–509.

Labaton, Stephen. "Denny's Restaurants to Pay $54 Million in Race Bias Suits." *New York Times*, May 25, 1994.

Lacayo, Celia. "Latinos Need to Stay in Their Place: Differential Segregation in a Multi-Ethnic Suburb." *Societies* 6, no. 3 (2016): 25. https://www.mdpi.com /2075-4698/6/3/25.

Lao-Montes, Agustín. "Afro-Latin@ Difference and the Politics of Decoloniza- tion." In *Latin@s in the World-System: Decolonization Struggles in the Twenty- First Century U.S. Empire*, ed. Ramón Grosfoguel, Nelson Maldonado- Torres, and José David Saldívar, 78–79. Boulder, CO: Paradigm, 2005.

Larkin, Brian Patrick. "The Forty-Year 'First Step': The Fair Housing Act as an Incomplete Tool for Suburban Integration." *Columbia Law Review* 107, no. 7 (2007): 1617–54.

Latinx Racial Equity Project. https://latinxracialequityproject.org. Accessed July 26, 2021.

LaVeist-Ramos, Thomas Alexis, Jessica Galarraga, Roland J. Thorpe Jr., Caryn N. Bell, and Chermeia J. Austin. "Are Black Hispanics Black or Hispanic? Exploring Disparities at the Intersections of Race and Ethnicity." *Journal of Epidemiological Community Health* 66 (2012): 1–5.

LeDuff, Charlie. "At a Slaughterhouse, Some Things Never Die: Who Kills, Who Cuts, Who Bosses Can Depend on Race." *New York Times*, June 16, 2000.

Lee, Gary, and Robert Suro. "Latino-Black Rivalry Grows: Los Angeles Reflects Tensions Between Minorities." *Washington Post*, Oct. 13, 1993.

Lee, Sonia S.. *Building a Latino Civil Rights Movement: Puerto Ricans, African Amer- icans, and the Pursuit of Racial Justice in New York City*. Chapel Hill: University of North Carolina Press, 2014.

Lee, Sonia S., and Ande Diaz. "'I Was the One Percenter': Manny Diaz and the Beginnings of a Black-Puerto Rican Coalition." *Journal of American Ethnic History* 26, no. 3 (2007): 52–80.

Lefebvre, Henri. *The Production of Space*. Translated by Donald Nicholson-Smith. Oxford, UK: Blackwell, 1991.

"Legality of Segregating Prisoners by Race." Interview with Ramona Ripston and Paul Butler. NPR, Feb. 13, 2006. https://www.npr.org/templates/story/story .php?storyId=5203572.

Li, Michael, and Yurij Rudensky. "Rethinking the Redistricting Toolbox." *Howard Law Journal* 62, no. 3 (2019): 713–37.

Limón, Noerena, Christa Murillo, Jaimie Owens, Alejandro Becerra, Meghan Lucero, and Emilio Abarca. *2019 State of Hispanic Homeownership Report.* San Diego: National Association of Hispanic Real Estate Professionals, 2019. https://nahrep.org/downloads/2019-state-of-hispanic-homeownership -report.pdf.

Lindo, Roger. "Miembros de las diversas razas prefieren a los suyos: Así lo afirma una investigación de la Universidad de California de Los Angeles." *La Opinión*, Nov. 20, 1992.

Literte, Patricia E. "Competition, Conflict, and Coalition: Black-Latino/a Relations Within Institutions of Higher Education." *Journal of Negro Education* 80, no. 4 (2011): 477–90.

Llanos-Figueroa, Dahlma. *Daughters of the Stone.* New York: Thomas Dunne Books, 2009.

Lloréns, Hilda. "Identity Practices: Racial Passing, Gender, and Racial Purity in Puerto Rico." *Afro-Hispanic Review* 37, no. 1 (2018): 29–47.

Llorens, Hilda, Carlos G. García-Quijano, and Isar P. Godreau. "Racismo en Puerto Rico: Surveying Perceptions of Racism." *CENTRO: Journal of the Center for Puerto Rican Studies* 29, no. 3 (2017): 154–83.

Lofland, Lyn H. *A World of Strangers: Order and Action in Urban Public Space.* New York: Basic Books, 1973.

Logan, John. *How Race Counts for Hispanic Americans.* Albany: State University of New York, Lewis Mumford Center for Comparative Urban and Regional Research, 2003. http://mumford.albany.edu/census/BlackLatinoReport /BlackLatinoReport.pdf.

López, Antonio. "Cosa de Blancos: Cuban-American Whiteness and the Afro-Cuban Occupied House." *Latino Studies* 8, no. 2 (2010): 220–43.

López, Canela. "It's Time for Non-Black Latinx People to Talk About Anti-Blackness in Our Own Communities—And the Conversation Starts at Home." *Insider*, June 26, 2020. https://www.insider.com/anti-blackness-non -black-latinx-spaces-racism-2020-6.

López, Gustavo, and Ana Gonzalez-Barrera. "Afro-Latino: A Deeply Rooted Identity Among U.S. Hispanics." Pew Research Center, Mar. 1, 2016. https://www.pewresearch.org/fact-tank/2016/03/01/afro-latino-a-deeply -rooted-identity-among-u-s-hispanics.

López, Gustavo, and Jens Manuel Krogstad. "How Hispanic Police Officers View Their Jobs." Pew Research Center, Feb. 15, 2017. https://www.pewresearch .org/fact-tank/2017/02/15/how-hispanic-police-officers-view-their-jobs.

López, Nancy. "Killing Two Birds with One Stone? Why We Need Two Separate Questions on Race and Ethnicity in the 2020 Census and Beyond." *Latino Studies* 11 (2013): 428–38.

López, Nancy, and Howard Hogan. "What's Your Street Race? The Urgency of Critical Race Theory and Intersectionality as Lenses for Revising the U.S. Office of Management and Budget Guidelines, Census and Administrative

Data in Latinx Communities and Beyond." *Genealogy* 5, no. 3 (2021): 75. https://doi.org/10.3390/genealogy5030075.

López, Nancy, Edward Vargas, Melina Juarez, Lisa Cacari-Stone, and Sonia Bettez, "What's Your 'Street Race'? Leveraging Multidimensional Measures of Race and Intersectionality for Examining Physical and Mental Health Status Among Latinx." *Sociology of Race and Ethnicity* 4, no. 1 (2017): 49–66.

Loveman, Mara, and Jeronimo Muniz. "How Puerto Rico Became White: Boundary Dynamics and Intercensus Racial Reclassification." *American Sociological Review* 72, no. 6 (2007): 915–39.

"Lunchtime Brawl Involving 40 People Breaks Out at LA High School 'After Tensions Flared Between Black and Hispanic Students at Prom.'" *Daily Mail*, May 10, 2016. https://www.dailymail.co.uk/news/article-3582947/Lunchtime -brawl-involving-40-people-breaks-LA-high-school-tensions-flared-Black -Hispanic-students-prom.html.

Lyons, Christopher J. "Defending Turf: Racial Demographics and Hate Crime Against Blacks and Whites." *Social Forces* 87, no. 1 (2008): 357–85.

Machicote, Michaela. "Dear Latines: Your Antiblackness Will Not Save You." *Latinx Talk*, Nov. 11, 2020. https://latinxtalk.org/2020/11/11/dear-latines -your-antiblackness-will-not-save-you.

Maciag, Michael. "Residential Segregation Data for U.S. Metro Areas." *Governing*, Jan. 10, 2019. https://www.governing.com/gov-data/residential-racial -segregation-metro-areas.html.

Márquez, John D. *Black-Brown Solidarity: Racial Politics in the New Gulf South.* Austin: University of Texas Press, 2013.

Marrero, Pilar. "El odio en acción." *BBC Mundo*, Aug. 29, 2001. http://news.bbc .co.uk/hi/spanish/specials/newsid_1513000/1513820.stm.

Marrow, Helen B. *New Destination Dreaming: Immigration, Race, and Legal Status in the Rural American South.* Stanford, CA: Stanford University Press, 2011.

Martínez, George A. "African-Americans, Latinos, and the Construction of Race: Toward an Epistemic Coalition." *Chicano-Latino Law Review* 19 (1998): 213–22.

Massagli, Michael. "What Do Boston-Area Residents Think of Each Other?" In *The Boston Renaissance*, ed. Barry Bluestone and Mary Huff Stevenson, 144–64. New York: Russell Sage Foundation, 2000.

Massey, Douglas S., and Brooks Bitterman. "Explaining the Paradox of Puerto Rican Segregation." *Social Forces* 64, no. 2 (1985): 306–31.

Massey, Douglas S., and Nancy A. Denton. *American Apartheid: Segregation and the Making of the Underclass.* Boston: Harvard University Press, 1993.

McClain, Paula D., Niambi M. Carter, Victoria M. DeFrancesco Soto, Monique L. Lyle, Jeffrey D. Grynaviski, Shayla C. Nunnally, Thomas J. Scotto, J. Alan Kendrick, Gerald F. Lackey, and Kendra Davenport Cotton. "Racial Distancing in a Southern City: Latino Immigrants' Views of Black Americans." *Journal of Politics* 68, no. 3 (2006): 571–84.

McConnaughy, Corrine M., Ismail K. White, David L. Leal, and Jason P. Casellas. "A Latino on the Ballot: Explaining Coethnic Voting Among Latinos and the Response of White Americans." *Journal of Politics* 72, no. 4 (2010): 1199–211.

McDonald, Archie P., ed. *The Mexican War: Crisis for American Democracy.* Lexington: D. C. Heath, 1969.

Medrano, Marianela. *Regando esencias [The Scent of Waiting]*, *Colección Tertuliando*, no. 2, New York: Ediciones Alcance, 1998.

Melendez, Edwin, Clara Rodriguez, and Janis Barry Figueroa, eds. *Hispanics in the Labor Force: Issues and Policies*. New York: Plenus Press, 1991.

Melendez, Miguel "Mickey." *We Took the Streets: Fighting for Latino Rights with the Young Lords*. New Brunswick, NJ: Rutgers University Press, 2003.

Miller, Joshua L., and Ann Marie Garran. *Racism in the United States: Implications for the Helping Professions*. 2nd ed. New York: Springer, 2017.

Millet, Ricardo. "Case Study of Black-Brown Bridging: A Study Commissioned by the Marguerite Casey Foundation." Unpublished manuscript, 2010.

Mindiola, Tatcho, Jr., Yolanda Flores Niemann, and Nestor Rodriguez. *Black-Brown Relations and Stereotypes*. Austin: University of Texas Press, 2002.

Minority Rights Group, ed. *No Longer Invisible: Afro-Latin Americans Today*. London: Minority Rights Publications, 1995.

Mirabal, Nancy Raquel. *Suspect Freedoms: The Racial and Sexual Politics of Cubanidad in New York, 1823–1957*. New York: NYU Press, 2017.

Monforti, Jessica Lavariega, and Gabriel Sanchez. "The Politics of Perception: An Investigation of the Presence and Sources of Perception of Internal Discrimination Among Latinos." *Social Science Quarterly* 91, no. 1 (2010): 245–65.

Moore, Solomon. "Hundreds Hurt in California Prison Riot." *New York Times*, Aug. 9, 2009. https://www.nytimes.com/2009/08/10/us/10prison.html.

Mora, G. Cristina, Reuben Perez, and Nicholas Vargas. "Who Identifies as 'Latinx'? The Generational Politics of Ethnoracial Labels." *Social Forces*, 2021.

Morales, Ed. "Brown Like Me?" *Nation*, Mar. 8, 2004.

Morales, Ed. *Latinx: The New Force in American Politics and Culture*. New York: Verso, 2018.

Morales, Erica. "Parental Messages Concerning Latino/Black Interracial Dating: An Exploratory Study Among Latina/o Young Adults." *Latino Studies* 10, no. 3 (2012): 314–33.

Morales, Maria Cristina. "The Utility of Shared Ethnicity on Job Quality Among Latino Workers." *Latino Studies* 9 (2011): 439–65.

Morales Carrión, Arturo. *Auge y decadencia de la trata negrera en Puerto Rico (1820–1860)*. Barcelona: Centro de Estudios Avanzados de Puerto Rico y el Caribe, 1978.

Moran, Tim. "Hate Crime Charges Dropped Against Northwestern Chapel Vandals." *Patch*, Nov. 28, 2016. https://patch.com/illinois/evanston/hate-crime -charges-dropped-against-northwestern-chapel-vandals.

"MS-13 on Long Island: What We Know About the Gang." *Newsday*, July 18, 2017. https://projects.newsday.com/long-island/ms-13-long-island-know-gang.

Muñoz Vásquez, Marya, and Idsa E. Alegría Ortega. *Discrimen por razón de raza y los sistemas de seguridad y justicia*. San Juan: Comisión de Derechos Civiles de Puerto Rico, 1998.

Murguia, Edward, and Tyrone Forman. "Shades of Whiteness: The Mexican American Experience in Relation to Anglos and Blacks." In *White Out: The Continuing Significance of Racism*, ed. Ashley "Woody" Doane and Eduardo Bonilla-Silva, 63–84. New York: Routledge, 2003.

Murguia, Edward, and Edward Telles. "Phenotype and Schooling Among Mexican Americans." *Sociology of Education* 69, no. 4 (1996): 276–89.

Murr, Andrew. "A Gang War with a Twist: Gangbangers in L.A. on Trial for Deadly Hate Crimes." *Newsweek*, July 17, 2006.

"NAHREP Releases New State of Hispanic Homeownership Report." Chicago Association of Realtors, Aug. 9, 2019. https://chicagorealtor.com/nahrep -releases-new-state-of-hispanic-homeownership-report.

National Conference of Christians and Jews. *Taking America's Pulse: The Full Report of the National Conference Survey on Inter-Group Relations*. New York: National Conference of Christians and Jews, 1994.

National Survey of Latinos Report. Washington, DC: Pew Hispanic Center and the Kaiser Family Foundation, 2002.

Newman, Katherine S. *No Shame in My Game: The Working Poor in the Inner City*. New York: Alfred A. Knopf, 1999.

Ng, Christina. "Latino Gang Charged with Racial Cleansing Attacks in California Town." *ABC News*, June 9, 2011. http://abcnews.go.com/US/latino-gang -charged-racial-cleansing-california-town/story?id=13794815#.UHuGJ4bF271.

Nicholas, James C. "Racial and Ethnic Discrimination in Rental Housing." *Review of Social Economy* 36, no. 1 (1978): 89–94.

Nielsen, Laura Beth, and Robert L. Nelson. "Rights Realized? An Empirical Analysis of Employment Discrimination Litigation as a Claiming System." *Wisconsin Law Review* 2005, no. 2 (2005): 663–711.

Nieves, Yadira. "The Representation of Latin@s in the Media: A Negation of Blackness." *Afro-Latin American Research* no. 22 (2018): 29–38.

Noe-Bustamante, Luis, Mark Hugo Lopez, and Jens Manuel Krogstad. "U.S. Hispanic Population Surpassed 60 Million in 2019, but Growth Has Slowed." Pew Research Center, July 7, 2020. https://www.pewresearch.org /fact-tank/2020/07/07/u-s-hispanic-population-surpassed-60-million-in -2019-but-growth-has-slowed.

Noe-Bustamante, Luis, Lauren Mora, and Mark Hugo Lopez. "About One-in-Four U.S. Hispanics Have Heard of Latinx, but Just 3% Use It." Pew Research Center, Aug. 11, 2020. https://www.pewresearch.org/hispanic/wp -content/uploads/sites/5/2020/08/PHGMD_2020.08.11_Latinx_FINAL.pdf.

Nolasco, Vianny Jasmin. "Doing Latinidad While Black: Afro-Latino Identity and Belonging." PhD diss., University of Arkansas, Fayetteville, 2020.

Okamoto, Dina, and G. Cristina Mora. "Panethnicity." *Annual Review of Sociology* 40, no. 1 (2014): 219–39.

Opie, Frederick Douglass. *Upsetting the Apple Cart: Black-Latino Coalitions in New York City from Protest to Public Office*. New York: Columbia University Press, 2015.

Orosco, Cynthia, "Aprender a convivir: Negros e Hispanos." *La Opinión*, Apr. 14, 2001.

Orozco, Marlene, and Inara Sunan Tareque. *2020 State of Latino Entrepreneurship Report*. Palo Alto, CA: Stanford Graduate School of Business, 2020. https:// www.gsb.stanford.edu/sites/default/files/publication-pdf/report-2020-state -of-latino-entrepreneurship.pdf.

Ortiz, Paul. *An African American and Latinx History of the United States*. Boston: Beacon Press, 2018.

Ortiz, Teresa. *Never Again a World Without Us: Voices of Mayan Women in Chiapas, Mexico*. Washington, DC: EPICA Task Force, 2001.

Padgett, Tim. "Why Are So Many Latinos Obsessed with Demonizing Black Lives Matter? It's Complicated." WLRN, Oct. 5, 2020. https://www.wlrn.org/2020-10-05/why-are-so-many-latinos-obsessed-with-black-lives-matter-its-complicated-or-simple.

Padilla, Adriana E. Reader response to opinion editorial "Roots of Anger: Longtime Prejudices, Not Economic Rivalry, Fuel Latino-Black Tensions," by Tanya Katerí Hernández. Los Angeles Times, Jan. 11, 2007. https://www.latimes.com/archives/la-xpm-2007-jan-11-le-thursday11-story.html.

Padilla, Laura. "'But You're Not a Dirty Mexican': Internalized Oppression and Latinos." Texas Hispanic Journal of Law and Policy 7 (2001): 61–113.

Paquette, Carole. "Book Details Klan Role in Smithtown's Past." New York Times, Nov. 17, 1996. https://www.nytimes.com/1996/11/17/nyregion/book-details-klan-role-in-smithtown-s-past.html.

Parisi, Domenico, Daniel T. Lichter, and Michael C. Taquino. "Multi-Scale Residential Segregation: Black Exceptionalism and America's Changing Color Line." Social Forces 89, no. 3 (2011): 829–52.

Parker, Kim. "Multiracial in America: Proud, Diverse and Growing in Numbers." Pew Research Center, June 2015. https://www.pewsocialtrends.org/2015/06/11/multiracial-in-america.

Pastor, Manuel, Ashley K. Thomas, Preston Mills, Rachel Rosner, and Vanessa Carter. "Bridges Puentes: Building Black-Brown Solidarities Across the U.S." USC Dornsife Equity Research Institute, Nov. 2020. https://dornsife.usc.edu/assets/sites/1411/docs/Bridges_Puentes_Report_FINAL_02.pdf.

Peery, Nelson. "Witnessing History: An Octogenarian Reflects on Fifty Years of African American-Latino Relations." In Neither Enemies nor Friends: Latinos, Blacks, Afro-Latinos, ed. Anani Dzidzienyo and Suzanne Oboler, 305–12. Houndmills, UK: Palgrave Macmillan, 2005.

Perdomo, Willie. Where a Nickel Costs a Dime. New York: W. W. Norton, 1996.

Pérez, Ana Cecilia. "As Non-Black POC, We Need to Address Anti-Blackness." Yes! Solutions Magazine, July 6, 2020. https://www.yesmagazine.org/opinion/2020/07/06/non-black-poc-anti-blackness.

Pessar, Patricia R. A Visa for a Dream: Dominicans in the United States. Cranbury, NJ: Pearson, 1995.

Pew Research Center. Majority of Latinos Say Skin Color Impacts Opportunity in America and Shapes Daily Life. Nov. 2021. https://www.pewresearch.org/hispanic/wp-content/uploads/sites/5/2021/11/RE_2021.11.04_Latinos-Race-Identity_FINAL.pdf.

"Philando Castile Death: Mother Gets $3M over Police Shooting." BBC News, June 26, 2017. https://www.bbc.com/news/world-us-canada-40408004.

Piatt, Bill. Black and Brown in America: The Case for Cooperation. New York: NYU Press, 1997.

Prohías, Rafael J., and Lourdes Casal. The Cuban Minority in the U.S.: Preliminary Report on Need Identification and Program Evaluation. Boca Raton: Florida Atlantic University, 1973.

Prud'homme, Alex. "Race Relations Browns vs. Blacks." Time, July 29, 1991.

Quarshie, Mabinty, and Donovan Slack. "Census: US Sees Unprecedented Multiracial Growth, Decline in the White Population for First Time in History." USA Today, Aug. 13, 2021.

Quesada, Kayla Popuchet. "The Violent History of Latin America Is All About Promoting Whiteness (Opinion)." *Latino Rebels*, Sept. 9, 2020. https://www .latinorebels.com/2020/09/09/violenthistorylatinamerica.

Quinones, Sam. "Azusa 13 Street Gang Leader, Son Sentenced to Prison." *Los Angeles Times*, Jan. 15, 2013. https://www.latimes.com/local/la-xpm-2013 -jan-15-la-me-0115-gang-sentence-20130115-story.html.

———. "Last Suspect in Cheryl Green Hate-Crime Murder Gets 238 Years." *Los Angeles Times*, June 20, 2012. http://latimesblogs.latimes.com/lanow/2012 /06/last-suspect-in-cheryl-green-hate-crime-murder-sentenced-to-238 -years.html.

———. "Race, Real Estate, and the Mexican Mafia: A Report from the Black and Latino Killing Fields." In *Black and Brown in Los Angeles: Beyond Conflict and Coalition*, ed. Josh Kun and Laura Pulido, 261–300. Berkeley: University of California Press, 2014.

Quiñones Rivera, Maritza. "From Trigueñita to Afro-Puerto Rican: Intersections of the Racialized, Gendered, and Sexualized Body in Puerto Rico and the U.S. Mainland." *Meridians* 7, no. 1 (2006): 162–82.

Quiros, Laura, and Beverly Araujo Dawson. "The Color Paradigm: The Impact of Colorism on the Racial Identity and Identification of Latinas." *Journal of Human Behavior in the Social Environment* 23, no. 3 (2013): 287–97.

"Racial/Ethnic Composition, Cities and Communities, Los Angeles County: By Percentages, 2010 Census." *Los Angeles Almanac*. http://www.laalmanac.com /population/po38_2010.php. Accessed July 24, 2021.

Radio Caña Negra (podcast). https://open.spotify.com/show/70k9xA1ERqzVs4tYU8 Gcea?si=W9gx1onoRImHyziS50A9dw&dl_branch=1. Accessed July 26, 2021.

Rafael, Tony. *The Mexican Mafia*. New York: Encounter Books, 2007.

Ramirez, Mark D., and David A. M. Peterson. *Ignored Racism: White Animus Toward Latinos*. New York: Cambridge University Press, 2020.

Ramos, Paola. *Finding Latinx: In Search of the Voices Redefining Latino Identity*. New York: Vintage, 2020.

Ramos-Zayas, Ana Y. *National Performances: The Politics of Class, Race, and Space in Puerto Rican Chicago*. Chicago: University of Chicago Press, 2003.

Raphael, T. J. "California Prisons Struggle to Adapt to Desegregation." *PRI— The Takeaway*, Apr. 27, 2016. https://www.pri.org/stories/california-prisons -struggle-adapt-desegregation.

Recio, Sili. "Black and Ugly." *HuffPost*, Aug. 4, 2015. https://www.huffpost.com /entry/black-and-ugly-b_7927324.

Redd, Spring. "Something Latino Was Up with Us." In *Home Girls: A Black Feminist Anthology*, ed. Barbara Smith, 52–56. New Brunswick, NJ: Rutgers University Press, 1983.

Reiter, Bernd, and Kimberly Elson Simmons, eds. *Afro-Descendants, Identity, and the Struggle for Development in the Americas*. East Lansing: Michigan State University Press, 2012.

Reosti, Anna. "'We Go Totally Subjective': Discretion, Discrimination, and Tenant Screening in a Landlord's Market." *Law and Social Inquiry* 45, no. 3 (2020): 618–57.

Resto-Montero, Gabriela. "With the Rise of the Alt-Right, Latino White Supremacy May Not Be a Contradiction in Terms." *Mic*, Dec. 27, 2017.

https://www.mic.com/articles/187062/with-the-rise-of-the-alt-right-latino
-white-supremacy-may-not-be-a-contradiction-in-terms.

Reyes, Raul A. "Afro-Latinos Seek Recognition, and Accurate Census Count."
NBC News, Sept. 21, 2014. https://www.nbcnews.com/storyline/hispanic
-heritage-month/afro-latinos-seek-recognition-accurate-census-count-n207426.

"Riots Break Out Between Black, Latino Students at Victorville School." CBS
Los Angeles, Sept. 28, 2012. https://losangeles.cbslocal.com/2012/09/28
/riots-break-out-between-Black-latino-students-at-victorville-school.

Rivera, Maritza Quiñones. "From Triguenita to Afro-Puerto Rican: Intersections
of the Racialized, Gendered, and Sexualized Body in Puerto Rico and the
US Mainland." *Meridians* 7, no. 1 (2006): 162–82.

Rivera, Stephanie. "Poly High Violence Just Made News, But Parents Say It's
a Decades-Old Problem; They Want Solutions." *Long Beach Post*, May 28,
2019. https://lbpost.com/news/education/poly-high-beating-special-ed
-solutions.

Rivera-Rideau, Petra. "Expanding the Dialogues: Afro-Latinx Feminisms." Latinx Talk, Nov. 28, 2017. https://latinxtalk.org/2017/11/28/expanding-the
-dialogues-afro-latinx-feminisms.

Rochester, Shawn D. *The Black Tax: The Cost of Being Black in America*. Stirling,
NJ: Good Steward, 2018.

Rodríguez-Muñiz Michael. *Figures of the Future: Latino Civil Rights and the Politics
of Demographic Change*. Princeton, NJ: Princeton University Press, 2021.

Román, Miriam Jiménez. "Real Unity for Afro-Latinos and African Americans."
AfroLatin@ Forum. http://www.afrolatinoforum.org/real-unity-for
-afrolatinos.html.

Román, Miriam Jiménez, and Juan Flores. Introduction to *The Afro-Latin@
Reader: History and Culture in the United States*, ed. Miriam Jiménez Román
and Juan Flores, 1–15. Durham, NC: Duke University Press, 2010.

Rosado, Shantee. "Puerto Ricans, Dominicans, and the Emotional Politics of Race
and Blackness in the U.S." PhD diss., University of Pennsylvania, 2018.

Rosenblum, Alexis, William Darity Jr., Angel L. Harris, and Tod G. Hamilton.
"Looking Through the Shades: The Effect of Skin Color on Earnings by
Region of Birth and Race for Immigrants to the United States." *Sociology of
Race and Ethnicity* 2, no. 1 (2016): 87–105.

Roth, Wendy D. "Racial Mismatch: The Divergence Between Form and Function in Data for Monitoring Racial Discrimination of Hispanics." *Social
Science Quarterly* 91, no. 5 (2010): 1288–311.

Roth, Wendy D., and Nadia Y. Kim. "Relocating Prejudice: A Transnational
Approach to Understanding Immigrants' Racial Attitudes." *International
Migration Review* 47, no. 2 (2013): 330–73.

Royster, Deirdre A. *Race and the Invisible Hand: How White Networks Exclude Black
Men from Blue-Collar Jobs*. Berkeley: University of California Press, 2003.

Rubin, Joel. "Gang Member Gets Prison for Firebombing Black Families in
Boyle Heights." *Los Angeles Times*, June 3, 2019. https://www.latimes.com
/local/lanow/la-me-gang-firebombing-20190603-story.html.

Rushing, Beth, and Idee Winfield. "Bridging the Border Between Work and
Family: The Effects of Supervisor-Employee Similarity." *Sociological Inquiry*
75, no. 1 (2005): 55–80.

Russell, Suzanne C. "Perth Amboy Gang Tensions Worry Parents." *Home News Tribune*, Apr. 7, 2004.

Sacks, Michael Paul. "The Puerto Rican Effect on Hispanic Residential Segregation: A Study of the Hartford and Springfield Metro Areas in National Perspective." *Latino Studies* 9, no. 1 (2011): 87–105.

Saenz, Christina. "Who and What the Hell Is a White Hispanic?" *Latino Rebels*, Sept. 25, 2014. https://www.latinorebels.com/2014/09/25/who-and-what -the-hell-is-a-white-hispanic.

Salazar, Ruben. "Chicanos Would Find Identity Before Coalition with Blacks." *Los Angeles Times*, Feb. 20, 1970. Reprinted in *Border Correspondent: Selected Writings, 1955–1970*, ed. Mario T. García, 239–41. Berkeley: University of California Press, 1995.

————. "Negro Drive Worries Mexican-Americans." *Los Angeles Times*, July 14, 1963. Reprinted in *Border Correspondent: Selected Writings, 1955–1970*, ed. Mario T. García, 113–14. Berkeley: University of California Press, 1995.

Salinas, Cristobal, Jr., and Adele Lozano. "Mapping and Recontexualizing the Evolution of the Term 'Latinx': An Environmental Scanning in Higher Education." *Journal of Latinos and Education* 18, no. 4 (2019): 302–15.

Sampson, Robert J., and Stephen W. Raudenbush, "Seeing Disorder: Neighborhood Stigma and the Social Construction of 'Broken Windows.'" *Social Psychology Quarterly* 67 (2004): 319–42.

Sanchez, Gabriel R. "Latino Group Consciousness and Perceptions of Commonality with African Americans." *Social Science Quarterly* 89, no. 2 (2008): 428–44.

Sanchez, Gabriel R., and Patricia Rodriguez Espinosa. "Does the Race of the Discrimination Agent in Latinos' Discrimination Experiences Influence Latino Group Identity?" *Sociology of Race and Ethnicity* 2, no. 4 (2016): 531–47.

Santiago-Valles, Kelvin. "Policing the Crisis in the Whitest of All the Antilles." *CENTRO: Journal of the Center for Puerto Rican Studies* 8, nos. 1–2 (1996): 42–57.

Sawyer, Mark. "Racial Politics in Multiethnic America: Black and Latina/o Identities and Coalition." In *Neither Enemies nor Friends: Latinos, Blacks, Afro-Latinos*, ed. Anani Dzidzienyo and Suzanne Oboler, 265–79. Houndmills, UK: Palgrave Macmillan, 2005.

Sawyer, Mark Q. *Racial Politics in Post-Revolutionary Cuba*. Cambridge: Cambridge University Press, 2005.

Serrano, Daniel. *Gunmetal Black*. New York: Grand Central, 2008.

Schleef, Debra J., and H. B. Cavalcanti. *Latinos in Dixie: Class and Assimilation in Richmond, Virginia*. Albany, NY: SUNY Press, 2009.

Shroder, Susan. "Suspect Arrested in Carlsbad Hate Crime." *Hartford Courant*, Sept. 29, 2011. https://www.courant.com/sdut-suspect-arrested-in-carlsbad -hate-crime-2011sep29-story.html.

Siegel, Reva B. "A Short History of Sexual Harassment." Introduction to *Directions in Sexual Harassment Law*, ed. Catharine A. MacKinnon and Reva B. Siegel, 1–40. New Haven, CT: Yale University Press, 2004.

Sinnette, Elinor Des Verney. *Arthur Alfonso Schomburg: Black Bibliophile and Collector*. New York: New York Public Library and Wayne State University Press, 1989.

Slave Voyages (website). "Trans-Atlantic Slave Trade—Database." http://www .slavevoyages.org/estimates/bE6pXgi9.

Smith, Barbara Ellen. "Market Rivals or Class Allies? Relations between African American and Latino Immigrant Workers in Memphis." In *Global Connections and Local Receptions: New Latino Immigration to the Southeastern United States*, ed. Fran Ansley and Jon Shefner, 299–317. Knoxville: University of Tennessee Press, 2009.

Smith, Robert Courtney. *Mexican New York: Transnational Lives of New Immigrants.* Berkeley: University of California Press, 2006.

Smith, Sandra Susan, and Jennifer Anne Meri Jones. "Intraracial Harassment on Campus: Explaining Between- and Within-Group Differences." *Ethnic and Racial Studies* 34, no. 9 (2011): 1567–93.

Smith, Terry. *Whitelash: Unmasking White Grievance at the Ballot Box.* Cambridge: Cambridge University Press, 2020.

South, Scott J., Kyle Crowder, and Erick Chavez. "Migration and Spatial Assimilation Among US Latinos: Classical Versus Segmented Trajectories." *Demography* 42, no. 3 (2005): 497–521.

Spano, John. "Blacks Were Targeted, Witness Insists: A Highland Park Gang Member Testifies in a Civil Rights Conspiracy Trial That a 1999 Murder Was Part of a Racial Cleansing Campaign." *Los Angeles Times*, July 6, 2006.

Spiegel, Sarah. "Prison Race Rights: An Easy Case for Segregation." *California Law Review* 95 (2007): 2261–93.

Spivak, Gayatri Chakravorty. "Subaltern Studies: Deconstructing Historiography." In *Selected Subaltern Studies*, ed. Ranajit Guha and Gayatri Chakravorty Spivak, 3–32. New York: Oxford University Press, 1988.

Stack, John F., and Christopher L. Warren. "The Reform Tradition and Ethnic Politics: Metropolitan Miami Confronts the 1990s." In *Miami Now! Immigration, Ethnicity, and Social Change*, ed. Guillermo J. Grenier and Alex Stepick III, 174. Gainesville: University Press of Florida, 1992.

Stack, Liam. "Black Workers' Suit Accuses Job Agency of Favoring Hispanic Applicants." *New York Times*, Dec. 6, 2016. https://www.nytimes.com/2016/12/06 /us/lawsuit-alleges-discrimination-against-blacks-at-national-job-agency.html.

Steffensmeier, Darrell, Ben Feldmeyer, Casey T. Harris, and Jeffery T. Ulmer. "Reassessing Trends in Black Violent Crime, 1980–2008: Sorting Out the 'Hispanic Effect' in Uniform Crime Reports Arrests, National Crime Victimization Survey Offender Estimates, and U.S. Prisoner Counts." *Criminology* 49, no. 1 (2011): 197–251.

Straus, Emily E. "Unequal Pieces of a Shrinking Pie: The Struggle Between African Americans and Latinos over Education, Employment, and Empowerment in Compton, California." *History of Education Quarterly* 49, no. 4 (2009): 507–29.

Sued Badillo, Jalil, and Angel López Cantos. *Puerto Rico Negro.* Río Piedras, Puerto Rico: Editorial Cultural, 1986.

Swarns, Rachel L. "Bridging a Racial Rift That Isn't Black and White." *New York Times*, Oct. 3, 2006.

Tafoya, Sonya M. "Shades of Belonging: Latinos and Racial Identity." *Harvard Journal of Hispanic Policy* 17 (2004–5): 58–78.

Tanner, Adam. "Hispanics Battle Blacks in Major Calif. Prison Riot." Reuters, Jan. 20, 2007. https://www.reuters.com/article/us-prison-riot/hispanics -battle-blacks-in-major-calif-prison-riot-idUSN3144650620070101.

Telles, Edward. *Pigmentocracies: Ethnicity, Race, and Color in Latin America.* Chapel
  Hill: University of North Carolina Press, 2014.
Telles, Edward, Mark Q. Sawyer, and Gaspar Rivera-Salgado, eds. *Just Neighbors?
  Research on African American and Latino Relations in the United States.* New
  York: Russell Sage Foundation, 2011.
Telzer, Eva H., and Heidie A. Vazquez Garcia. "Skin Color and Self-Perceptions
  of Immigrant and U.S.-Born Latinas: The Moderating Role of Racial Social-
  ization and Ethnic Identity." *Hispanic Journal of Behavioral Sciences* 31, no. 3
  (2009): 357–74.
Thomas, Piri. *Down These Mean Streets.* New York: Alfred A. Knopf, 1967.
Torres, Arlene. "La gran familia Puertorriqueña 'ej preta de Beldá'" [The Great
  Puerto Rican Family Is Really Black]. In *Blackness in Latin America and the
  Caribbean, Volume 2: Social Dynamics and Cultural Transformation: Eastern
  South America and the Caribbean,* ed. Arlene Torres and Norman E. Whitten
  Jr., 285–97. Bloomington: Indiana University Press, 1998.
Torres, Julie. "Black Latinx Activists on Anti-Blackness." *Anthropology News,* Sept.
  3, 2020. https://www.anthropology-news.org/articles/black-latinx-activists
  -on-anti-blackness.
Torres Gotay, Benjamín. "Justicia desiste del caso contra estudiante de educación
  especial." *El Nuevo Día,* Feb. 12, 2018. https://www.elnuevodia.com/noticias
  /tribunales/nota/justiciadesistedelcasocontraestudiantedeeducacionespecial
  -2397941.
Torres-Saillant, Silvio. "Problematic Paradigms: Racial Diversity and Corporate
  Identity in the Latino Community." *Review of International American Studies*
  3, no. 1–2 (2008): 435–55.
Uhlmann, Eric, Nilanjana Dasgupta, Angelica Elgueta, Anthony G. Greenwald,
  and Jane Swanson. "Subgroup Prejudice Based on Skin Color Among
  Hispanics in the United States and Latin America." *Social Cognition* 20, no. 3
  (2002): 198–226.
Umemoto, Karen, and C. Kimi Mikami. "A Profile of Race-Bias Hate Crime
  in Los Angeles County." *Western Criminology Review* 2, no. 2 (June 2000).
  http://www.westerncriminology.org/documents/WCR/v02n2/umemoto
  /umemoto.html.
Unger, Todd. "Hate Crime Strikes Rio Rancho." *KOAT Action 7 News,* July 25,
  2012. https://www.koat.com/article/hate-crime-strikes-rio-rancho/5042100.
Uzogara, Ekeoma E. "Who Desires In-Group Neighbors? Associations of Skin
  Tone Biases and Discrimination with Latinas' Segregation Preferences."
  Group Processes and Intergroup Relations 22, no. 8 (2019): 1196–214.
Valcarel, Carmen Luz. "Growing Up Black in Puerto Rico." In *Challenging
  Racism and Sexism: Alternatives to Genetic Explanations,* ed. Ethel Tobach and
  Betty Rosoff, 284–94. New York: Feminist Press, 1994.
Valdes, Francisco. "Race, Ethnicity, and Hispanismo in a Triangular Perspective:
  The 'Essential Latino/a' and LatCrit Theory." *UCLA Law Review* 48, no. 2
  (2000): 305–13.
Valdes, Marcela. "The Fight for Latino Voters." *New York Times Magazine,* Nov.
  29, 2020.
Valdés, Vanessa K. *Diasporic Blackness: The Life and Times of Arturo Alfonso Schom-
  burg.* Albany, NY: SUNY Press, 2017.

Valentín, Luis J., and Carla Minet, "Las 889 páginas de telegram entre Rosselló Nevares y sus allegados." *Centro de Periodismo Investigativo*, July 13, 2019. http://periodismoinvestigativo.com/2019/07/las-889-paginas-de-telegram -entre-rossello-nevares-y-sus-allegados.

Vargas, Edward D. "Latinos and Criminal Justice, Policing, and Drug Policy Reform." Latino Decisions/LatinoJustice PRLDEF, Jan. 10, 2018. https:// latinodecisions.com/wp-content/uploads/2019/06/LJ_Posted_Deck.pdf.

Vargas, Nicholas. "Latina/o Whitening?: Which Latina/os Self-Classify as White and Report Being Perceived as White by Other Americans?" *Du Bois Review: Social Science Research on Race* 12, no. 1 (2015): 119–36.

———. "Off White: Colour-Blind Ideology at the Margins of Whiteness." *Ethnic and Racial Studies* 37, no. 13 (2014): 2281–302.

Vasquez, Jesse. "One Prison Taught Me Racism. Another Taught Me Acceptance." *Washington Post*, Oct. 1, 2018. https://www.washingtonpost.com /outlook/2018/10/01/one-prison-taught-me-racism-another-taught-me -acceptance.

Vigil, James Diego. "Ethnic Succession and Ethnic Conflict." In *Just Neighbors? Research on African American and Latino Relations in the United States*, ed. Edward Telles, Mark Q. Sawyer, and Gaspar Rivera-Salgado, 325–42. New York: Russell Sage Foundation, 2011.

Vilson, Jose. "My Skin Is Black, My Name Is Latino. That Shouldn't Surprise You." *Medium*, July 6, 2017. https://level.medium.com/my-skin-is-Black -my-name-is-latino-afrolatinidad-as-a-layered-Blackness-eb592b69ae12.

Wang, Hansi Lo. "The 2nd-Largest Racial Group in the U.S. Is 'Some Other Race.' Most Are Latino." *GPB News*. PBS, Sept. 30, 2021. https://www.wgbh .org/news/national-news/2021/09/30/the-2nd-largest-racial-group-in-the -u-s-is-some-other-race-most-are-latino.

West, Cornel. *Race Matters*. Boston: Beacon Press, 1993.

White, John Valery. "The Irrational Turn in Employment Discrimination Law: Slouching Toward a Unified Approach to Civil Rights Law." *Mercer Law Review* 53 (2002): 709–810.

Wilkerson, Isabel. *Caste: The Origins of Our Discontents*. New York: Random House, 2020.

Wilkinson, Betina Cutaia. *Partners or Rivals? Power and Latino, Black, and White Relations in the Twenty-First Century*. Charlottesville: University of Virginia Press, 2015.

Williams, Joyce E., and Liza Garza. "A Case Study in Change and Conflict: The Dallas Independent School District." *Urban Education* 41, no. 5 (2006): 459–81.

Yancey, George. "'Blacks Cannot Be Racists': A Look at How European-Americans, African-Americans, Hispanic-Americans and Asian-Americans Perceive Minority Racism." *Michigan Sociological Review* 19 (2005): 138–54.

Yancey, George. *Who Is White? Latinos, Asians, and the New Black/Nonblack Divide*. Boulder, CO: Lynne Rienner, 2003.

INDEX

absentee landlords, housing discrimination by, 97–98
Acevedo, Elizabeth, 5
adelantando la raza, 15, 18
adultification of Black youngsters, 51–52, 54–55
African(s): phenotype of, 6, 13, 17–18, 135, 141–42; racialized struggles of, 3, 56
African Americans: adverse effects of bias against, 11; coalitions with Latinos, 131–33; as competitors, 22; Dominicans and, 30–31; housing discrimination against, 93–95; Latino social distance from, 20–24; and Mexican Americans, 25–28; preference for Latinos over White non-Hispanics by, 22; presumed resentment and bias against Latinos by, 9; Puerto Ricans and, 29–30
African Diaspora, 3, 51
Africano, 135
Afro-Columbians, 5
Afro-Cubans: census classification of, 127; housing discrimination against, 90–91; in racial hierarchy, 128
Afro-Dominicans, 52–53, 63–64, 86–87
Afro-Latinos: adverse effects of bias against, 11; anti-Black racism of, 15; on census form, 125–31; defined, 4; discrimination against, 10–11; identity of, 4–5, 25–28,

61–62, 125–31, 138–43; Latin American and Caribbean racial stereotypes of, 12–16; Latino bias against, 9; marginalization of, 3–4; and racial Blackness, 5
Afro-Mexicans, 28, 79, 100–101
Afro-Peruvians, 4
Afro-Puerto Ricans, 29; employment discrimination cases against, 68–72; and family racial traumas, 17, 139–42
Aja, Alan, 90
Alexander, Andy, 115–16
Allapattah, Fla., 91
Allsup's Convenience Store (Carlsbad, N.M.), 43–45
alt-right podcast, 103
America First (podcast), 103
Andrews, Bernie, 42–43
anti-Black racism, in Latin America and Caribbean, 13–16
anti-Black violence, pervasiveness of, 2
antidiscrimination law: in educational settings, 48; and exclusion from public spaces, 34, 35, 36, 38; and future of racial equality, 133, 134–35; and housing discrimination, 58; and job discrimination, 70–71; and judges' failure to understand Latino anti-Blackness, 10–11, 68; in Puerto Rico, 14
apartment rentals, housing discrimination in, 86–87, 98–99
Arce, Julissa, 129

discrimination, 78–79; importance of stories to counteract, 121–22; and racism against Latinos, 12; terms of, 31–32

racial mixture, 7, 8, 13, 23, 80, 99, 140–44

racial order, 5

racial segregation, in prisons, 104–5, 106

racial slurs: of employees, 57, 58, 69–71, 73–75; in non-gang-affiliated violence, 116; in public schools, 50, 51

racial stereotypes: and caste system, 5; in employment discrimination, 64, 76, 77; in housing discrimination, 101; in Latin America and Caribbean, 12–13, 68; by Latino immigrants, 8–9; and Latino judges, 69, 71; of Latino police officers, 117; by Latino students, 47; by Latino teachers, 52–54; in Puerto Rico, 14–15; and racialized compliments, 14; sexualized, 62–63; and social distance, 21, 22; on Spanish-language television, 24

racial taxonomy of Latin American countries, 60–62, 127

racial territoriality, 114

Radio Caña Negra (podcast), 10

Ramona Gardens public housing complex, 107–8

Ramos, Alex Michael, 102–3

Reagan, Ronald, 136

real estate agents, and housing discrimination, 95–96

Recio, Sili, 51

Redd, Spring, 5

redistricting, 123–25

regions, racial attitudes among Latinos across, 25–31

rental agency, Latino-controlled informal, 86–87, 91

Republican National Hispanic Assembly, 26

residential segregation: in Boston, 133; in Chicago, 49; of Cubans, 100–101; in Florida, 91–92; and Latino-dominated networks of information housing rentals, 87, 89; in New York City, 31; and

physical violence, 111–14, 159n46; of Puerto Ricans, 100; and racial equality, 100, 158n45; and racial hostilities, 133; and skin color, 100–101; in Smithtown, N.Y., 98

restaurant(s), as sites of discrimination, 34–36, 37–40, 41–43

Restaurante Compostela (San Juan), 35–36

retail clothing store, as public space, 41–42

Reyes, Rosalind, 65–66

Richmond, Va., social distance in, 28

Rickyleaks, 15

Ríos, Palmira, 135, 136

Rivera, Maritza Quiñones, 18

Rodriguez, Antonio, 76–79

Rodriguez-Muñiz, Michael, 126

Rominger, Anna Maria, 99

Rosemond, David, 90–91

Rosselló, Ricardo, 15

routine traffic stops, police bias and violence in, 117–18

Saenz, Thomas, 124

salaries, 57, 79–80, 84–85

Salazar, Ruben, 25

Salvadorian(s), 20

Samohi High School (Santa Monica, Calif.), 49

Sanchez, Victor Rivera, 135–37

San Luis Obispo County, Calif., non-gang-affiliated violence in, 115

Santa Monica, Calif., Latino anti-blackness in schools in, 49

Santiago, Arturo, 115

Santiago, Milton Falero, 83

Sawyer, Mark, 37–38

#SayHerName campaign, 117

Schomburg, Arturo, 117

school(s), 46–55; "adultification" of Black youngsters in, 51–52; colleges as, 46–48; colorism in, 47; discipline in, 53–54; K-12, 48–55; Latino instructors in, 51–55; microaggressions in, 47; over-sexualization of Black students in, 54–55; physical violence in, 48–50; preschools as, 51; race-based bullying in, 50–51;

vandalism, 115, 116
Vargas, Nicholas, 122
Varrio Azusa 13 gang, 108
Varrio Hawaiian Gardens Latino
    gang, 108–9
Vasquez, Francisco, 106–7
Vasquez, Jesse, 105
Vasquez, Louis, 106
Villaraigosa, Antonio, 49
Vilson, José Luis, 1
violence, 102–19; everyday, 114–16;
    by Latino police officers, 117–19;
    by Latino white supremacists,
    102–4; pervasiveness of anti-Black,
    2; in prisons, 104–11; residential
    segregation and, 111–14, 159n46;
    in schools, 49—51; for turf de-
    fense, 113–14; unemployment and,
    112; by US-born *vs.* immigrant
    Latinos, 112–13
voting districts, and equality efforts,
    123–25, 132
Voting Rights Act (1965), 123

wage structure, 57, 79–80, 84–85
War Against Poverty, 30
Washington, Harold, 132
Washington Heights, N.Y., 19, 52
Waters, Alma, 38
Webb, Maybell, 65
West, Cornel, 75
White identity politics, 103
White Latino privilege, 121

Whiteness: Latino, 120–22, 128–29,
    130; Latino esteem for, 121
White non-Hispanics, decline in
    population of, 2
White power organizations, Latinos
    in, 7
White privilege: and census catego-
    ries, 129, 130; in employment,
    78, 80
White supremacist(s): in electoral
    politics, 124–25; and Latin Ameri-
    can racial hierarchy, 16; Latino, 2,
    7, 11, 102–4; in prison gangs, 104;
    violence by, 102, 115
Winston-Salem, N.C.: Latino-African
    American racial coalition building
    in, 132; Latinos and Blacks in, 28
Winter Park, Fla., non-gang-affiliated
    violence in, 116
worker-based coalitions, 132
working conditions, 57, 71, 73–74
Wright, Aaron, 38

Yancey, George, 103
Yanez, Jeronimo, 118
Yang, Debra Wong, 109
Young, Cruz, 63–64
Young Lords, 30, 132
Young Lords Party, 132

Zenón, Héctor Bermúdez, 35–36
Zimmerman, George, 103
Zimmerman, Robert, 103

ABOUT THE AUTHOR

Tanya Katerí Hernández is the Archibald R. Murray Professor of Law at Fordham University School of Law, where she is an associate director of the Center on Race, Law, and Justice as its head of Global and Comparative Law Programs and Initiatives. Hernández, who holds an AB from Brown and a law degree from Yale, is an internationally recognized comparative race law expert. As a Fulbright Scholar she lectured at the Université Paris Ouest Nanterre La Défense in Paris and the University of the West Indies Law School in Trinidad. Her fellowships include being a Law and Public Policy Affairs fellow at Princeton University, a faculty fellow at the Institute for Research on Women at Rutgers University, a faculty fellow at the Fred T. Korematsu Center for Law and Equality, and a scholar in residence at the Schomburg Center for Research in Black Culture. Professor Hernández is a fellow of the American Bar Foundation, the American Law Institute, and the Academia Puertorriqueña de Jurisprudencia y Legislación. *Hispanic Business Magazine* selected her as one of its annual one hundred most influential Hispanics. She serves on the editorial boards of the *Revista Brasileira de Direito e Justiça* (*Brazilian Journal of Law and Justice*) and the *Latino Studies Journal* published by Palgrave-Macmillan Press.

Professor Hernández's scholarly interest is in the study of comparative race relations and antidiscrimination law, and her work in that area has been published in numerous university law reviews such as those of Cornell, Harvard, NYU, UC Berkeley, and Yale, and in news outlets like the *New York Times*, among other publications. Her previous books are *Racial Subordination in Latin America: The Role of the State, Customary Law and the New Civil Rights Response* (including Spanish and Portuguese translation editions), *Brill Research Perspectives in Comparative Law: Racial Discrimination*, and *Multiracials and Civil Rights: Mixed-Race Stories of Discrimination*.